R. Olson

Software Project Management
STEP BY STEP

Software Project Management
STEP BY STEP

Milton D. Rosenau, Jr.
Marsha D. Lewin

Lifetime Learning Publications
Belmont, California
A Division of Wadsworth, Inc.

London, Singapore, Sidney, Tokyo, Toronto, Mexico City

Production Service: *Bernie Scheier & Associates*
Copy Editor: *Sylvia Stein*
Illustrator: *John Foster*
Compositor: *Thompson Type*

© 1984 by Wadsworth, Inc. All rights reserved. No part of this book may be reproduced, stored in a retrieval system, or transcribed, in any form or by any means, electronic, mechanical, photocopying, recording, or otherwise, without the prior written permission of the publisher, Lifetime Learning Publications, Belmont, California 94002, a division of Wadsworth, Inc.

Printed in the United States of America
1 2 3 4 5 6 7 8 9 10——88 87 86 85 84

Library of Congress Cataloging in Publication Data

Rosenau, Milton D., 1931–
Software project management—step by step

   Bibliography: p. Includes index.
   1. Computer programming management. I. Lewin, Marsha D., 1941–   II. Title.
QA76.6.R677   1984   001.64′2′068   84-5773
ISBN 0-534-03379-2

Contents

Preface ix

1 The Concept of Computer Software Project Management 1

Distinguishing Characteristics of Projects 1
The Project Management Process 7
The Life Cycle Concept 9
Typical Problems 9
Highlights 10
Further Reading 11

Part 1 Defining Software Project Goals 13

2 The Triple Constraint 15

The Notion of the Triple Constraint 15
Obstacles to Satisfying the Triple Constraint 16
Corrective Steps 21
Project Outcomes 24
Typical Problems 24
Highlights 25
Further Reading 25

3 Acquiring Successful Software Projects 27

Strategic Issues 27
The Proposal Process 31

Typical Problems 42
Highlights 43
Further Reading 43

4 Negotiations and Contracts 45
Negotiating the Contract 45
International Projects 51
Typical Problems 54
Highlights 54
Further Reading 55

Part 2 Planning a Software Project 57

5 The Crucial Role of Planning 59
Planning 59
The Need for Plans 60
Planning Issues 64
"The Plan" 68
Planning for the Project Life Cycle 71
Typical Problems 73
Highlights 73
Further Reading 74

6 Planning the Software Performance Dimension 76
Statement of Work 76
Work Breakdown Structure 77
Typical Problems 81
Highlights 82
Further Reading 82

7 Planning the Schedule 84
Bar Charts 84
Milestones 86
Network Diagrams 86
Bar Chart Formats of CPM Diagrams 107
Typical Problems 108
Highlights 109
Further Reading 110

8 Planning the Cost Dimension 111
Cost Estimating 111

Project Cost System   119
Typical Problems   124
Highlights   125
Further Reading   125

9 The Impact of Limited Resources   127

Resources   127
Time Versus Cost Trade-Off   134
Contingency   136
Other Computer Uses for Planning   140
Cost/Schedule Control System Criteria   141
Typical Problems   142
Highlights   143
Further Reading   144

Part 3 Leading the People   145

10 Computer Software Project Organization Options   147

Three Principal Organizational Forms   147
Other Organizational Forms   152
The Informal Organization   154
Typical Problems   155
Highlights   155
Further Reading   155

11 Organizing the Project Team   157

Degree of Association with the Project   157
Sources of Personnel   160
Compromise   161
Control   164
Task Assignments   165
Typical Problems   166
Highlights   166
Further Reading   167

12 Organizing the Support Team   168

Involvement and Commitment   168
Coordination   171
Interaction with Support Groups   172
Subcontractors   174
Typical Problems   175

Highlights 177
Further Reading 177

13 The Role of the Computer Software Project Manager 178

Influence Rather Than Authority 178
Effective Managerial Behavior 180
Theories of Motivation 187
Implications of Motivational Theory 190
Stimulating Creativity 192
Detecting Burnout 194
Practical Tips 194
Typical Problems 195
Highlights 195
Further Reading 196

Part 4 Monitoring Project Progress 199

14 Monitoring Tools for Software Projects 201

Controlling to Achieve Objectives 201
Control Techniques 201
Reports 203
Multiple Projects 207
Typical Problems 209
Highlights 209
Further Reading 209

15 Software Project Reviews 211

The Necessity for Reviews 211
The Conduct of Reviews 212
Periodic Reviews 215
Topical Reviews 219
Typical Problems 224
Highlights 225
Further Reading 225

16 Cost Reports 227

Computer Cost Reports 227
Control 229
Typical Problems 235
Highlights 236
Further Reading 236

17 Handling Changes 238
Reasons for Changes 238
Adopting Changes 242
Typical Changes 246
Highlights 247
Further Reading 247

18 Coping with Unexpected Problems 249
The General Approach 249
Decision Trees 252
Matrix Array 255
Problem-Solving Meeting Styles 259
Typical Problems 260
Highlights 260
Further Reading 261

Part 5 Completing the Software Project 263

19 Computer Software Project Completion 265
Project Staffing Cycle 265
Computer Consequences 270
Increasing the Odds of Success 272
Typical Problems 274
Highlights 274
Further Reading 275

20 What You Have to Do After You Thought You Were Done 276
Continuing Service and Support 276
Ownership Rights 277
Audits 278
People Issues 279
Feedback 279
Typical Problems 280
Highlights 280
Further Reading 280

Part 6 Other Issues 283

21 Small Computer Software Projects 285
Defining Small Projects 285

Simplified Management   286
Problems   286
Typical Problems   290
Highlights   291
Further Reading   291

22   Where Do You Go from Here?   293

Summary   293
Other Sources of Help   294
The Future of Project Management   295
Continuing Project Management Skill Development   296
A Final Thought   298

Appendix 1   Abbreviations Often Used in Computer Software Project Management   299

Appendix 2   Glossary of Terms Commonly Employed in Project Management   304

Index   311

Preface

WHO THIS BOOK IS FOR

This book is intended specifically for the person who has just started to manage or work on computer software projects. This book is for you if you are

- A programmer, systems analyst, or software engineer working with others on a software project
- A computer scientist or software manager who finds himself or herself thrust into a position with project management responsibility
- An engineer working on equipment that requires software or computer programming support
- A recently appointed manager of a project requiring computer software development or maintenance.

In short, you will benefit if you have an interest in or need for the successful *management* of computer software projects in which you've had very little or no direct experience. No matter what your previous skill, if you're now responsible for getting something done by a specified date and with a limited budget, this book will help you grasp and master key practical skills for successful computer software project management. Now you must not only demonstrate (and continue to practice) your professional skill, but must also take responsibility for schedule and budget, using physical and human resources over which you may have little or no real control.

THE APPROACH TO COMPUTER SOFTWARE PROJECT MANAGEMENT

Although no treatment can or should trivialize a subject as complex as project management, this book is specifically designed to make it as simple as possible. Managing a computer software project does not mean performing all the analysis, programming, and testing for the project. It does mean managing others and interfacing with the rest of the organization. We stress those *management* skills, rather than *technological* skills such as systems analysis or programming, which are required to successfully complete a software project. Thus, other books have chapters or sections about system requirements, software requirements, preliminary design, detailed design, programming, coding and debugging, unit test, integration, system test, validation, acceptance, documentation, installation, user training, and postimplementation audit or review. This book discusses these topics, but within the context of defining the project goal, planning the work to be done, leading (or managing) people, monitoring and measuring progress, and completing software projects.

In many ways, software development has changed little in twenty years (certainly compared to hardware). We have more development methodologies, configurations, and job classifications. We can quote numbers of lines of code generated and talk of structure, modularity, integrity, and redundancy. But we still rely on the individual programming talent to convert user intentions into automated products and services. Managing those talents is what this text is all about.

This book draws upon a variety of software development types: management information and accounting systems, operating and application systems, defense, large and small projects. We do not aim to make this a comprehensive manual for all possible programming efforts. Rather, we draw as wide a panorama as we can to show the reader the magnitude of the field of software development. There is no single algorithm for managing the software development process; but there are some guidelines that, together with common sense, can increase your chances of being the manager of a successful project.

We subscribe to the principles of software engineering and its life cycle concept for project management and control. Your organization will have its own methodology and definitions; what you learn in these next pages can and should be applied to your formal methodologies for immediate usefulness. We wish you success, few bugs, and a project that is delivered ahead of schedule, below budget, with better performance than planned.

HOW THIS BOOK IS ORGANIZED

Software Project Management—Step by Step provides a step-by-step approach that we have found effective in our combined fifty years of industrial experience and in teaching thousands of seminar students, working adults of all ages from a wide variety of industries. By taking you through the project management process, this book will equip you with detailed tools that you can immediately apply to your first (or next) project and that will help you overcome the pitfalls that typically bedevil software projects.

The step-by-step approach divides the project management process into five general activities and emphasizes the importance of satisfying the three constraints imposed by performance specifications, schedule, and budget.

The first management activity is *defining*, and under it we discuss the Triple Constraint, how to acquire successful software projects, and negotiations and contracts.

The second activity is *planning*. We discuss the crucial role of planning, planning the performance, schedule, and cost dimensions, and the impact of limited resources.

The third management activity is *leading*. Here we cover computer software project organization options, organizing the project and support teams, and the role of the computer software project manager.

Under *monitoring*, the fourth management activity, we discuss control tools, project reviews, cost reports, handling changes, and coping with unexpected problems.

The fifth activity is *completing* the project, and we discuss completion and what you must do after you think you've finished.

USEFUL AND UNIQUE FEATURES OF THIS BOOK

The emphasis here is on management of computer software projects for the person with less than five years experience in such a managerial role. Specific helpful features include the following:

- Each short chapter is devoted to a single topic and can be absorbed in one to three hours. Thus, the entire book can be mastered in a single month, making it uniquely useful for the working adult.
- The book covers the subject matter chronologically, from a project's beginning to its end. It covers proposal and negotiation activities that are required if you must sell the work to others (inside or outside your organization) to get the work authorized. Even if you have been directed to manage (or contribute to) a project that is already authorized, this material is useful because it will force you to consider whether you have enough initial information to be successful.
- The Triple Constraint of performance specification, time schedule, and money budget is stressed.
- Typical problems are highlighted in each chapter.
- Useful references in each chapter point to other recent publications.
- Because the computer software profession and many of the books that you may rely upon for technological assistance use numerous abbreviations (often unexplained), this book contains an appendix with an extensive list of these abbreviations.
- There is also an appendix with a glossary of key project management terms.

We have also included a number of forms to assist the reader in grasping the information necessary for particular tasks within the software development process. Organizations generally have their own forms and conventions, but their content should be similar.

Milton D. Rosenau, Jr.
Santa Monica, CA

Marsha D. Lewin
Los Angeles, CA

Acknowledgements

We wish to express our thanks to thousands of seminar students, the various university and other sponsors of these seminars, our countless clients, and our many colleagues in industry who provided so many helpful suggestions and illustrative materials.

We also appreciate the efforts of Graceanne W. Chally, who did the tedious work of creating the word processor disc files.

It is a pleasure to acknowledge our copy editor, Sylvia E. Stein, who has done an outstanding job of clarifying our material, and the reviewers whose constructive comments have produced a more complete, more lucid book.

Finally, no effort such as this goes without the supportive effort of our families—spouses Ellen and Andy, son David—whose patience and understanding we so greatly appreciate.

Software Project Management
STEP BY STEP

1

The Concept of Computer Software Project Management

This chapter differentiates computer software project management from other computer software work and from other managerial activity by examining how projects differ from other activities. It describes the sequence of five managerial activities that characterizes project management.

DISTINGUISHING CHARACTERISTICS OF PROJECTS

Origin

Imagine you are a systems analyst whose boss has asked you to manage a software project, or a computer programmer who has been asked to set up a new financial report, or a member of a professional or community group who has volunteered to arrange the annual meeting. How would you go about it? How does this activity differ from others in which you engage? Is it similar to going to your work place each day? In what ways does it differ?

At this point, you probably want more information about the project. For instance, is it small or large? What do you mean by small or large—the quantity of materials to be studied, the deadline, or the budget? How does project magnitude alter your approach?

2 The Concept of Computer Software Project Management

Projects are one-of-a-kind undertakings that originate when something has to be done.

This hypothetical project illustrates some of the characteristics that distinguish projects from other activities. Projects originate because something not done before must be done. Computer software projects originate because new software has to be developed or existing software has to be modified.

Although going to work on some mornings may seem to be a major undertaking, it is not usually considered a project. Going to work is an activity that repeats a prior activity, namely, going to work the day before. This aspect of the definition of a project is not clear-cut. For instance, if you worked for a payroll service bureau and your project had been to write a program that issues checks for a client company, at some point writing a second or third or fourth payroll check program in the same language for the same machine ceases to be a project and becomes a repetitive activity. As a general rule, if the payroll check programs are different from one another, then each is a project. If each check program is virtually identical, we have a production line for such programs and are not engaged in a project per se.

Product

There are hardware and software projects.

There are many ways to characterize projects. "Hardware project" and "software project" are common terms, depending on whether the final result is a tangible product (hardware) or a computer program accompanied by a report or some other form of documentation (software).

Thus, the product or end result of a project is a second characteristic. A project is not an ongoing activity, but rather an undertaking that ends with a specified accomplishment. In the first hypothetical example, this would be the completion of the software project.

Marketplace

Projects can be categorized by their source of sponsorship, as shown in Table 1-1. One of the fringe benefits of being a good project manager is that the tools and techniques applied on the job also have utility for personal undertakings. Figure 1-1 is a time-oriented critical path network (discussed in more detail in Chapter 7) that one of us used when we moved from one house to another. Because the escrow period was only thirty days, scheduling of many activities in the correct sequences was critical, and this particular tool was very useful.

If the customer is a governmental entity, there will probably be very formal procedures. If your company's vice-president of marketing wishes to develop a real-time decision support system for his or her own information, the process may be very informal.

Whether a software project is done under contract to another organization or not affects how formal the process is. But even for a software project for your own organization, or even your own department, it's smart to pretend the project is being undertaken for another organization. This pretense helps assure that you will introduce enough formality to manage the project successfully. For instance, a project undertaken for another organization requires a contract with

For whom a project is done affects how it is done.

TABLE 1-1. Project types

Source	Example
Personal or family	Move to a new home Make list for greeting cards Establish household budget
Organization sponsored—for the organization itself	Set up a new computer Put a new tax withholding schedule into operation Market a new spreadsheet analysis program
Customer sponsored—done by your organization under contract	Write a software program to issue payroll checks Provide firmware Deliver a computer with software as a turnkey system
Subcontracted—tasks performed by other organizations for your organization	Develop a materials control program Provide working firmware Deliver a microcomputer system to support litigation work
Government sponsored—done by a governmental entity	Automate Social Security payments Audit income tax returns Process orders at Library of Congress

a clear, detailed statement of what is to be done, by when, and for how much; such a job specification is sometimes left out of internally sponsored projects.

The nature of the competition is also important. The only software development group in a region is in a favorable situation. A software development group that is one of many in some small city is in a very different and less favorable competitive situation. Inside your own organization (company, government bureau, or university), management can choose to buy software from a supplier (either standard or custom modified) or ask you to develop it. Buying software from a third party is becoming increasingly common, espe-

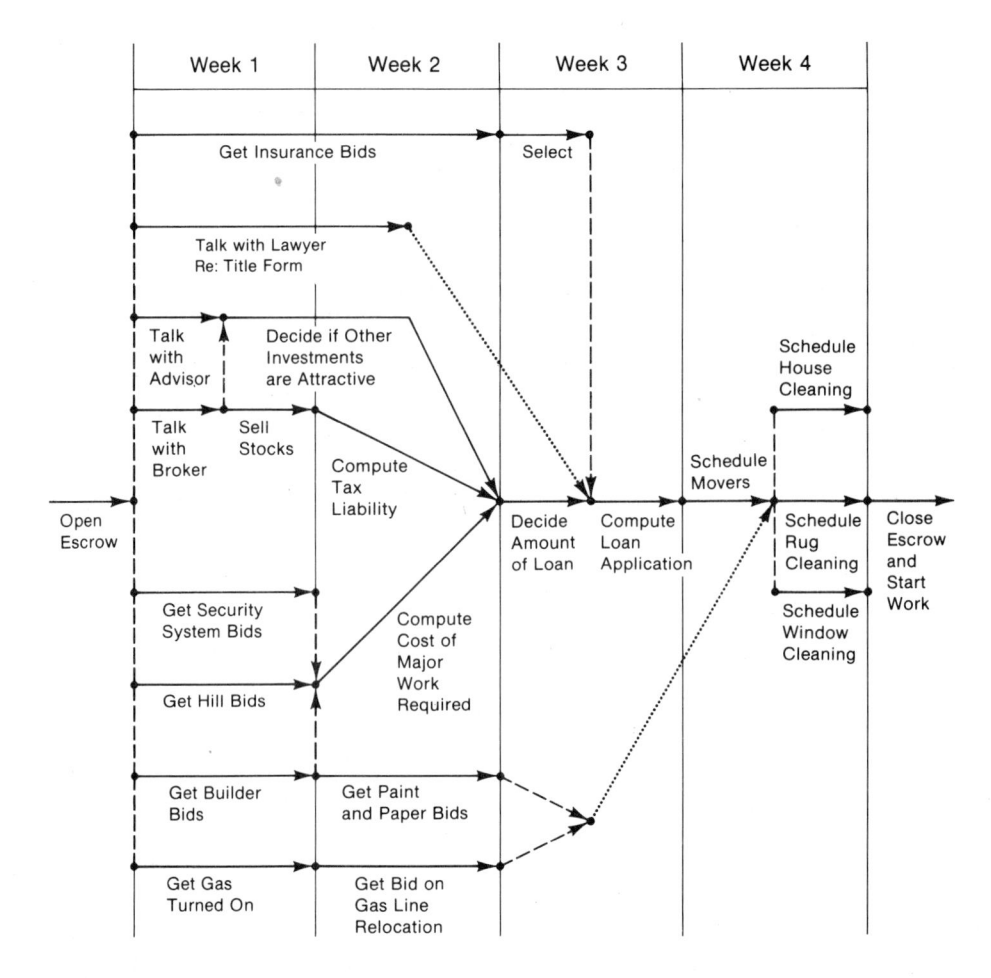

Figure 1-1. Example of project management tool applied to a personal project.

cially in companies with a heavy backlog of projects. Or management can devote its limited resources to something entirely different, such as building expansion. Thus, you are always in some kind of competition, and it is important to be professional and competent in managing your project.

Once an organization of a project manager has successfully concluded a project, a company-sponsored software project, for instance, it will be much easier to undertake a second project of that sort. Although there are similarities in managing all kinds of projects, successfully completing a company-sponsored software project is very different from successfully completing a customer-sponsored firmware project.

In general, projects are done by someone or some organization for someone else or for some other organization.

Project Size

"Program" is commonly used synonymously with "project." Thus, the expression "program management" is often used interchangeably with "project management." Some organizations use "task management" as well. Program management, project management, and task management are generally identical. But programs are usually larger than projects, and projects are usually larger than tasks. Other terms are also used, such as job, work order, and subtask; and these generally refer to still smaller projects. Thus, there is some connotation of size when terms other than project management are used. Nevertheless, the techniques and methodology are essentially the same, differing only in detail. We shall use "project" throughout the rest of this book.

The software written for the space program required many years and millions of dollars. The successful implementation of automated teller machines in the banking industry has resulted from millions of dollars expended in both hardware and software development. Conversely, a computer programming project may be completed in a few hours or days. Hence, size and complexity do not distinguish a project from another activity. They do, however, affect project success.

Resources

Projects are accomplished by resources, namely, people and things. Many of the required resources are only marginally under the effective control of the project manager. For example, the computer hardware needed is often controlled by a separate operations group.

Managing projects means managing people.

The project manager must organize the correct human resources to take advantage of the available physical resources. Then the project manager has to deal with the constraints and emotional problems inherent in their use while trying to accomplish the project initiator's technical performance goals within the schedule and budget. Managing people is often the most difficult aspect of managing a project, especially for recently appointed managers whose academic training is primarily technical (for example, computer science, mathematics, or engineering). Such technologists tend to be more comfortable with things and numbers than with people. What is particularly important in a computer software project is its ultimate use by humans. Often, in the human (user) to machine (computer) translation, the original intent is lost. Thus, the project manager is responsible not only for the management of the people who report to him or her, but for the human interface with people who must ultimately use the system.

The project manager's goal is to utilize organizational resources to achieve the project's objectives. However, the project manager will often be frustrated by the many other directions in which the organization seems to be (and often is) moving (see Figure 1-2). These multiple directions arise because of personal aspirations and interests, because of various parochial interests by different components of the organization, and because there are many projects being carried

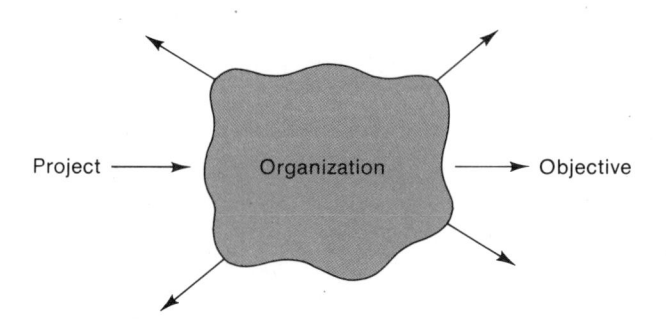

Figure 1-2. The competition for organizational resources impacts a project.

Source: "Project Management." Lecture notes by Milton D. Rosenau, Jr. Copyright © 1981 by the Association for Media-based Continuing Education for Engineers, Inc. (AMCEE). Reprinted by permission.

out simultaneously. Multiple directions are due to simple differences in terminology, which may cause wasted efforts due to misunderstandings. For example, a user requesting "immediate response" meant within the hour, but the programmer coded a sophisticated two-second maximum response time to an inquiry.

Because of the tremendous importance of these "people issues," we discuss organizational options and their influence on resource control and availability in Chapter 10. This organizational discussion is then followed by an extensive review of effective actions you can take as project manager to lead both the project and support teams.

Project management entails working with people you have not chosen, many of whom have different skills and interests.

THE PROJECT MANAGEMENT PROCESS

Project management, which requires five different managerial activities, can be most simply structured as a five-step process:

1. Define—defining the project's goals
2. Plan—planning how you and your team will satisfy the Triple Constraint (goal) of performance specification, time schedule, and money budget (the plan depends on the mix of human and physical resources to be used.)
3. Lead—providing managerial guidance to human resources, subordinates, and others (including subcontractors), that will result in their doing effective, timely work
4. Monitor—measuring or controlling the project work to find out how progress differs from plan in time to initiate corrective action (this often leads to replanning, which may force a goal [definition] change, with a consequent need to change resources.)
5. Complete—making sure that the job that is finally done conforms to the current definition of what was to be done and wrapping up all the loose ends

Projects require five steps, which may overlap.

The first two steps are not necessarily separate and sequential, except when the project initiator issues a firm, complete, and unambiguous statement of the desired project output, in which case the organization that will carry out the project may start to plan how to achieve it. It is more common to start with a proposed work definition, which is then jointly renegotiated after preliminary planning elucidates some consequences of the initially proposed work definition. In fact, the resources to be dealt with in the leading phase often must be considered before planning can be finished (see Figure 1-3A). For instance, you might need people familiar with COBOL if the plan is to write a business application on a mainframe computer; you would use other people familiar with PASCAL if the project was to be done using a microcomputer. Similarly, as you will see in later chapters, replanning is almost always required, thus frequently amending the negotiated definition (see Figure 1-3B). Ultimately, the project can be completed when the work that is done satisfies the current requirement (see Figure 1-3C).

Successful project management is the accomplishment of the performance specification (that is, objective or technical goals), on schedule, and within the budget.

Nevertheless, the five-step managerial activity process covers each required action and is a useful conceptual sequence in which to consider project management. Thus we have organized this book according to it.

The Triple Constraint, an extremely important notion for project management, provides the defining parameters of a project. It consists of three dimensions:

1. Performance specification
2. Time or schedule
3. Budget or money

All projects are defined and characterized by a Triple Constraint.

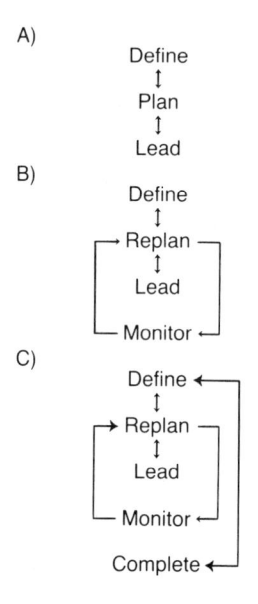

A)
```
Define
  ↑
 Plan
  ↑
 Lead
```

B)
```
       Define
         ↑
   ┌→ Replan ─┐
   │     ↑    │
   │   Lead   │
   │          │
   └─ Monitor ←┘
```

C)
```
       Define ←─┐
         ↑     │
   ┌→ Replan ─┐│
   │     ↑    ││
   │   Lead   ││
   │          ││
   └─ Monitor ←┘│
       Complete ←┘
```

Figure 1-3. The five phases are interdependent.

THE LIFE CYCLE CONCEPT

A natural sequence of events occurs in the process of developing computer software. The separation of the total project into easily managed interrelated phases has become standard practice. The number of phases differs from company to company and author to author. However, as a practical matter, a phase in the software project life cycle is delineated by:

- A unique audience or set of audiences involved
- Completion of milestone documents or products by the end of that phase
- Separate and distinct uses of information prepared
- Dependency on preceding phases

In this book, we use a six-phase life cycle as shown in Figure 1-4. Each phase has a unique mix of reviewers, milestone documents, and purpose throughout which the five project management steps of defining, planning, leading, measuring, and completing occur.

Use a project life cycle concept that lets you divide the software development process into manageable parts.

TYPICAL PROBLEMS

> Failure to identify a project for what it truly is usually leads to missed specifications, late completion, and/or a budget overrun. One expert is quoted as saying, "I don't
> *continued*

CONTROLS	SOFTWARE DEVELOPMENT LIFE CYCLE PHASES	MILESTONE DOCUMENTS	REVIEWS BY
PROJECT (WORK) PLAN	CONCEPTS	CONCEPTS & OBJECTIVES	SENIOR MANAGEMENT
	DEFINITION	REQUIREMENTS	USER
	FEASIBILITY	SYSTEM ARCHITECTURE PRODUCT SPECIFICATIONS	USER, DEVELOPMENT DEVELOPMENT MANAGEMENT
	SYSTEM DESIGN	GENERAL SYSTEMS DESIGN APPLICATION DESIGN SPECIFICATIONS	DEVELOPMENT
	DETAILED DESIGN	DETAILED DESIGN SPECIFICATIONS	DEVELOPMENT
	IMPLEMENTATION	TEST SPECIFICATIONS USER DOCUMENTS OPERATIONS MANUALS	QUALITY ASSURANCE USER

Figure 1-4. The software development life cycle.

know of anything riskier as a business investment than developing software; it is hard to produce on schedule, within budget, and without flaws and bugs" (*Business Week*, October 19, 1981, p. 103). The solution is to recognize there is a project when something must be done and then to organize to complete the project in the least disruptive way.

Writing specifications for software is extremely difficult. Misinterpretations frequently occur over terminology used differently by users and programmers, as well as by programmers and systems analysts. The field of software engineering is attempting to control and may someday eliminate the ambiguity and inaccuracy of software specifications.

The fact that humans are involved in projects and must be worked with is often especially troubling for technically trained project managers. Such managers expect, but do not get, completely logical or rational behavior from these people (or, for that matter, from themselves). Although many project management tools are completely rational (for instance, many of the planning and monitoring tools discussed in this book), project management in an overall sense is not an exact science.

HIGHLIGHTS *Projects are temporary, one-of-a-kind undertakings with a specific objective that are accomplished by organized application of appropriate resources.*

Four distinguishing characteristics of projects are origin, product, marketplace, and resources.

Size or complexity do not distinguish projects from other activities.

Project management is the process of achieving project objectives in any organizational framework despite countervailing pressures.

There are five steps to project management: define, plan, lead, measure, and complete.

The Triple Constraint defines a project: performance specification, time or schedule, and budget or money.

FURTHER READING

R. D. Archibald. *Managing High-Technology Programs and Projects.* New York: Wiley-Interscience, 1976.
> *Chapter 2, section 3, is a good short discussion of the distinguishing characteristics of project management.*

C. W. Burrill and L. W. Ellsworth. *Modern Project Management.* Tenafly, NJ: Burrill-Ellsworth Associates, 1981.
> *Chapter 1, pages 1–13, summarizes the concept of a data-processing project.*

H. B. Einstein. "Project Management." *The Magazine of Bank Administration* (April 1982).
> *This is a brief article on project management with a useful view of the project life cycle.*

E. Jenett. "Guidelines for Successful Project Management." *Chemical Engineering* (July 9, 1973), pp. 70–82.
> *This is a really fine article with an excellent summary definition of projects. Although it treats the construction industry specifically, this is a valuable short article for all project managers.*

H. O. Lubbes. "The Project Management Task Area." *IEEE Computer* (November 1983), pp. 56–62.
> *Although specific to Department of Defense Software procurement, this is a good discussion of the need to set clear project goals.*

R. H. Thayer, A. Pyster, and R. C. Wood. "Validating Solutions to Major Problems in Software Engineering Project Management." *IEEE Computer* (August 1982), pp. 65–77.
> *This study of software engineering managers stresses the importance of planning, organizing, and controlling to project success.*

Part 1
DEFINING SOFTWARE PROJECT GOALS

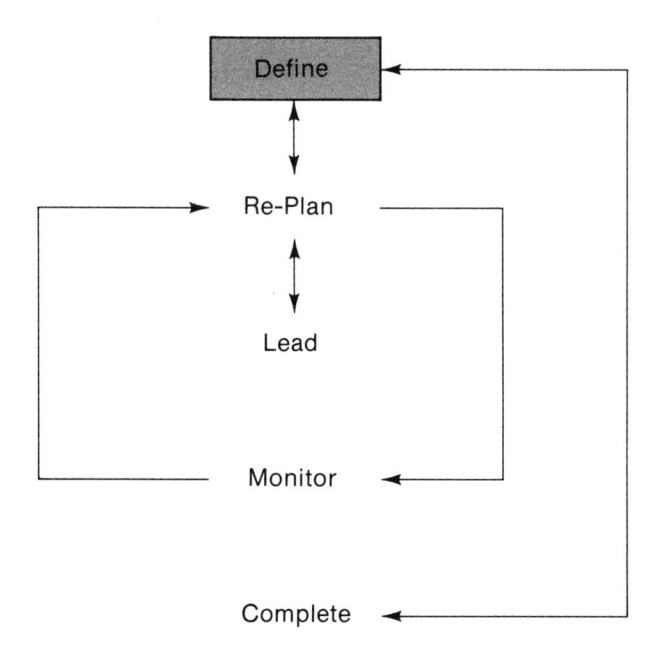

```
        Define ◄─────────────┐
          ▲                   │
          ▼                   │
    ┌─► Re-Plan ──────┐       │
    │     ▲           │       │
    │     ▼           │       │
    │    Lead         │       │
    │                 │       │
    │   Monitor ◄─────┘       │
    └─────┘                   │
                              │
        Complete ◄────────────┘
```

2

The Triple Constraint

This chapter introduces the concept of the Triple Constraint as a project definition, identifies some of the obstacles to satisfying it, and describes some steps to achieving it. The consequences of various project outcomes are considered from the point of view of satisfying the Triple Constraint.

THE NOTION OF THE TRIPLE CONSTRAINT

Figure 2-1 illustrates the Triple Constraint, a very important concept we shall emphasize throughout the book. Successful project management means accomplishing the performance specifications on or before the time schedule and within the budgeted cost. The cost is usually measured in dollars (or francs or marks) but may sometimes be measured in the number of labor hours or perhaps labor hours in each of several labor rate categories, such as senior programmer, junior programmer, and so forth, plus the expense of computer time. Unfortunately, the Triple Constraint is very difficult to satisfy because most of what occurs during the project conspires to pull the performance below specification and to delay the project, putting it behind schedule, which usually makes it exceed budget. The successful project manager is alert to these problems and satisfies the Triple Constraint.

OBSTACLES TO SATISFYING THE TRIPLE CONSTRAINT

The Triple Constraint defines projects: performance specifications, time schedule, and money (or labor hour) budget.

Projects encounter a wide variety of problems. Some of the principal ones are enumerated in the following sections, organized by the dimension of the Triple Constraint most affected. Sometimes only general symptoms are evident, rather than specific problems with a single dimension of the Triple Constraint. Although Figure 2-1 shows these three dimensions to be orthogonal axes, hence mutually exclusive, project management is not that ideal. For instance, a system may perform poorly compared to expectation in relation to the money invested, may have slow response time, may be perceived as relatively inflexible, or may lack desired features. Similarly, a late project, for example, will usually also overrun the budget. Thus, items listed as causes of time problems may also cause cost problems.

Performance Problems

There are many reasons the performance specification is difficult to achieve. We shall discuss three of them. First, there may have been poor communication between the com-

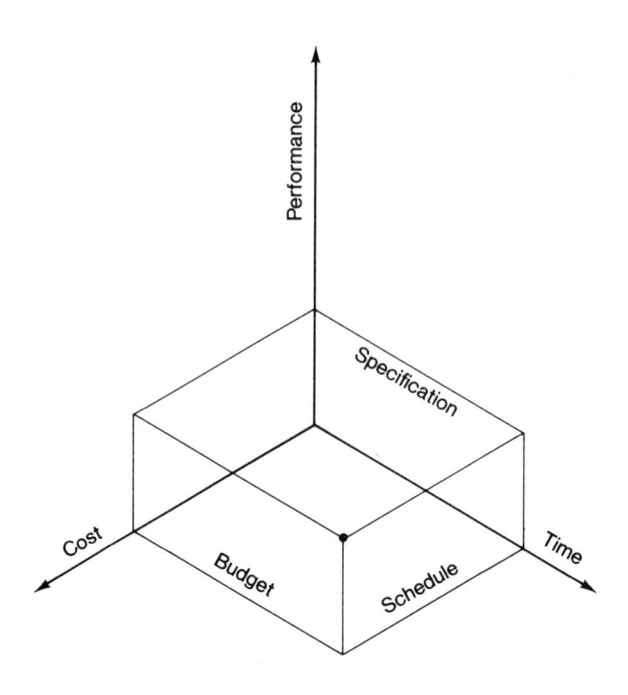

Figure 2-1. The Triple Constraint.

puter program user and the software developer. That is, they have different perceptions of the specification or the wording is ambiguous. For instance, "security" means different things to different people or in different contexts. To an older person, it may mean having enough money. A politician will think of the nation's economic or military position. An investor will think it means stocks or bonds. A person reading this book will normally use the word to mean protection of sensitive data within a computer's memory.

Clarify unclear specifications.

A second problem arises because the user's (or customer's) or the developer's (or contractor's) assumptions may have been too optimistic. Their goals may have been too ambitious, which is not uncommon.

Third, the developer or contractor may do a poor job or make mistakes in programming, thus failing to meet the contract performance. Unfortunately, workers (and managers) make errors occasionally, and these errors may cause a performance deficiency.

Software specifications, whether verbal, diagrammatical, or tabular, are an attempt to define unambiguously a software implementation that is to be written by someone else, usually for use by yet another party. It is difficult to define an as-yet unseen, unused software product to satisfy future as well as current user requirements. Ambiguity creeps in when the specification is reviewed and implemented from someone else's point of view (for example, a programmer).

A further complication with regard to the performance dimension is its multidimensionality. That is, it includes functional characteristics of the computer program, interface requirements, and quality standards.

Time Problems

Schedule problems arise for several reasons, the most insidious being an overemphasis on the performance dimension at the expense of a balanced view of the Triple Constraint. For instance, computer scientists or mathematicians, who are commonly appointed project managers, tend to concentrate on the technology and to strive for technical innovations or breakthroughs. A computer programmer may emphasize work on a clever algorithm or use a new programming language rather than simply patching an existing program. This preference for "elegant" solutions rather than practical implementation is accomplished at the expense of the schedule, and it frequently has unfavorable cost repercus-

Technical excellence usually interferes with meeting the schedule.

sions. To put this another way, "better" is the enemy of "good enough."

Even where a fascination with technology is not overwhelming, technically trained people tend to assume the performance specification is sacrosanct, whereas they consider it permissible to miss the schedule or budget objectives. Conversely, the user might be satisfied (if not ecstatic) to achieve 90 percent of the performance specifications, provided both the schedule and the budget are met. For example, on a planetary exploration project, it is vital to be ready by the "launch window," a restricted range of dates, even if one of several on-board software capabilities must be omitted. Or, if the income tax law is changed, it is absolutely necessary to reprogram the withholding schedules by the statutory date, regardless of how technically elegant the computer program is.

A second source of difficulty in meeting the schedule arises because resources are not available when required. These resources may be either equipment (such as a remote terminal or computer access) or personnel (a well-qualified programmer, for example). This absence of planned resources forces the project manager to find substitutes, which may require a subcontract to get some programming work done. Or it may mean using marginally qualified people who take longer to complete a systems analysis than the well-qualified person previously assumed to be available. Not all programmers are interchangeable; specifying the precise type of technical resource required early in the project will increase the probability of obtaining him or her—for example, a COBOL programmer analyst with two years' insurance industry experience rather than a junior programmer.

Third, a project can get into schedule difficulty because those assigned to it are not interested in their tasks. In this case, they may choose to work on other things or work halfheartedly on the project. This problem is particularly acute in projects that are well over the original schedule, thus usually forcing personnel to have been working on crash schedules for months. There is a limit to the flow of adrenalin that enables programmers to work around the clock in the hopes of finally completing the project. The manager must beware of burnout in employees who have been working the problem for too long—their productivity lags and the number of errors usually increases.

Fourth, schedule problems often occur because of personnel changes during the course of the project. New technicians or managers can cause a delay in schedule as they assimilate the terminology, task, and personalities.

Fifth, schedule problems can arise because the performance specification is raised—for instance, increased efforts that lead to additional work are accepted. A common occurrence that illustrates this is a customer asking for a few extra items in a printed report. The project manager may misperceive this as trivial because a report is already being printed. If he or she agrees to provide these items, which were not part of the original proposal, the project manager is agreeing to do additional work without changing the schedule (or cost). There is, however, additional work called for to arrange for the additional items to be printed, and it does not take many changes of this sort first to produce a one-day schedule slippage and then a one-week slippage and so on until the project is in serious schedule difficulty.

The time schedule should change if the performance specifications change.

Cost Problems

Cost problems arise for many reasons. When a project is in trouble on its time dimension, it will often be in trouble on its cost dimension as well because resources are not being used as efficiently as planned.

A second cause is the "liars contest" that often occurs during contract negotiation (if the project is done for another organization). Imagine you have bid $10,000,000 to deliver a software program to optimize the siting of shopping centers. During negotiations, you were told that, unless you lower your price to $9,500,000, the contract will be awarded to another company. In your desire to obtain the work, you and your management agree to minor wording changes, which appear to reduce the scope of work a bit and permit you to justify a substantial cost reduction. When you make this kind of price reduction without fundamental work reductions, you have built in a cost overrun at the very beginning of the project. A professional, experienced project manager will never agree to this kind of negotiation unless he or she knows the money will be restored later in contract changes. This is a potential cost problem for which the less experienced project manager must be very alert.

Beware of the liars contest.

This liars contest also happens inside an organization. In this case, the project has to be sold to upper management, and you are competing with other organization managers for authorization. Chapters 3 and 4 are primarily about doing work under contract for another organization, but they cover much that is important for managers of projects being done inside their own organizations. As we said in Chapter 1, it is smart to pretend your customer and the users are from another organization and to define the project with all the formality you would use for such an external contract. In fact, with all the internal politics in many corporations, a strong argument can be made that formality is even more important on internal projects; certainly our consulting experience has proven that to be true.

A third source of cost difficulties arises because many of the initial cost estimates are simply too optimistic. They do not reflect the inefficiencies that will occur in scheduling resources to perform the work or the fact that less-well-qualified people may be assigned to do the work.

Frequently, mistakes are made in the cost estimating. Like design mistakes, these are unfortunate, and careful scrutiny and review can minimize this occurrence.

A fifth reason for cost problems is simply an inadequate cost consciousness on the part of the project manager or a failure to have an adequate cost management system. This is never excusable.

Funding is required per plan.

Sixth, funding may not occur according to plan, and this may produce problems. Suppose your project is to run for three months and the customer originally proposes to fund you with $100,000 per month (that is, provide progress payments). The first month has gone according to plan and you have received your $100,000. At the start of the second month, your customer informs you they have only $50,000 available for that month but they will have $150,000 available the third month. You will still get $300,000, but you cannot apply the planned resources during the second month and must rush to catch up during the final month. Obviously, this would be a less efficient way to operate and means your costs will be higher than originally planned. When confronted with this sort of refunding proposal by a customer, therefore, the prudent project manager will insist on a budget increase if the performance specifications and schedule are not to be changed.

Seventh, larger budgets are generally required if a project is to be implemented in phases. The additional funding accommodates training of new personnel, who must replace those who have left the project, and inclusion of additional features temporarily required for a particular phase but not for permanent use.

CORRECTIVE STEPS

At seminars, one of us sometimes asks the following question: "Your organization wants to obtain a microcomputer system with custom software. What steps should you take to have suppliers provide such a system?" The participants, working in small groups, usually develop a list such as the following:

- Determine user requirements
- Define results you want
    Review assumptions
    Analyze cost-benefit trade-off
- Establish modularity, security, integrity, maintainability requirements
- Define milestone documents and reviews
- Identify key personnel, computer resources required
- Issue request for proposal (RFP)
    Vendor survey and evaluations
    Vendor selection
- Negotiate contract
- Monitor contract and negotiate changes
- Design system architecture
- Separate applications from systems functions
- Determine design and development methodology
- Determine change control mechanism
- Plan conversion
- Determine hardware system
- Determine programming languages to be used
- Plan installation and testing
- Plan facilities and configuration
- Recruit and train personnel for operation and maintenance
- Conduct acceptance tests
    Software and documentation
    Training
- Get post mortem feedback

Whenever you start a computer software project, under contract to another organization or for your own organization, it is crucial to ask yourself whether the initiation has been thought through this carefully. The entire thrust of such careful project structuring is to assure really clear, complete, and continuing communication between the user (whether or not the user is the customer) and the developer.

Another seminar question is: "What actions can users take to help project managers satisfy the Triple Constraint?" In this case, participants identify items such as the following:

Commit to success

Participate fully in defining requirements

Budget adequately

Provide adequate clerical and user resources

Provide knowledgeable contact

Be receptive to change

Know what is wanted

Provide user availability

Deliver test data in a timely fashion

Provide timely and complete evaluation of test results

Adhere to contract

Be flexible

Clearly set (maintain) priorities

Provide timely and complete feedback

Sell new system to rest of user community

Be patient and tolerant

Once again, you can see how important it is to work closely with the users.

The key to preventing performance problems (or at least minimizing them) is a performance specification that meets the following criteria:

1. Complete as to all functions to be performed and documentation to be furnished
2. Unambiguous as to meaning and requirements
3. Consistent with data inputs and outputs
4. Feasible, for instance, as regards speed of operation
5. Measurable (or testable)
6. Comprehensible by people responsible for measurement or tests

If the computer software is to store and process personnel data, there are laws regulating access to such files; completeness then requires that these legal requirements be clearly delineated at the time of project definition. If the user's needs are not well understood by the developer (or the user, for that matter), the specification will be poor, and frequent changes will be required.

The issue of computer software maintenance is also important. Two issues regarding maintenance concern us: maintenance of the system being developed and maintenance as a design issue. Regarding the first, experience teaches us that new software will require maintenance. The cost of this maintenance may equal the original cost or even be three times this original development cost. There are two keys to coping with this reality. First, do not ignore maintenance. Use judgment to decide what it may cost and factor this cost into any cost-benefit analysis that is performed to justify a computer software project's initiation. Second, make each maintenance task into a separate project to be initiated later, when justified on its own merits. This approach avoids open-ended (thus endless, and hence overrun) projects. Strive for a complete, clear, and specific end point.

Second, maintainability is an important design consideration that affects performance, cost, and schedule. Computer software can be designed for ease in subsequent maintenance or for speed of development. That trade-off usually means versatility for greater cost against inflexibility implemented more quickly. For example, a request for a one-time report need not be written so that it can be reused for many subsequent reports in different order, printing some additional information or selecting different items to print. An accounting system for the stock brokerage industry certainly should be designed, however, so that changes in margin requirements can be easily implemented as they are mandated by the Federal Reserve. The requirement for versatility must be established with the user to enable efficient use of programming and design resources within budget.

Sometimes when you start a project, you and the user agree that it is impossible to define all the specifications completely. Whenever this happens, it is crucial to agree specifically and in detail on what will be done by a given date. For instance, you may be undertaking a meteorology software project requiring high speed computing for which the use of parallel processing architecture is planned. There are many unknowns in such a project. Therefore, you may agree to work for one year to establish the complete, final specifications for the software. The second phase work can be the rest of the project, which is now aimed at specific, achievable goals. As mentioned earlier, however, be sure to increase your budget to accommodate this phased implementation.

When you can't set all project specifications, employ phased implementation.

PROJECT OUTCOMES

A project may end anywhere in the three-dimensional space illustrated by the Triple Constraint. Whether a deviation from the Triple Constraint point is acceptable depends on the project. For example, a project might be late. If the project is to collect data on a space shuttle launch, then lateness would be an intolerable outcome, regardless of the software cost. As suggested earlier, schedule compliance is the overriding concern for statutorily required projects as well.

In other situations, the budget may be the most important issue. When a contractor accepts a fixed price contract to deliver working software, he or she will lose money if the budget is overrun. Conversely, on a cost reimbursable contract, the customer must pay for the overrun. In either situation, ability to pay is crucial.

Project specifics determine the relative importance of each dimension of the Triple Constraint.

Third, there are situations in which the performance specification may not be missed. Once again, the project specifics will determine whether this is crucial. When savings and loan institutions were allowed to provide interest-bearing checking accounts, the supporting computer processing systems had to be tested out and ready by the date the customers started opening these new accounts. In other cases, for instance, where there are required legal safeguards on access to computer-based personnel data, the law must be complied with.

TYPICAL PROBLEMS

> The project initiator's emphasis is almost always unclear initially, and project personnel tend to assume their own biases in ranking the relative importance of each dimension. This can easily lead to a disastrous outcome, which can be avoided by adequate discussions between the user and the manager at the project's inception.
>
> The other major problem, mentioned earlier, is the myopic attention to the performance dimension by technical personnel. It can be overcome, or at least reduced, if the project manager clearly conveys the user's emphasis and its rationale.

HIGHLIGHTS

The Triple Constraint defines all projects.

The Triple Constraint consists of performance specifications, a time schedule, and a money or labor hour budget.

Obstacles that prevent satisfying the Triple Constraint are not mutually exclusive.

Project specifics determine the relative importance of each dimension of the Triple Constraint.

Adequate and clear discussions among the customer, the project manager, and the technical personnel can help avoid many common problems.

FURTHER READING

R. D. Archibald. *Managing High-Technology Programs and Projects.* New York: Wiley-Interscience, 1976.
   Chapter 1, section 5, has a brief discussion of some causes of poor project outcomes.

V. G. Hajek. *Management of Engineering Projects.* New York: McGraw-Hill, 1977.
   Chapter 1, section 1, has a short discussion of some disciplines and functions needed to be successful with projects.

H. Kerzner. *Project Management: A Systems Approach to Planning, Scheduling and Controlling.* New York: Van Nostrand Reinhold, 1979.
   Chapter 1, section 1, enumerates the social and environmental issues impacting project success.

H. Klein. "Future of Struggling Anacomp May Hinge on Sales of Long-Delayed Bank Software." *Wall Street Journal* (January 4, 1984), p. 25.
   This short article illustrates the importance of timely completion of software.

T. Manuel. "Parallel Processing." *Electronics* (June 16, 1983), pp. 105–106.
   This short article introduces some of the issues in parallel processing architecture.

M. L. Markus. "Power, Politics, and MIS Implementation." *Communications of the ACM* (June 1983), pp. 430–444.

This is an excellent presentation of theories explaining people's resistance to management information systems and hints on monitoring that resistance.

P. W. Metzger. *Managing a Programming Project,* 2nd ed., Englewood Cliffs, NJ: Prentice-Hall, 1981.

Chapter 2, pages 16–49, provides a good discussion of many specific issues to be considered in the definition phase of a software project.

3

Acquiring Successful Software Projects

Proposals bridge the defining and planning phases of projects. This chapter examines the strategic issues that govern writing successful proposals. Although we focus on proposals written for external organizations, all the same principles apply to proposing to undertake projects within your own organization. Project proposals constitute the definition embodied in the contract or work authorization. A good proposal includes a thorough plan for work performance that embodies the Triple Constraint. This chapter also discusses the proposal process in detail.

STRATEGIC ISSUES

Framework

Figure 3-1 illustrates the strategic framework for obtaining winning projects. It does not matter whether the projects originate outside the organization by a customer or within the organization. However, many organizations dissipate their energies in preparing losing proposals, which

1. Cannot win against the competition
2. Will have an unfavorable outcome with regard to the Triple Constraint
3. Can be successful but are insignificant or irrelevant to the proposing organization

Concentrate on meaningful prospective winners.

Therefore, the basis of a successful strategy is to filter out losing projects. These include projects inconsistent with the organization's long-term goals or with the current and near-term resources within or otherwise available to the organization. Such filters might reject consumer project efforts in an industrial product company. Similarly, the filters could reject a fixed price contract for a technical development in a conservative company that will not normally undertake a fixed price contract for something not previously accomplished. And this same screening should reject development of a batched MIS system when the company has announced on-line capabilities to be provided within two years to assist its nationwide expansion program.

Filtering out the huge number of possible projects the organization might have addressed leaves a much smaller number of projects that are appropriate for the organization to consider. It can then address some or perhaps all of these in proposal efforts to which it applies adequate and appropriate resources. The result of this process is that an organization submits only very well founded proposals for consideration. This result is most likely to be achieved if the organization has a careful review process, often called the "bid/no bid" decision.

In summary, avoid projects that are inconsistent with your organization's long-term goals or current and near-term resources, unlikely to win the proposal competition, unlikely to satisfy the intended Triple Constraint, or insignificant or irrelevant.

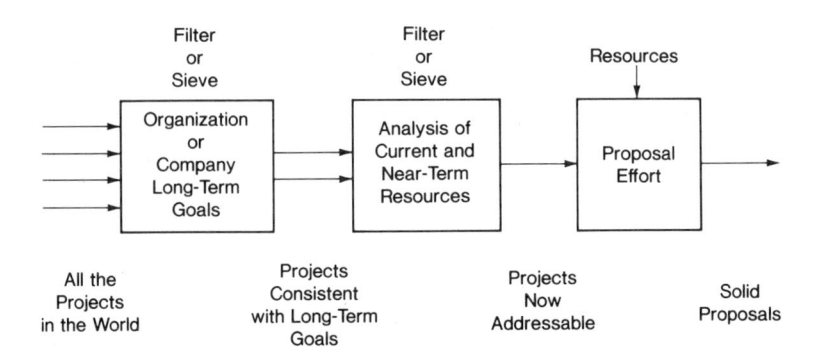

Figure 3-1. Strategy to obtain winning projects.

Bid/No Bid Decisions

The decision to bid on a proposal opportunity, whether to an external organization or within the organization itself, must be taken within the context of the organization's strategic framework. This framework is of course specific to the organization at that particular time. The company that rejects consumer product projects today may have the interest and capability to undertake these projects five years from now. There are many issues involved in this decision, four of which we discuss.

Clear criteria are vital.

The Requirement

The first issue is whether there is a real requirement. If a requirement exists, it is important to decide whether the funds are really available. It is possible that there is a real requirement but no funds. An automated employee applicant system, allowing retrieval of resumes received, might be enormously valuable for the personnel department. However, the company is not likely to expend its funds on such a system if it still needs to automate its billing procedures. Contractors occasionally seek subcontractor proposals for "window dressing" to satisfy someone or otherwise justify an alternative approach they propose to take. Clearly, it is not worth responding to such requests for a proposal because the effort will not result in a winning project.

It is also important to examine the priority or importance of the proposed project. In this connection, the relationship of a particular proposal opportunity to present and future programs is also an important issue. Many small "paper study" projects, not attractive per se, actually are very attractive because they can lead in the future to large production programs. Some software projects can be sold effectively, causing delays in more expensive work, if they provide learning opportunities and require no additional capital outlays.

Project Value

The project's social, ecological, and energy impacts might be highly significant to an organization in deciding whether or not to bid on a project. Presumably, a project to build special hardware and software for handicapped children would have high social impact. Similarly, a project that offers the opportunity to apply important new technology or otherwise enhance the organization's reputation might have high nonmonetary value. Control Data Corporation's decision to build plants in the inner Twin Cities to help provide jobs for the metropolitan disadvantaged was such an effort. In general, projects may be significant because they offer education and training, partial achievements of a larger goal, or experience with new approaches. The expected sales of a commercial new product project effort and the profits of such an effort would also be significant issues.

Finally, many projects are merely a hidden obligation for an organization to accept future financial commitments for new capital or facility investments. This must be discovered before any money is spent so as to be certain that future major financial commitments are within the organization's resources and ability as well as being consistent with the project's prospective value. Many defense contractors have learned how tight their belts must be when a large development contract ends and there are computer systems and programmers without work.

Response Ability

The organization must have the ability.

The central issue here, also illustrated in Figure 3-1, is the organization's present capability first to prepare a winning proposal and second to perform the proposed work. If some capabilities are not actually present, there must be a viable plan to make them available when they are needed.

Winning the Competition

First an organization must ask whether there was advance information about the project available to it. This is particularly true about efforts arising from a customer organization and being presented to a contracting company as a request for a proposal (RFP), but it is also relevant for efforts within an organization. Lack of advance information often indicates that someone else has a head start or the request was hastily created and lacks substance.

A second issue concerns the customer. Is it an individual (yourself, a friend, or someone else) or a commercial organization? If the latter, is it your organization or an external organization? If it is your own company, has your superior ordered you to carry out the project or must your project proposal compete with other project proposals management is considering for funding? If the customer is a governmental organization, a city, county, state, or federal (domestic or foreign) entity, there will probably be detailed specifications, formal quality standards, perhaps the necessity for surety bonds, and very often rigid and formalized inspection procedures; there may also be geographic location requirements on the bidder. Who are the key personnel within the customer organization? Are they known to your organization? What history do you have with them or with their organization? Is your organization's reputation with the prospective customer favorable?

Your organization must have enough money to write the proposal and to sustain the postproposal selling and negotiating efforts. Therefore, you must know whether money to invest in this kind of activity is available. You must expect the project to earn more money than the proposal costs because you will not win every job on which you propose.

There are situations in which you will be the sole source recipient of an RFP, for instance, when your boss tells you to carry out a project within your organization. There is thus no competition, but how you perform the job is still important. It may be better to decline an effort when it is offered sole source if you are convinced the performance you can provide will be at best marginal or if required resources will be inadequate.

All competition has to be analyzed. Some relevant issues are the competition's technical and managerial competence, its ability to produce the requested project output, an estimate of its interest in the particular type of project, its need (or degree of "hunger"), and its prior relationship with the customer or organization.

Although you will not win every proposal, you must be willing and able to satisfy any commitments you propose to undertake.

The decision tree approach described in Chapter 18 is particularly helpful in assessing the worthiness of bidding on a particular task or set of tasks.

In summary, avoid projects or proposals for projects that are inconsistent with your organization's long-term goals or its current and near-term resources, are unlikely to win the proposal competition or satisfy the intended Triple Constraint, or are insignificant.

THE PROPOSAL PROCESS

Informal requests or the more formal RFP may trigger the proposal process. If you have informal requests as your starting point, you should spend some time in the conceptual phase (see Figure 1-4), in which the ground rules and objectives of the effort under consideration by the user can be addressed. In fact, the earlier you are called in to make a

Understand the proposal process.

proposal, the more conceptual work you must do to establish the users' requirements.

If receipt of an RFP initiates a proposal effort, then some requirements analysis has already been done, although it might be conflicting, ambiguous, or inaccurate. Most proposals must respond specifically to the requirements as stated in the RFP; however, successful bids often point out areas where requirements can best be met in other ways. In general, where design solutions are included in the RFP, go back to the customer and make sure that your company really has a chance to be considered. We have seen cases where the RFP consisted merely of hardware and software specifications copied from a vendor, who, not surprisingly, was awarded the contract because his was the only system that could satisfy the RFP!

The proposal process entails more than writing the proposal (see Figure 3-2). That's the meat of the proposal sandwich. It also requires preparation work and postsubmission work. The goal of the preproposal work is to learn about the customer's problem and bias, which allows you to set a proposal theme. The proposal theme provides a focus to direct everyone contributing to the proposal, which increases odds of producing a coherent, winning proposal. Thus, the overall proposal process includes the following:

The Proposal Sandwich

The Finish
Post Submission Efforts

The Meat
The Proposal Document

The Foundation
Pre-Proposal Work

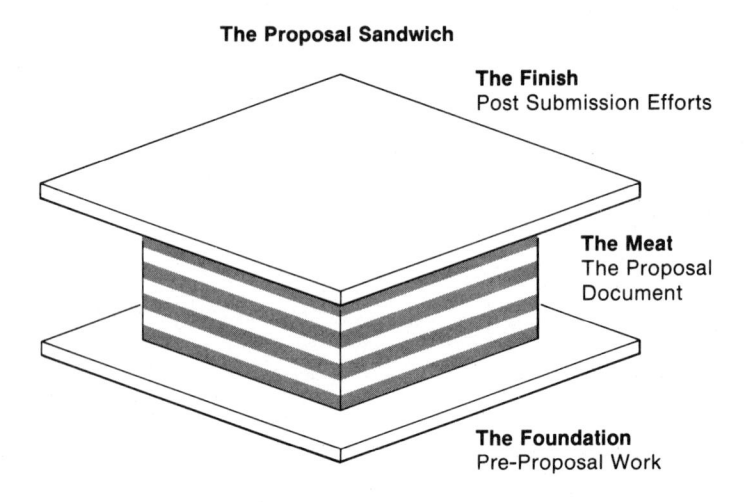

Figure 3-2. The proposal sandwich.
Source: "Project Management." Lecture notes by Milton D. Rosenau, Jr. Copyright © 1981 by the Association for Media-based Continuing Education for Engineers, Inc. (AMCEE). Reprinted by permission.

1. Authorization (which formally considers the issues previously discussed)
2. Selection of a dominant theme
3. Preparation of the statement of work
4. Development of a plan to satisfy the Triple Constraint (an effort for which checklists may be helpful)
5. Adjustment to remove inconsistencies and inadequacies
6. Approval
7. Submission
8. Postsubmission follow-up, including presentations and contract negotiations

Authorization

The proposal process often starts before an RFP, in which case the effort is frequently called the preproposal effort. Regardless of when the proposal process is initiated, this activity must be authorized. A form such as that in Figure 3-3 can be used for this purpose. In preparing a proposal, an organization is going to commit a certain amount of effort and money to it. This investment should be made only when it seems the opportunity then available has a good chance of paying off and only if it is consistent with the organization's goals.

Another point to consider at the time of proposal authorization is the individual who will manage it. Ideally, the proposal manager should be the intended project manager.

A proposal itself can be considered a project with a Triple Constraint, in which case the performance objective is submission of a winning proposal and price, in accordance with the required submission schedule, for a cost acceptable in view of the probable (financial) return to your organization.

Consider, then begin.

Theme Fixation

Except in those very formal RFPs in which contact with the prospective customer is either prohibited or heavily constrained (for instance, some government RFPs), it is vital to spend time with your customer (or software user) fixing the theme and central focus of your proposal effort. This includes clarifying which dimension(s) of the Triple Constraint should be emphasized.

34 Acquiring Successful Software Projects

PROPOSAL AUTHORIZATION	NUMBER	REVISION

TITLE

JOB
- PERFORMANCE REQUIRED
- ESTIMATED STARTING DATE | ESTIMATED DURATION
- ESTIMATED BID PRICE $ | ESTIMATED SUBCONTRACT TO OTHERS %
- IS JOB FUNDED? | WHAT IS FOLLOW-ON POTENTIAL?
- ESTIMATED NEED FOR CAPITAL AND FACILITY EXPENSE IF JOB IS OBTAINED
- CUSTOMER ORGANIZATION
- KEY CUSTOMER PERSONNEL
- CONTRACT FORM | SPECIAL CONSIDERATIONS | SECURITY CLASS

COMPETITION
- COMPETITORS
- COMPETITORS' STRENGTHS
- SIGNIFICANCE TO COMPETITORS IF THEY LOSE
- OTHER COMPETITOR WORK FOR CUSTOMER
- OUR UNIQUE ADVANTAGES

PROPOSAL
- WHAT IS TO BE SUBMITTED?
- DUE DATE | PROPOSAL COST (DETAIL BELOW)
- PROPOSAL MANAGER | OTHER KEY PROPOSAL PERSONNEL

ACTIVITY / EFFORT	PROJECT DEPT. (HOURS)	SUPPORT GROUP A (HOURS)	SUPPORT GROUP B (HOURS)	SUPPORT GROUP C (HOURS)	NONLABOR (DOLLARS)
PREPROPOSAL					
BIDDERS' CONFERENCE					
PROPOSAL PREPARATION					
CUSTOMER PRESENTATION					
CONTRACT NEGOTIATION					
OTHER					
TOTAL HOURS					
TOTAL COST					

FUNDING NEEDED	JAN	FEB	MAR	APR	MAY	JUN	JUL	AUG	SEP	OCT	NOV	DEC
MONTHLY												
CUMULATIVE												

APPROVALS
GROUP A	DATE	MARKETING MANAGER	DATE	VICE-PRESIDENT—FIN.	DATE
GROUP B	DATE	DIVISION CONTROLLER	DATE	EXEC. VICE-PRESIDENT	DATE
GROUP C	DATE	DIVISION MANAGER	DATE	PRESIDENT	DATE
PROPOSAL MANAGER	DATE	VICE-PRESIDENT—OPERAT.	DATE	CHAIRPERSON OF BOARD	DATE

Figure 3-3. Typical proposal authorization form.

There are several reasons theme fixation is important. In the first place, many customers are in fact organizations and the "customer" is comprised of people who view the contemplated undertaking in slightly different ways. It is necessary to understand these subtle differences and either harmonize them or deduce who has the most influence. This is especially true of complex software programs, where there may be many users and many levels of users (for example, managers and clerks), each with his or her own requirements for the system.

In addition, the customer's statement of the problem in the RFP may be imperfect or incomplete. Working with the customer can correct this problem as well as demonstrate your organization's competence. In the course of this dialogue with your customer, you will have opportunities to launch trial balloons representing your initial approach to the proposal. You will learn your customer's preference, which will permit you to adjust your thinking to produce a proposal that is more responsive to your customer's prejudices and predilections.

It is also important that everybody in your organization understand the chosen theme so their contributions are consistent with it. This theme will be used throughout your written proposal. It might be technical sophistication and elegance, early delivery, the fact that the unit you propose to furnish is a proven item, or that you have a team ready to put to work on the job. If everyone in your organization understands what the theme is, your proposal should be acceptable to your prospective customer.

Statement of Work

Content

The statement of work (SOW) must describe the job to be done. It should designate any specifications that will be applied. It should identify measurable, tangible, and verifiable acceptance criteria so there is no uncertainty whether the final item is in fact acceptable.

As we said in Chapter 2, when it is not possible to be this precise at the earliest phase of a job, because the final product is not assuredly realistic or clearly attainable, it is important to undertake a two-phase project effort. The first phase, perhaps extending to a customer review, is quoted completely,

Project goals must be specific, measurable, and attainable.

then the whole job is quoted only approximately, in a nonbinding fashion. The whole job quote represents the proposer's best estimate of project requirements. The first-phase quotation, however, is firm and includes sufficient effort to construct acceptance criteria for the rest of the job. However, beware of customers who will use your quotation as an RFP for bids by other companies or who decide to—and can—do the task themselves because you have provided such a complete roadmap for the task at hand!

Clarification

After it is drafted, the SOW should be reviewed with the customer prior to further work on the proposal itself. Ambiguous words should be avoided and it is desirable to be quantitative, using numbers and dimensions whenever possible.

Make the SOW precise and measurable.

A SOW such as "provide an operating system" can be ambiguous. The contractor might interpret it as being satisfied by providing a single-user operating system when the customer expected a multiuser operating system. A common SOW ambiguity is "fast response time." In a batched environment, thirty seconds may seem instantaneous, but in an on-line environment, more than a two-second response time seriously degrades user performance.

Software can often be designed in different ways at vastly different costs. If the SOW is predicated upon a particular architecture, be sure to specify that choice to avoid confusion and subsequent misunderstandings.

Plan

A proposal is a bridging step in the overall project process, being involved in both the "define" and "plan" phases of a project. The proposal will contain a plan; additionally, the act of writing the proposal forces the organization to think through and attempt to simulate the entire project. The project plan is as much a part of the proposal as the SOW. It should include either an absolute or relative schedule, itemized reviews, and specified deliverable documents.

Simulation

Simulation is used in many situations. Servomechanism engineers, for instance, will simulate on paper, and perhaps further using a digital or analog computer, the performance of a servomechanism before attempting to build even the breadboard. In doing this simulation, they are investigating how the servomechanism might perform if it is built according to certain specifications.

Computer systems engineers will simulate, through performance analysis, queue lengths and traffic patterns on large distributed data-processing networks so that they can better estimate the hardware configurations they will require to adequately service the network under consideration. Trade-offs are made between the value of prompt service to users under extremely heavy loads and the costs of the additional hardware required to accomplish that speed. A major purpose of these simulations is to identify any potential problem areas in the prospective system before building it. If a design won't work on paper, it won't work when it's built.

In the case of project planning, where the project plans are a simulation of how the project will be carried out, there are similar reasons for engaging in simulation. It is important to decide how to establish a price for the proposed work. A detailed simulation, that is, a plan, makes it more likely that the price will be sufficient. If the plan has been thoroughly prepared, it will also convince the customer that your organization understands the proposed job, which helps in negotiating your contract. If the project schedule is unrealistic on paper, the project won't be completed on time.

Simulation aids prediction.

The Triple Constraint

Because the Triple Constraint is so important to planning and planning is so important to the proposal process, Part 2 is devoted to planning. But it is important to understand that the project plan devised during the proposal process and presented in the proposal is a plan to satisfy the Triple Constraint. You use the work breakdown structure (WBS) to describe your approach to the performance dimension. The WBS specifies all work activities required to be performed to complete a job as short tasks with quantifiable inputs, outputs, schedules, and assigned responsibilities. You use network diagrams or in some cases a bar chart, in which each activity corresponds to a WBS element, to describe your approach to the time dimension. You use a complete cost breakdown for each activity to describe your approach to the money dimension and defend your price.

These three planning elements are prepared in the order presented. First, the WBS is used to describe those things that will be undertaken to satisfy the performance specification. After that is complete, it is possible to prepare a network diagram for each of these designated elements in the WBS. Initially, each of these items should be estimated in a "natu-

The plan has three dimensions.

ral" time frame; then these activities' logical relationships to each other can be established. If, as usually happens, this produces an unacceptably long program, it is then important to decide which activities will be scheduled to be completed in periods shorter that the "natural" time. That is, some of the project activities must be carried out faster than is desirable. After this has been done, prepare cost estimates for each activity. Note that it is not desirable to prepare the cost estimates prior to determining the time to be allowed for a given activity. These issues will be treated in more detail in later chapters.

Checklists

Checklists are designed to help assure that nothing that will have to be dealt with during the course of the job has been forgotten or omitted from consideration in the proposal. A checklist should contain items such as the following:

- Applications requirements
- Systems requirements
- System inputs
- System outputs
- Detailed architectural design
- Design specifications
- Review procedures
- Hardware requirements
- Personnel capabilities
- Milestone reviews
- Milestone documents
- Product specifications
- Project plan
- Operator instructions
- User instructions
- Technical interface manuals
- Hardware reference manuals
- Release information
- Systems reference manual
- Functional specifications
- Security plan
- System test and acceptance specifications
- Feasibility studies
- File and data requirements
- Cost/benefit analysis
- System design
- Program design
- System conversion plan
- Shipment and delivery
- Turnover to operations
- Postimplementation reviews
- Supplies
- Training aids
- Library
- Project index
- Change control system
- Data base administration

This checklist is not exhaustive and may not contain the most significant or most important items for your project. It is meant to suggest the kind of items that might appear in a checklist.

The best way to develop a checklist is to create your own over a period of years. One way is simply to enter items on file cards whenever they occur to you during the course of project work. You may later sort out these cards alphabetically, by time phase, or by some other logical method. Having developed a checklist from your own experience, you will perform better on future projects because you will not forget items likely to be significant. Thus, you will consider their impact on a project during the proposal phase. They will not emerge as unexpected developments during performance of the project.

Take advantage of experience.

Adjustments

Adjustments are often required after a proposal has been partially prepared. Perhaps someone discovers that two departments contributing to the proposal have duplicated their efforts or have made differing assumptions about some significant item. Or perhaps someone discovers new information or corrects some oversight.

When an adjustment is required, all participants must join in deciding how to make it. The proposal manager should not assume this responsibility. Two benefits accrue from participants making the adjustment. First, the experts are considering the problem and presumably making the most sensible adjustment. Second, having contributed to the adjustment, other participants gain a sense of involvement in the decision and tend to perform the job better when the proposal has been converted into a project undertaking.

Approval

As with the initiation of the proposal effort, the conclusion of the proposal requires managerial action within an organization. There will typically be a sign-off control sheet (Figure 3-4). Normally, each organization has a procedure that specifies the signature authority of given managerial levels, and such a procedure indicates which managers or officers must sign the control sheet signifying their approval for proposal submission. The sign-off control sheet must contain a brief description of the Triple Constraint contained in the

PROPOSAL SUBMISSION APPROVAL	COMPANY PRIVATE
PROPOSAL TITLE	NUMBER
CUSTOMER	CONTRACT FORM

SUMMARY STATEMENT OF WORK

SCHEDULE FOR JOB		
COST	FEE	TOTAL BID PRICE

DOCUMENTS, REPORTS, MODELS, ETC., SUBMITTED
SUMMARY OF OUR RISKS
KEY PEOPLE PROMISED
FINANCIAL COMMIITMENTS REQUIRED
WARRANTY
ACCEPTANCE CRITERIA
REMARKS

MARKETING MANAGER	DATE	VICE-PRESIDENT—FIN.	DATE
DIVISION CONTROLLER	DATE	EXEC. VICE-PRESIDENT	DATE
DIVISION MANAGER	DATE	PRESIDENT	DATE
VICE-PRESIDENT—OPERAT.	DATE	CHAIRPERSON	DATE

Figure 3-4. Typical proposal submission approval form.

proposal document being submitted. The sign-off control sheet is retained in the proposing organization's files and is not submitted to the customer.

It is important not to take the approval of senior managers for granted. Therefore, it is important to give these people timely briefings throughout the proposal preparation effort as to the scope of the proposal, the risks and benefits of the project, and the nature of the resources to be committed to the resulting project. Although the proposal authorization document constitutes one such involvement of senior management, it alone will not suffice. The number and frequency of such briefings during proposal preparation depend on the organization, its rules and procedures, and the proposal manager's good judgment. As a general rule, senior management support is as crucial to proposal success as it is to project success.

Plan ahead for the proposal approval.

Submission

The time comes to submit the proposal to the designated recipient, who may require it bear a postmark by a certain date or be received at a given office and date stamped by a particular time. Such standards are overriding and must be complied with.

Postsubmission

Mailing or delivering the proposal is not the end of a winning proposal effort. At the very least, the winning organization must negotiate a contract with the customer. Sometimes several proposing organizations are deemed qualified and negotiations are carried out with two or more of them prior to selecting the winning contractor.

In many proposal situations, the negotiation phase is preceded by a presentation to the customer. Such a presentation may be elaborate, requiring special graphics and models, and may entail extensive time and effort.

More work follows submission.

To recapitulate, the following are steps in the proposal process: Establish your organization's business strategy; understand your resources; get the authorization (bid/no bid); make the preproposal effort; receive the RFP; attend the bidder's conference; fix the theme; prepare the statement of work; plan the job; adjust the proposal; approve the proposal; submit the proposal; present the proposal to the customer; and negotiate the contract. The proposal contains a statement of work, which is the basic project definition. To prepare the proposal, it is necessary to do some, but not all, of the project planning. Much of this planning is commonly included in the proposal.

TYPICAL PROBLEMS

> The first problem encountered in proposing winning projects is attempting to do virtually the entire job during the proposal. That is, in trying to prepare a solid proposal, you spend too much time working through the plan for the project. You can overcome this by recognizing that risk must be balanced and plan only enough to reduce the project's uncertainty to an acceptable level. A related problem is inadequate project planning in the proposal. The solution here is to keep planning until it becomes too time-consuming. This is obviously a judgmental issue for which personal experience must provide guidance.
>
> Another problem is the last-minute rush to complete the proposal in time to submit it. The solution to this problem is to have a schedule and adhere to it. Visible multiple authorship in a proposal, usually because of failure to allow editing time, is a problem you can readily avoid.
>
> Third, be sure to solicit support from the customer's top management. Normally this will be done as part of the preproposal process to ensure that your effort in preparing the proposal will not be wasted. There is nothing more frustrating than to prepare a proposal only to have no contract awarded at all, when senior management decides to table the development effort.
>
> Most RFPs are specific. However, some requirements as stated in the RFP are flexible because the client is unwilling to pay your cost for the features requested. Wherever possible the proposal should indicate alternatives available to the client that would be more cost-effective. For example, the client may have requested a custom-coded accounting system, but you may know of a commercially available package with the desired features for significantly less money.
>
> *continued*

> Fifth, beware of treating internal assignments casually. These projects often have highly political implications. Failure to establish unambiguous requirements and cost/benefit analyses on the promise of "this is just what we've needed" has left more than one data-processing manager defending the commitment of resources to a pet project that has no organizational support. If you can't get a separate budget to accomplish a task or more than a single user-manager's support, you might want to reevaluate the worth of the project and your stake in it.

HIGHLIGHTS

Organizations must filter out losing projects.

Winning projects arise from good proposals, thoughtfully initiated to be consistent with the organization's goals.

Four issues involved in the decision to bid on a proposal opportunity are the nature of the requirement, the value of the project to the bidder, the bidder's response ability, and its ability to win.

The proposal defines what the project will accomplish.

A checklist may be helpful to avoid overlooking required work.

The proposal process includes authorization, theme selection, SOW preparation, plan development, adjustment, approval, submission, and postsubmission follow-up.

Internal projects should be treated with the same rigor as external projects.

Project proposals describe the Triple Constraint with a work breakdown structure, activity network diagram or bar chart, and cost estimate for each activity, which then serve as a project plan.

FURTHER READING

C. W. Burrill and L. W. Ellsworth. *Modern Project Management.* Tenafly, NJ: Burrill-Ellsworth Associates, 1981.
> Chapters 9–11, pages 199–239, discuss project selection, cost/benefit analysis, and risk analysis for software projects.

M. D. J. Buss. "How to Rank Computer Projects." *Harvard Business Review* (January–February 1983), pp. 118–125.
   This is a succinct discussion of initiating internally sponsored projects that will have broad support.

V. G. Hajek. *Management of Engineering Projects.* New York: McGraw-Hill, 1977.
   Chapter 4 contains a good description of the content of a proposal for an aerospace system project.

H. Kerzner. *Project Management: A Systems Approach to Planning, Scheduling and Controlling.* New York: Van Nostrand Reinhold, 1979.
   This shows a typical proposal preparation and submission schedule on page 375 but has very little discussion.

F. W. McFarlan, J. L. McKenney, and P. Pyburn. "The Information Archipelago—Plotting a Course." *Harvard Business Review* (January–February 1983), pp. 145–156; F. W. McFarlan and J. L. McKinney. "The Information Archipelago—Governing the New World." *Harvard Business Review* (July–August 1983), pp. 91–99; J. L. McKenney and F. W. McFarlan. "The Information Archipelago—Maps and Bridges." *Harvard Business Review* (September–October 1982), pp. 109–119.
   These three articles deal with various aspects of integrating computer systems and related equipment into organizations so as to minimize risks and maximize benefits.

P. W. Metzger. *Managing a Programming Project,* 2nd ed. Englewood Cliffs, NJ: Prentice-Hall, 1981.
   Pages 174–176 enumerate ten points about proposals.

4

Negotiations and Contracts

Negotiations between the customer and the contractor convert the final definition of work into a contract. This chapter emphasizes the importance of appropriate contract forms and the necessity to start the proposal process with attention to this issue. It also discusses the special case of projects involving a foreign customer.

NEGOTIATING THE CONTRACT

Preproposal Negotiations

Contract negotiation really begins in the proposal phase because the expected contract form must be consistent with the job to be undertaken. If there is any reason to believe the customer will require a fixed price contract (Table 4-1), for instance, and the job calls for a major technological advance you are not certain you can achieve, it would not be prudent to continue in the preproposal and proposal effort. Hence, one objective of preproposal activity and discussions with a customer prior to major proposal expense is to assure that the contract form they intend to issue is consistent with the contract your company or organization is willing to negotiate considering the work to be undertaken. In addition, negotiations are designed further to improve the likelihood of the customer organization and contracting organization having the same perception of the job.

Make a proposal only if the contract will be acceptable.

Customer and Contractor Perceptions

The perceptions of both contracting parties must be harmonious. It is always possible that an RFP or the responding proposal will not be completely clear. If the preproposal process did not remove these potential misperceptions, the negotiation process offers the last opportunity to do so. Specifically, the final deliverables, software and/or hardware, must be well defined, and the criteria for measuring or judging acceptance and completion must be straightforward.

Contractual Forms

At the simplest level, there are no contracts. This is typical of self-financed efforts such as a project to paint your own house. This situation also prevails in efforts supported by your own organization, such as development of MIS software within a company.

When one organization enters into a contract with another organization, there is a variety of possible contractual forms (see Table 4-1). In the first of these, very common in commercial situations, the contract is a so-called fixed price (FP) or firm fixed price (FFP) contract. This has the lowest financial risk to the customer because the maximum financial obligation is specified; conversely, the FP form has the highest

TABLE 4-1. Common contractual forms.

Abbreviation	Definition
FFP	Firm fixed price—the price and fee are predetermined and do not depend on cost
FP	Fixed price—same as FFP
CPFF	Cost plus fixed fee—the customer agrees to reimburse the contractor's actual costs, regardless of amount, and pay a negotiated fixed fee independent of the actual costs
CPIF	Cost plus incentive fee—similar to CPFF except the fee is not preset or fixed but rather depends on some specified incentive
T AND M	Time and material—the customer agrees to pay the contractor for all time and material used on the project, including a fee as a percentage of all project costs

financial risk for the contracting organization but offers the highest potential reward if the estimated costs can be underrun. There are variations on this in which the price allows for escalation or redetermination due to some set of factors, such as inflation. Or there may be an FP contract with an incentive fee based on some performance aspect, perhaps early delivery.

An FP contract is preferable when there is virtually no uncertainty about your ability to satisfy the performance specification on schedule and for, at most, your estimated costs. Such situations typically occur when you have done essentially the identical or very similar project work previously and you have the appropriate human and physical resources available.

Another class of contractual arrangements is those in some way cost reimbursable. Here the customer bears an obligation to reimburse the contractor for all costs incurred; so the customer has a high financial risk and the contractor has a correspondingly low risk. Typical contracts of this sort are cost plus a fixed fee (CPFF) or cost plus an incentive fee (CPIF). Time and material (T and M) contracts are also a form of cost reimbursable contract.

Contracts entered into with the U.S. Department of Defense are governed by complex regulations, the Defense Acquisition Regulations (DAR). In the case of FP contracts, the government is never obligated to pay more than the specified amount. However, if the contractor performs very well and manages to underrun the cost budget substantially, the government has the right to reduce the amount paid to the contractor below the price specified in the contract. Thus, FP contracts are a one-way street to the government's advantage.

The contract form puts risk on either the customer or the contractor.

In software development, especially with microcomputers, some other contractual variations are now occurring more frequently. For instance, some people are negotiating for a "piece of the action," hoping others will buy the developed software. Thus, a contract may include provision for royalties on future sale of the software.

Selecting the Best Contract Form

Certain contract forms work better—to the advantage of both contractor and customer—than others in given situations. Whenever possible, you should try to arrange a contract that will have the best chances of suiting both parties in the long run. If, for example, you are stuck on a fixed price contract and suffering from cost overruns that the contractor bears, you'll probably be working with a demotivated group, which will exacerbate your problems.

Generally, FP contracts work well in situations where there is very little new work being done; the costs can be estimated precisely, based on prior performance, such as installation of a prepackaged general ledger system. CPFF is appropriate where the exact resources and costs cannot be clearly estimated and both parties are willing to share the risk. This would be true of a real-time interactive distributed network based upon special-function terminals that have never been used before. CPIF would suit a situation where early delivery would be of great enough value to the customer—perhaps for market advantage, such as being able to calculate new discount brokerage commission rates before the competition can do so—that he or she would pay the contractor more. We use T and M during the requirements analysis phase, after which the scope of the task can be determined and estimated more precisely with one of the other contractual forms.

Negotiations

In a typical negotiation, the customer attempts to increase the performance specification while reducing the schedule and budgeted cost. If it is a competitive solicitation, the customer will often play off one prospective contractor against another to try to maximize his or her apparent benefit. Therefore, one should expect the customer to behave in this way.

In addition, negotiators should understand clearly how far, if at all, their management is prepared to deviate from the terms and conditions offered in the submitted proposal it approved. Second, good planning aids negotiators in that there is a complete work breakdown structure, with an attendant activity schedule and cost estimate for each element of it. These help negotiators understand the job being negotiated and can usually help explain and/or defend it to the prospective customer.

Rehearse negotiations.
In preparing for negotiations, it is frequently desirable for your organization to conduct a trial run with someone playing the customer. In short, be well prepared and know your minimum acceptable position. Also, because only one negotiating team member should talk at once, you can rehearse who will respond to particular issues if they are raised.

Depending upon project size, appropriate members of the negotiating team might include an industry applications specialist (familiar with the particular legal and processing requirements) and individuals experienced in the proposed hardware, languages, and operating system. It is important to have knowledgeable negotiators to avoid concessions that render the project less profitable.

During actual negotiations, it is usually to your advantage first to define the job (the detailed statement of work, specifications, and test criteria) and the schedule. After that, you can negotiate the exact contract form, including any detailed terms and conditions, and the final price. The effective negotiator always "horse trades" and never makes a unilateral concession.

Expect the negotiated contract price to be less than your proposed price.

Nevertheless, there is often give and take in the negotiation process, and some changes may be agreed to. Whenever there is a change in one element of the Triple Constraint, there must be changes in other elements. For instance, a customer may offer to provide customer furnished equipment (CFE) to reduce the expected cost of some activity within the proposed project. In the case of the government, this is called government furnished equipment (GFE). When this occurs, language on the performance axis must be changed to stipulate the performance specifications the CFE must meet and when it will be available. When both these things have been accomplished, it is possible to agree to substitute the CFE for contractor procured items and offer a reduction in the proposed schedule or budget. However, CFE must be completely and unambiguously stated and its impact must be evaluated. For example, a contractor receiving serial CFE interface cards and printers when parallel interfaces and printers were planned for will have serious performance problems that were not anticipated and must now be corrected.

After two dimensions of the Triple Constraint have been specified, the third can be determined.

When the negotiations are concluded, the binding direction on the project is that specified in the contract. Only contract change notices suitably signed and agreed to by both parties can permit changes. The authority for signing change orders must also be specified. Such changes should not occur outside the contracting mechanism, despite agreements reached by members of the contractor's and customer's support teams (for instance, when two programmers meet and agree that additional functions would be desirable in their respective modules). Verbal redirection, which can easily occur because of the many individuals involved, is not binding until the contract is amended, as shown in Figure 4-1. Renegotiations such as these require the same amount of

A negotiated change in one dimension of the Triple Constraint should be accompanied by changes in the other dimensions.

planning and preparation as the original negotiations. It is not uncommon to have several renegotiations during a long or complex project.

Legal Aspects

There is a myriad of legal aspects in project contracts. Discussions with suitable people in your organization are often helpful.

In the case of U.S. government contracts, there is a host of special regulations. A typical government contract will include the following:

1. Customer's name and address $\Big\}$ Authorized
2. Contractor's name and address $}$ signatures
3. Statement of supplies (items), services, and prices
4. Description or specification of what is required (statement of work)
5. Preservation, packaging, and packing instructions
6. Delivery or performance period
7. Inspection and acceptance terms
8. Contract administration data

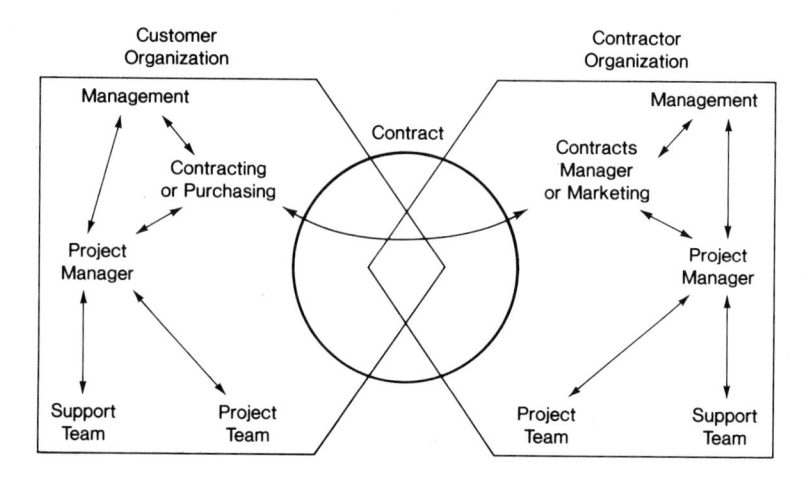

Figure 4-1. Interpretation of the Triple Constraint must be controlled through the contract.

9. Special provisions (funding limitations or customer furnished equipment)
10. General provisions (reference to DAR or overtime payment terms)
11. List of required documentation

Misrepresentation of costs is illegal and can produce serious consequences. In addition, in the case of fixed price contracts, failure to deliver can expose the contractor to very serious cost penalties far beyond absorbing the cost of his own effort. Such penalties may not only include termination but may obligate you to pay the costs of a substitute the government hires to deliver after you are in default.

Know government regulations on contracts before contracting with a government agency.

If any patents are obtained in the course of the program, the government may own them. In addition, there are frequently highly proscribed procedures specifying how much of the work throughout the project must be performed. Costs are frequently subject to audit when the job is completed, and the amount finally paid to the contractor is frequently reduced.

In the case of commercial contracts, restrictions are far less one-sided. Force majeure (that is, an act of God) may permit a contractor to escape any penalty for failure to deliver on time. In addition, the suitably drawn contract will specify disputes that are to be settled by arbitration rather than by the courts. This is far simpler, quicker, and less costly to both parties. Nevertheless, antitrust regulations and many other laws limit the kind of commercial arrangements into which two companies may enter. Ownership or licensing of software must be specified, as well as the number of copies that can be legally made. Where highly proprietary software of another party (for example, special operating system source code) is involved, the contract may spell out the procedural safeguards required to prevent illegal access to that information.

Understand the legal implications.

INTERNATIONAL PROJECTS

International projects are not fundamentally different from domestic projects. In practice, however, the travel lure of a remote and apparently salubrious destination seems to affect human judgment. Furthermore, international projects expose a contracting organization to special problems related to language, currency, and unfamiliar business practices.

Remoteness

Recognize the travel lure.

The other party in an international project is typically located in some remote area of the world. The far-off hills often look green. When two project opportunities are available to a company or organization at the same time, the one that originates in Zurich will receive far more attention than the one that originates in Cleveland, and this is independent of the intrinsic merits of the project opportunity. This is the "travel lure," and it is a problem you must recognize and identify for what it is. Conversely, some occasional political occurrences, such as those experienced by Electronic Data Systems employees in Teheran in 1980, have dampened traveling's lure, and this can inhibit pursuit of good opportunities.

Sometimes you should undertake a project involving a foreign customer or partner. When this is the case, it is often desirable to get more information about the foreign organization or the business in which it is engaged. If your organization has an office in the country, that is the best source of information. The foreign organization's country may have an information office in the United States, which may be able to provide useful information. The United States embassy or trade centers in the foreign country may have information, as may the U.S. Department of Commerce or the World Bank.

Having gathered all the information you can without leaving the United States, you may then have to succumb to the travel lure and go to the foreign country to discuss the project or negotiate. It is generally prudent, although not always feasible, to go several days before the initial meeting to compensate for jet lag.

Business Practices

The business practices governing project performance as well as negotiations and discussions leading to the project will typically be those dictated by the customer's country. For instance, Japanese tend to discuss a project at great length to try to achieve consensus. When this has been done, a handshake or verbal agreement is binding.

Staffing requirements will frequently require some of the work be reserved for the customer's nationals. Sometimes nationals of a third country are stipulated or prohibited, for a variety of reasons. Permits or "red tape" enter into business practices, and these will often absorb far more time than expected. In some cases, export or import controls can impose severe restrictions; so it is always important to understand these issues early.

Language

Usually, the customer's language will prevail, and the contract will be written in it. If you are using a translation, it is prudent to have several prepared because the original host language document is the controlling document and interpreters are likely to interpret it differently. If you find wording differences, you can explore their significance with a language expert.

Be prepared for unfamiliar customs, language, and currency.

Regulations

As software systems become international in nature, certain problems are emerging. First, regulations regarding data privacy and reporting methods vary from country to country. This has great implications for the magnitude of a programming effort that, for example, would have to accommodate American and European regulations: Labor costs may differ among locations; and data communications and hardware costs are usually much higher abroad than here. In addition, if security and privacy are critical for the system, care must be taken to ascertain that they are attainable and enforceable. Lastly, with the uncertainty in various parts of the world today, the chances for successful completion of the project must be carefully weighed against the level of political instability in such parts of the world as the Middle East, South America, and Asia.

Software requirements vary from country to country.

Price

As with language, it is common for the customer's currency to be the stipulated medium of financial settlement. Because currency rates fluctuate, it may be desirable to insure your company against these fluctuations. This is done with a hedge contract. Alternatively, you may use letters of credit to satisfy the future payment obligations. In any event, your price must allow for the extra expense of doing business at a great distance.

TYPICAL PROBLEMS

The most common negotiation problem is deciding how to cope with the inevitable price squeeze the customer will try to inflict. Several things help:

1. A good plan, well explained
2. A clear understanding of where you have inserted negotiating "cushion" or "fat" (as distinct from contingency, which is discussed in Chapter 9) and a negotiating plan on how to horse trade it
3. Management guidance, or clearance, on how much you can give up
4. A reputation for having met prior commitments

Finally, if you are forced to surrender schedule or price, be sure to try to alter the performance specifications or obtain CFE.

Security of hardware and software is a big issue in many foreign countries. To avoid reproduction of your products by unauthorized parties abroad, spell out preventative, enforceable security measures clearly in the contract. Otherwise the foreign business may not be worth the risks.

HIGHLIGHTS   *A proposal should be made only if a reasonable contract can be negotiated.*

There are several contractual forms, including fixed price, firm fixed price, cost plus fixed fee, cost plus incentive fee, and time and material.

Both parties must be prepared to make concessions during negotiations.

Government contracts include numerous special regulations.

International projects introduce special problems, such as unfamiliar business practices, language, currency, distance, higher costs, and legal requirements governing software.

FURTHER READING

M. D. J. Buss. "Managing International Information Systems." *Harvard Business Review* (September-October 1982), pp. 153–162.
> This excellent article describes issues involved in international information systems projects.

R. H. Clough and G. A. Sears. *Construction Project Management*, 2nd ed. New York: Wiley-Interscience, 1979.
> Chapter 1 discusses contracting and negotiating issues in the construction industry.

R. Fisher and W. Ury. *Getting to Yes*. Harmondsworth, Middlesex, England: Penguin, 1983.
> This very readable, short book provides techniques for negotiating an agreement without giving in.

J. L. Graham and R. A. Herberger, Jr. "Negotiations Abroad—Don't Shoot from the Hip." *Harvard Business Review* (July-August 1983), pp. 160–168.
> This article contains very practical advice on international negotiations.

V. G. Hajek. *Management of Engineering Projects*. New York: McGraw-Hill, 1977.
> Chapters 7–10 provide the best (extensive and thorough) treatment of contracts, negotiations, and legal issues.

V. Maieli. "Sowing the Seed of Project Cost Overruns." *Management Review* (August 1972), pp. 7–14.
> This is a general discussion of the causes of cost overruns, with very useful pointers on traps to avoid during negotiations.

J. Main. "How to be a Better Negotiator." *Fortune* (September 19, 1983), p 141.
> This short article touches on some of the points in the Fisher and Ury book.

M. Silverman. *Project Management—A Short Course for Professionals*. New York: Wiley Professional Development Programs, 1976.
> Chapter 4 provides a fairly extensive coverage of negotiations and contract forms.

Part 2

PLANNING A SOFTWARE PROJECT

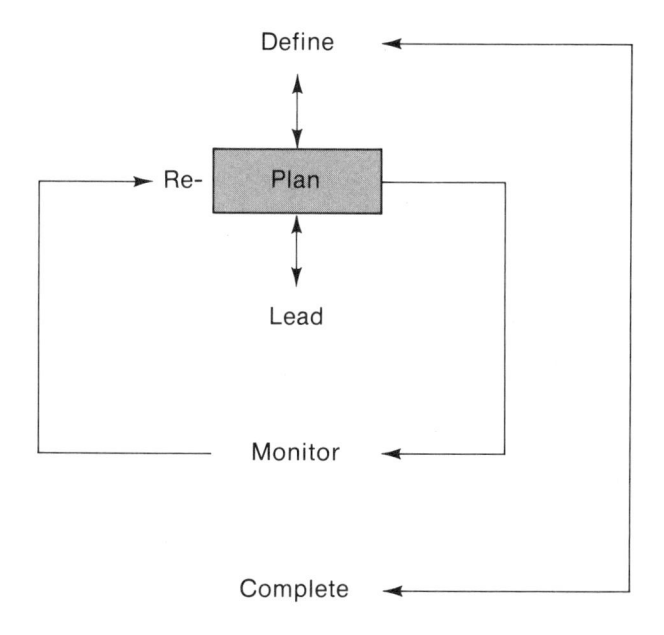

```
         Define
           ↕
Re-→   [ Plan ]  ──┐
           ↕        │
         Lead       │
                    │
       Monitor ←────┤
                    │
      Complete ←────┘
```

5

The Crucial Role of Planning

The planning phase of the project management process is crucial. Plans are the simulation of a project, comprising the written description of how the Triple Constraint will be satisfied. Therefore, project plans are really three plans: one for the performance dimension (the work breakdown structure), one for the schedule dimension (preferably a network diagram but occasionally a milestone listing or bar chart), and one for the cost dimension (a financial estimate). This chapter covers plans in general, reiterates the need for plans, describes how these three kinds of plans are made, reviews several planning issues, and discusses "the Plan," a document or series of documents embodying the project's planning agreements. The life cycle approach introduced in Chapter 1 is integrated with project planning.

PLANNING

In broadest generality, plans depend on three factors:

1. Knowing where you are now (or will be when whatever is being planned for will start)
2. Knowing where you want to get
3. Defining which way you will get from where you are to where you want to be

Plans require goals.

These three factors are illustrated in Figure 5-1. The old saying, "When you don't know where you want to go, any road will get you there," is true. You can have a plan only if you have a destination in mind.

Many data-processing and management information systems projects are initiated because of the organization's long-range plan. For example, a company decides to expand nationally and undertakes automated inventory system development by region rather than nationally to monitor its future direction. Thus, plans are frequently hierarchical, with short-range plans established within the context of long-term plans. For instance, project task plans are components of the overall project plan. When the long-range plan covers five or ten years, changes obviously occur, priorities must be altered, and projects are added or canceled in response to the dynamic environment.

THE NEED FOR PLANS

Plans aid coordination and communication, provide a basis for control, are often required to satisfy requirements, and help avoid problems.

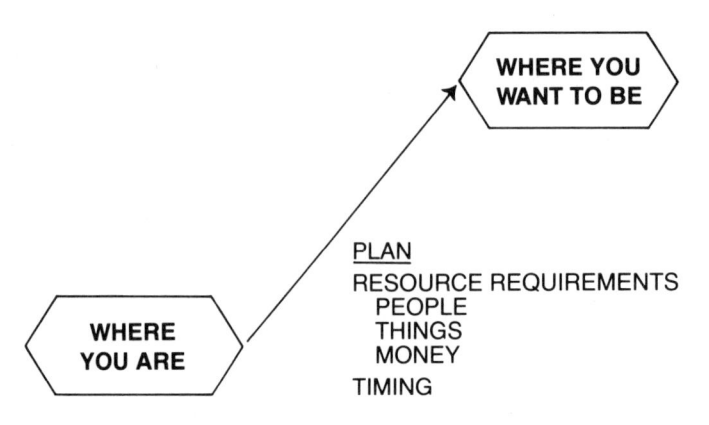

```
                              WHERE YOU
                              WANT TO BE

                    PLAN
                    RESOURCE REQUIREMENTS
                        PEOPLE
    WHERE              THINGS
    YOU ARE             MONEY
                     TIMING
```

Figure 5-1. Planning.
Source: "Basic Management Skills for Engineers and Scientists." Lecture notes by Milton D. Rosenau, Jr. Copyright © 1982 by the University of Southern California. Reprinted by permission.

Coordination and Communication

Most projects involve more than one person. Typically, an expert is asked to perform in the area of his or her expertise. For instance, an expert on systems architecture works on that high-level task, not on writing the detailed program specifications nor the code. The project plan is a way to inform everyone on the project what is expected of him or her and what others will be doing. Plans are a vehicle to delegate portions of the Triple Constraint down to the lowest (task or subtask) reporting level. If the people responsible for these tasks also participate in making the plans, they will have an added impetus to adhere to them. Thus, there is a "Golden Rule" for planning:

Let others plan their work.

> Get the persons who will do the work to plan the work.
>
> • They should know more about it than anyone else.
> • It's *their* task, not *yours*.

Your project plans matter. Even if your project can be performed in your office, other people in the organization, for instance, your boss, will want to know where your project is headed, what you are doing, and for how long you will be doing it. Thus, project plans constitute an important communication and coordination document and may motivate people to perform better.

Basis for Control

Plans are also the basis of your project controls (see Figure 5-2). It is a characteristic of projects that they do not go in accordance with plan. What you do not know when you start is where your project will go off plan. Deviations from plan, detected by monitoring progress, constitute your early warning signal during project performance that there are problems to be resolved. That should cause replanning to occur.

There are plans for all three dimensions of the Triple Constraint.

If you are developing a software package for new hardware whose scheduled delivery has slipped, you might want to develop your software on a similar hardware system and then convert it to the original hardware after the latter is finally delivered. Even though there is more work involved, you can prevent some delays and uncertainties.

Plans are a detailed description, formulated before the project is carried out, for accomplishing its various aspects.

Deviations may indicate the project will not reach its intended destination.

Figure 5-3 illustrates how all the techniques covered in Part 2 are related. The work breakdown structure (WBS) leads to a network diagram. Each activity or task on the network is then time-phased and checked for resource allocation to be certain it is consistent. When this is done, it is possible to construct a schedule bar chart indicating the time frame for each activity or task of the entire project. The costs for these tasks are then estimated and, when work is being performed on them, costs are reported back by a specific task in each of the expense categories. Part 4 discusses how this detailed variance information can be used to help manage the project.

Requirement Satisfaction

Plans are sometimes created merely to satisfy requirements imposed by others, perhaps a customer or your boss. In such a situation, plans are often created under duress rather than because they are perceived to be valuable, even essential, in achieving project objectives.

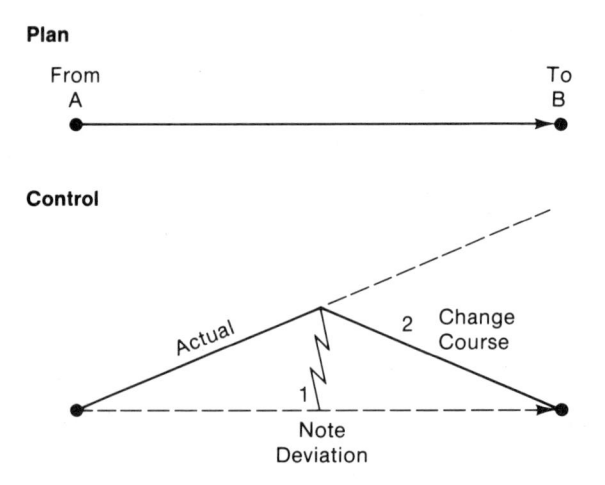

Figure 5-2. Plans are the basis for control.

Source: "Project Management." Lecture notes by Milton D. Rosenau, Jr. Copyright © 1981 by the Association for Media-based Continuing Education for Engineers, Inc. (AMCEE). Reprinted by permission.

Plans so created are frequently not followed. All too often they are generated and then discarded because they were prepared only to meet the requirement to prepare a plan. When there is such a requirement and the plans are prepared slavishly rather than thoughtfully, it is a waste of time for those who prepare them and those who read them.

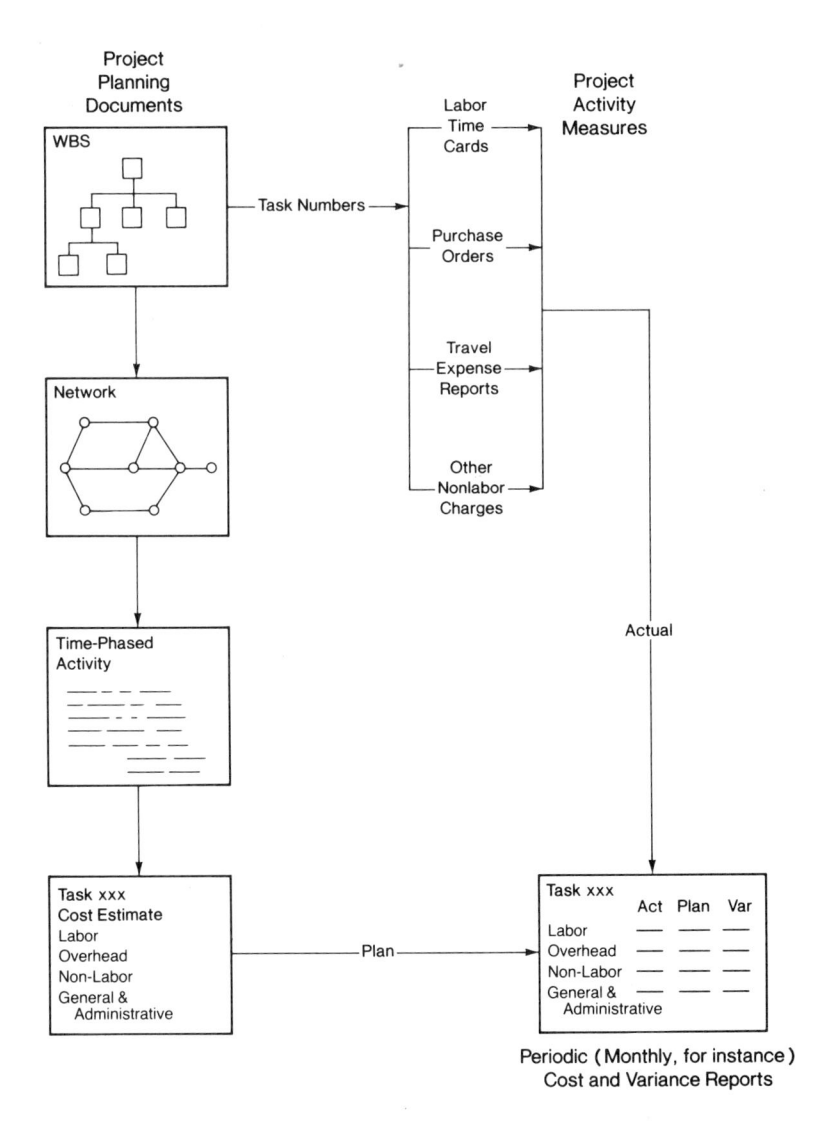

Figure 5-3. Overview of how project planning documents are used in project monitoring phase.

Problem Avoidance

Project management is frequently a race with disaster. All too often the last crisis has scarcely been resolved before the current one begins, and then the project manager is too busy to anticipate and try to head off the next one.

Planning is crucial; a good plan is essential.

A good plan helps you avoid problems during project performance (but plans cannot prevent problems). Consider the following example of a schedule and cost problem. Your software project requires end-user documentation. You assume this documentation will require sixty pages and twenty figures, and the technical documentation group, which will prepare it, agrees to do so in one week for $1,200. When you later ask them to prepare a one-hundred-twenty-page documentation report with forty figures, you will be told you will get it two weeks later and it will cost $2,400. Obviously, you cannot "plan" for a two-hundred-page documentation report with one hundred figures because the price in your proposal may be too high for you to win the job. You must make the best plans and estimates you possibly can and then try to adhere to them. For instance, as you get to the end of the project and must finalize the documentation, assign writing to the participants in such a way that they all clearly understand the planning goal. Constrain the writing efforts to adhere to plans. If you do this, the documentation should be approximately sixty pages and twenty figures.

PLANNING ISSUES

Uncertainty and Risk

Plans relate to future events. That is, your plans are a simulation of how things will occur in the future. There are necessarily uncertainties about the future, some of which may be somewhat predictable and thus partially controllable, but many of which are unpredictable.

You can reduce (but not eliminate) these predictable uncertainties by using checklists, thoroughly discussing the plans with experts, and involving your entire team. Nevertheless, uncertainties will remain because there are always unpredictable factors when you are doing something new. You can allow for these unknowns by inserting contingency in your plans, but you cannot eliminate them. For instance, thorough plans could not have prevented the New York City power outage that destroyed much computer data and disrupted computer service in the late 1960s. Clearly, however, plans can be no better than your present understanding. If you have done something similar before, you can plan it better than if it is entirely new to you and your team. For instance, previous experience with a batch processing system is not terribly helpful for planning a real-time software project.

Assumptions, such as which people will be able to work on your project, are involved in planning. The plan for programming looks a lot different when the best programmer will do the work than when a junior person will do the work. Because assumptions are involved in your planning, it is important to include contingencies, which we discuss in Chapter 9. Good plans are quantitative rather than qualitative and as precise as possible.

A Choice Between Options

In preparing plans, as in carrying out project work, you are frequently confronted with options. Your plan may be considered the record of your choice between these options and will normally depend on how much risk you are willing to take or how much contingency allowance is included in your plans. Figure 5-4 illustrates this kind of choice. It shows two possible activity sequences. Which you choose depends on what is important to you, in this case, a short schedule (option 2) or the higher assurance of accuracy (option 1).

Participants in your project will frequently present a plan that seems absurd to you. It may in fact be absurd. But perhaps the person who prepared it is simply emphasizing activities you are not stressing.

Co-workers' plans may reflect an emphasis that differs from yours.

A common project activity, ordering required materials, illustrates this problem. Sensible choices are to order these materials as early as possible (to be certain they are available when required) or as late as possible (to reduce the possibility of having to change selection or to help your organization's cash flow). It is very important to discuss the perceptions of everyone involved in the undertaking.

Or imagine your boss asks you at 9 A.M. to join her on a 5 P.M. transcontinental flight to attend an important meeting. You agree and advise her you will meet her at the airport. This arrangement allows you to drive past your house en route to the airport and pack your suitcase. Your plan might be as shown in Figure 5-5. In this case, the sequence of activities A, B, and C may not seem to matter. And it does not in terms of your time. But it is desirable to start your secretary's assignment as early as possible so he can perform activity D while you do activities B and C. Thus you should perform activity A first, but you can do C before B (or vice versa) without any schedule delay.

Hazards

There are innumerable hazards in preparing project plans. One follows from the preceding discussion. In an attempt to gain time in the early phases of a project or

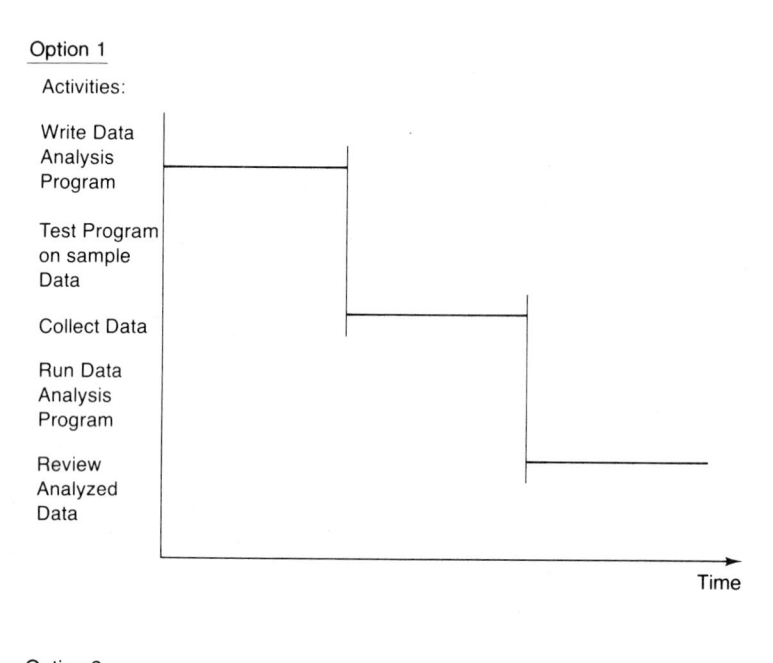

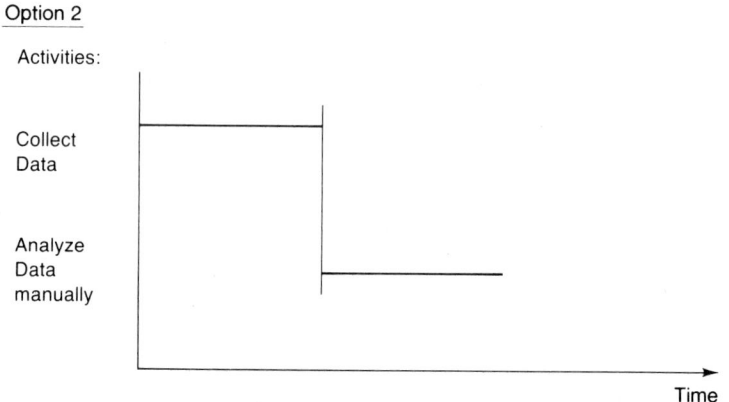

Option 1
Activities:
Write Data Analysis Program
Test Program on sample Data
Collect Data
Run Data Analysis Program
Review Analyzed Data

Option 2
Activities:
Collect Data
Analyze Data manually

Figure 5-4. Two possible schedule sequences.

because you are addicted to your own ideas, you may tend to do much of the planning yourself. You should avoid doing so for the same reason you do not like to be told to carry out somebody else's plan: It is demotivating. In fact, it is important to involve the people who will actually be doing the work so they plan as much of their work as possible. This is especially true where design is a part of the project and the system architects or designers must be consulted for their evaluations.

In addition, poor planning frequently occurs. Other than sheer laziness, the basis of almost all poor planning is a misunderstanding of the Triple Constraint point. Taking the time to create plans allows you to identify your perception of

Planning their own work can motivate people.

Activities:

A. Tell secretary to make travel reservations

B. Call spouse to tell about trip

C. Pack briefcase

D. Have secretary obtain and deliver tickets

E. Go home, pack suitcase, go to airport

Time

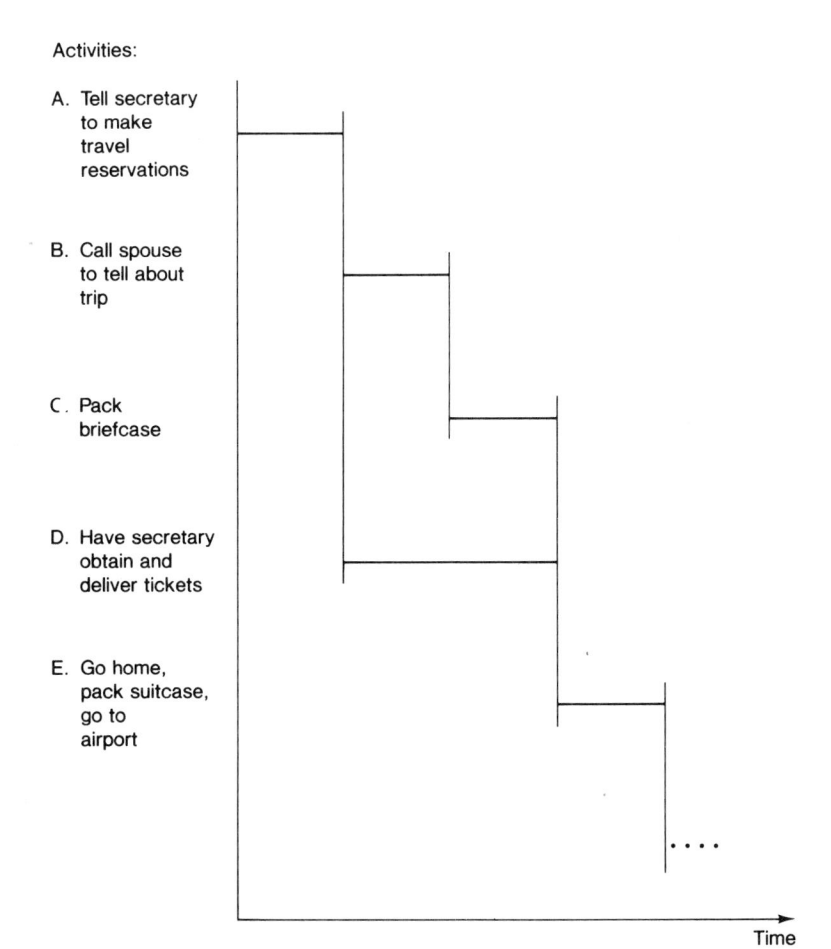

Figure 5-5. Option for trip preparation.

the Triple Constraint point and shows if and where it differs from somebody else's.

Occasionally, a tool commonly called a planning matrix is used. It lists activities to be carried out along one side of a piece of paper and designates involved personnel along the perpendicular side. Where these rows and columns intersect at a check mark, the designated personnel are involved in the designated activity. This kind of document may be helpful to some managers, but it is a misnomer to call it a planning matrix rather than an involvement matrix. To put it another way, a planning matrix may be a helpful document, but it is not a plan; it is a result of planning.

Currentness

Keep everyone current on revisions.

Once you have decided to plan your project and have issued the plans, people should take them seriously. They can do so only if they know the plans are current. Therefore, it is very important to know who has copies of them. When you revise plans, be absolutely certain to provide revisions to all people who have copies of previous plans. When you do this conscientiously, everyone involved in your project will know you take planning seriously. They will know the plans they have reliably indicate the project intention.

"THE PLAN"

In many projects, there is a book called "the Plan," "the Project Work Plan," or "the Project Plan." It may be one or a series of thick notebooks.

Issues Addressed

Plans expand upon the Triple Constraint.

"The Plan" addresses many topics. It frequently describes what is to be delivered as a result of the project and any specifications for those items. It may include video screen formats, a documentation tree, and project development guidelines. If there will be acceptance tests, it will describe them in detail. In general, the purpose of this kind of plan is to describe what is to be done, by when, and for how much—in other words, to expand upon the Triple Constraint. It is relevant throughout the software project life cycle (see Figure 5-6).

The project (work) plan's purpose is to provide the strategy and identify the resources required to implement a software product. It should specify the significant milestones (performance), required resources (cost), and predicted completion dates (schedule). The Plan is the document against which progress is reported throughout the project life cycle. It is rewritten and refined at least twice during the life cycle (or even more often if the work it identifies is significantly altered), as shown in Figure 5-7. Each iteration of the Plan replaced the previous version, with greater precision on each dimension of the Triple Constraint.

Topics Covered

Typically, the Plan will cover the following topics:

- Project summary
- Environment (external contingencies such as hardware, operating system, support facilities, contingencies on development of other products)
- Computing and personnel resources required
- Milestones (documents and reviews, testing, integration, local and field acceptance, customer training)
- Identification of key contacts in customer and contractor organization (an organization chart is often helpful)
- Project standards and procedures

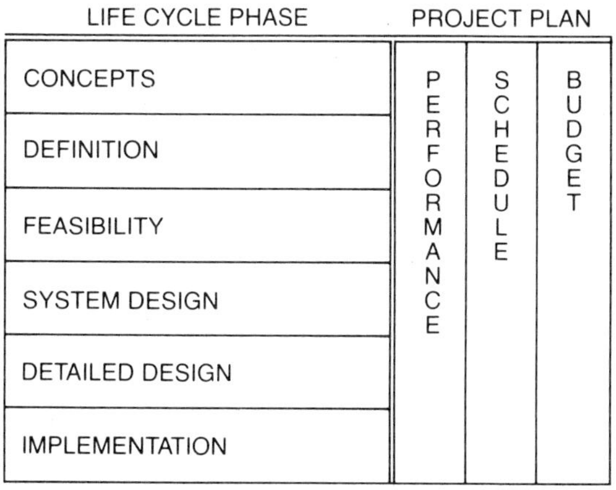

LIFE CYCLE PHASE	PROJECT PLAN		
CONCEPTS	P E R F O R M A N C E	S C H E D U L E	B U D G E T
DEFINITION	^	^	^
FEASIBILITY	^	^	^
SYSTEM DESIGN	^	^	^
DETAILED DESIGN	^	^	^
IMPLEMENTATION	^	^	^

Figure 5-6. Project planning spans the entire software project life cycle.

- Graphic representation of decomposition of architecture into coding level entities (This functional decomposition becomes more detailed with each plan revision.)
- Work breakdown structure
- Network diagram of activities with schedule dates
- Budget for all activities
- Statement of philosophy (regarding reviews, interfaces, Triple Constraint)
- Change control methodology

Activation

Spend no more time planning than you would spend correcting problems resulting from having no plan.

Project plans require activation. First, obtain whatever higher level approvals are required, including those of the customer. Second, disseminate "the Plan" to all involved personnel. In very large projects, dissemination may require a chart room in which the walls are covered with charts displaying the plans for and status of various activities, including financial progress and resource allocation. Chart rooms are not required for smaller projects.

Project plans may vary from fairly simple one-page statements to records with overwhelmingly intricate levels of detail. There is an appropriate level for each project undertaking. There is no magic formula that establishes the right level of detail; in general, never spend more time planning than it would take to correct any problems encountered because

LIFE CYCLE PHASE	PROJECT PLAN
CONCEPTS	
DEFINITION	
FEASIBILITY	VERSION #1
SYSTEM DESIGN	VERSION #2
DETAILED DESIGN	VERSION #3
IMPLEMENTATION	

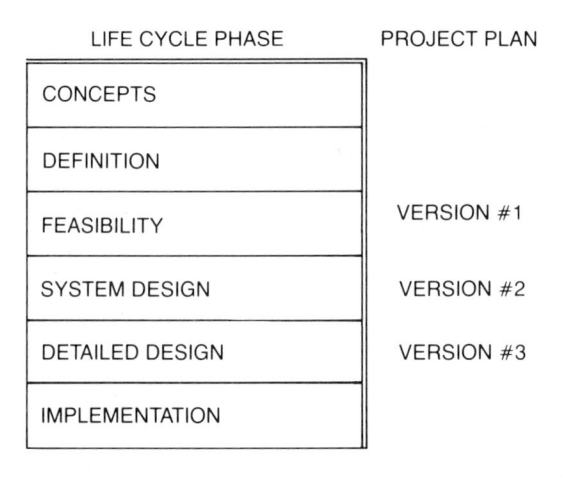

Figure 5-7. When to revise the project plan.

planning had not been undertaken. That is, a basic purpose of planning is to avoid problems. Also, project plans should contain just enough information to be useful to the level of management for which the plan is intended. Critical information is often lost because too much data is presented, and senior management doesn't have time to sift through it all.

PLANNING FOR THE PROJECT LIFE CYCLE

The life cycle provides the framework with which planning can be accomplished, defining a roadmap from concept to finished product, with milestones along the way so that the project can be monitored successfully. The purpose is to divide the software development project into manageable phases, each one of which represents a natural segment in terms of the task accomplished, the types of people involved, and the talents required.

The life cycle organization enables controlled planning.

Table 5-1 shows the six phases, the chief activity and documents inputted from each, and the reviewer involvement. The names of the documents or review panels are not as important as is the actual communication between the parties responsible for the work of that phase. This process of completing one phase and moving on to the next is not a discrete process; as changes are made, let's say, in the detailed design specifications because of hardware requirements, there may be a change required to the preceding product specifications. To monitor the effects on work done earlier, change control is an important part of any software development effort and must be addressed as part of the project planning effort. We deal with this more in Chapter 17.

The phases are not all of the same duration. Depending on the particular product you're producing, you might spend longer on feasibility (for newly applied technology) or on implementation (which may be the longest phase for a multi-installation customer due to the many individual acceptance tests required). You will need different types of talent at different phases. For requirements analysis you will need someone able to assess the business' and users' true as well as stated needs—a systems analyst. For architecture you will want someone familiar with software operating and application systems as well as with hardware. This sequencing of different types of talents often produces communication problems during the life cycle, as user needs are continually translated from one "language" to another. As the project manager, you must keep the user involved to ensure that you are still on target and to ensure critical user support when the software is developed.

As you set up your development life cycle, keep the following suggestions in mind:

1. Provide concurrent, not after the fact, documentation.
2. Make those milestones significant.
3. Be sure review boards are appropriately composed.
4. Hire talent appropriate to each phase.
5. Remember that phase completion is iterative.

TABLE 5-1. Attributes Of Each Life Cycle Phase.

Software Development Life Cycle Phases	Milestone Documents	Reviews By	Chief Activity
Concepts	Concepts & objectives	Senior management	Lay out a conceptual approach
Definition	Requirements	User	Define user's needs
Feasibility	System architecture Product specifications	User and development Development management	Define product(s) to meet user's needs
System design	General systems design Application design specifications	Development	Define software component to create products for user
Detailed design	Detailed design specifications	Development	Define programmable software entities
Implementation	Test specifications User documents Operations manuals	Quality assurance User	Code & test programmed software entities, assemble into products for use

TYPICAL PROBLEMS

> There are three pervasive problems with planning. First, a separate plan is required for each of the three dimensions of the Triple Constraint. These three plans must be integrated and consistent.
>
> Second, taking enough time to plan is costly. There is an old saying about this: "We don't have enough time to plan now; but we'll have lots of time to fix it up later." In fact, a little inexpensive planning early usually avoids a lot of very costly fixing later. This is analogous to testing computer software—a lot of up-front design is much cheaper than trying to remove programming bugs later. Also, planning in the form of design and analysis before undertaking programming and testing usually results in faster implementation. It is difficult to decide how much planning is appropriate, but the inexperienced project manager usually does far too little.
>
> Third, plans are frequently ignored because they are perceived as an irrelevant requirement of management. The solution is obvious: Write meaningful plans you intend to follow and keep current, and be sure everyone understands you have done so.

Plans are used for the following purposes:

HIGHLIGHTS

- *Simulate how the project will be carried out*
- *Write the proposal*
- *Negotiate the contract*
- *Coordinate and communicate*
- *Increase participants' motivation*
- *Control the project*
- *Satisfy requirements*
- *Avoid problems*
- *Record the choice between options*

Plans delegate portions of the Triple Constraint to the lowest reporting level.

Plans help keep projects on course.

If formulated only to meet someone's requirements for them, plans are virtually useless.

Everyone involved must receive every plan revision.

Planning notebooks, a series of planning notebooks, or a chart room may be needed.

Never spend more time on a plan than would be required to correct problems resulting from a lack of a plan.

Never spend more resources on a plan than on the actual development effort itself.

Plans reflect the balance between risk and contingency for both controllable and uncontrollable future events.

FURTHER READING

R. D. Archibald. *Managing High Technology Programs and Projects.* New York: Wiley-Interscience, 1976.
> Chapter 7, sections 1–4, briefly covers many of the issues in this chapter and contains a complete enumeration of applicable techniques.

P. Bruce and S. M. Pederson. *The Software Development Project.* New York: Wiley-Interscience, 1982.
> This book provides a thorough treatment of all the items for which planning is required in a computer software project.

C. W. Burrill and L. W. Ellsworth. *Modern Project Management.* Tenafly, NJ: Burrill-Ellsworth Associates, 1981.
> Chapter 2, pages 15–25, provides a brief discussion of planning in the DP environment.

D. I. Cleland and W. R. King. *Systems Analysis and Project Management,* 2nd ed. New York: McGraw-Hill, 1975.
> Chapter 15 provides a quick summary of the material in this and the next three chapters, set in the context of organizational planning.

P. W. Metzger. *Managing a Programming Project,* 2nd ed. Englewood Cliffs, NJ: Prentice-Hall, 1981.
> The portion of Chapter 2, pages 21–49, on project planning is especially useful for computer projects but has general utility as well.

R. S. Pressman. *Software Engineering.* New York: McGraw-Hill, 1982.

Chapters 1–4, pages 1–93, contain a thorough discussion of planning for computer software projects.

M. L. Shooman. *Software Engineering.* New York: McGraw-Hill, 1983.

Chapter 6, pages 408–512, contains a large amount of material on software project management techniques, but is somewhat mathematical.

W. R. Synott and W. H. Gruber. *Information Resource Management.* New York: Wiley-Interscience, 1981.

Chapter 11, pages 273–312, on project selection and management, identifies many issues to be considered in planning computer software projects.

S. Woolridge and K. London. *The Computer Survival Handbook*, 1st rev. ed. Ipswich, MA: Gambit, 1979.

This book is subtitled How To Talk Back to Your Computer, *and that sets the tone of a breezy (but knowledgeable) discussion of many factors to consider when planning a computer project.*

6

Planning the Software Performance Dimension

The goal of a performance dimension plan is to be sure that everything required to satisfy the performance specification is done. This chapter deals with planning for the performance dimension of the Triple Constraint. The statement of work is a useful aid, but the principal tool discussed is the work breakdown structure.

STATEMENT OF WORK

The statement of work (SOW) is that portion of the contract that explicitly enumerates what the project organization will do for and deliver to the customer or user. In projects within your organization, the SOW may be contained in a memo or work authorization rather than a contract. The SOW must always be accompanied by a project schedule and budget to be meaningful. Thus, a plan for the performance dimension of the Triple Constraint is primarily a listing of every activity that must be performed and every result that must be obtained. The SOW frequently contains explicit acceptance criteria, review schedules, and test specifications.

The work breakdown structure (WBS) subdivides the

SOW into smaller work packages, each of which should be understandable and achievable. If a WBS task is not understandable, it should be broken down into smaller work packages, to arrive at a level where the required work is capable of being done. Thus, the project's performance specification will be satisfied when each work package has been completed satisfactorily.

WORK BREAKDOWN STRUCTURE

Purpose

The work breakdown structure (WBS) is a convenient method for dividing a project into small work packages, tasks, or activities. A WBS reduces the likelihood of something dropping through a crack. To put it another way, it assures that all the required activities are logically identified and related.

The WBS identifies all the work required to complete a project.

Figure 6-1 is a WBS for a computer software project. There is no magic formula for constructing a WBS. Suppose the

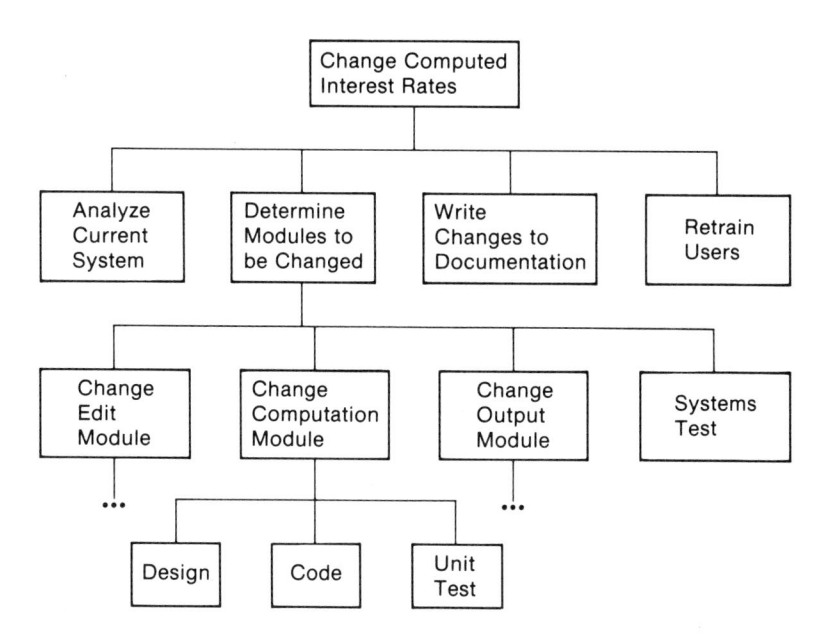

Figure 6-1. A WBS for a computer software project to change interest rates.

project also required new remote terminals for the display of output data. The WBS box for that task (labeled, perhaps, "provide data output terminals") could be shown either at the second level (logically between "determine modules to be changed" and "write changes to documentation") or at the fourth level under "change output module." Project logic and corporate organization will dictate the kind of detail that appears.

Figure 6-1 shows three modules in the project. The more modules you have in your project, the smaller and cheaper each module becomes. However, the more modules you have, the more money and time is spent in arranging for these to be properly interfaced with each other. Conversely, if you have only one module, there is no interfacing cost, but the module itself is large and expensive. Therefore, there is a happy midpoint that must be found by experience. One yardstick is if a single individual is working on the module, you need not break it down further unless it crosses a project life cycle phase. All phases, milestones, and reviews should stand alone.

Use the appropriate level of detail in a WBS.

Your software design alternatives (for instance, top down or structured design) will dictate the logic of some parts of the WBS. If you intend to use structured walkthroughs or step-by-step peer reviews, these are sufficiently important to warrant a task and entry on the WBS.

Figure 6-1 shows four levels of detail, but there is no standard number of levels to use. In general, probably at least three or four should be shown, but it might sometimes be appropriate to show five or ten or even more. The breakdown might occur using earlier or later activities, particular organizational involvements, or almost anything that makes reasonable sense. In general, it is best to structure the WBS on tangible, deliverable items, both software and hardware. If validation and verification were specified enumerated deliverables, along with systems analysis, program development, documentation, and training, then testing might better be shown at level two rather than at level four under each module.

The WBS must be tied to time and money plans.

The WBS defines the work packages and will be tied to attendant schedules and budgets for the work performers. Thus, it is desirable for the lowest level packages to correspond to small work increments and short time periods. It is often helpful to indicate who the task leader is by putting his or her name in the box for the task. In any event, the WBS can clarify organizational responsibility on a project and identify critical personnel or talents required early on in the project.

In addition to using the WBS for planning, task authorization forms, such as the one in Figure 6-2, should be used to clarify the statement of work for each task. If the task budget is a constraint, the task authorization form should have a blank for this. Note that the task authorization form has a block where the task leader accepts the task, which assures compliance with the Golden Rule discussed in Chapter 5.

If not specified in the project statement of work, the programming language and operating system choices should be indicated on the appropriate task authorization. It is clearly

TASK AUTHORIZATION			PAGE *1* OF *1*
TITLE *CHANGE INTEREST RATES*			
PROJECT NO. *B2361-84*	TASK NO. *27*	REVISION NO. *1*	DATE ISSUED *6-10-84*

STATEMENT OF WORK:

Change Interest Calculation Subsystem to compute simple daily interest on all passbook accounts from 5¼ to 5½% starting with all transfers, deposits, and withdrawals made after 1/1/85. Test successfully using standard testdata package.

APPLICABLE DOCUMENTS:

B 234
B 236
C005 → 027

SCHEDULE
START DATE: *7-1-84*   COMPLETION DATE: *1-1-85*

COST:

ORIGINATED BY:	DATE:	ACCEPTED BY:	DATE:
APPROVED BY:	DATE:	APPROVED BY:	DATE:
APPROVED BY:	DATE:	APPROVED BY:	DATE:

Figure 6-2. A task authorization form for computer software projects.

important to have project team agreement on whether the programming goal is run time efficiency and compatibility with other programs (which is most appropriate if the program is to be used repetitively) or whether the goal is to get the fastest solution (which is appropriate if the program is for a one-time solution to a mathematical or engineering problem) or if you are designing a single or multiuser product. Such a choice also affects memory size, which has to be considered in planning. Obviously, you don't want to leave these matters to chance. These choices will also affect schedule and cost plans. Therefore, these plans logically cannot be started until programming language and operating system choices are specified.

Helpful Hints

In preparing a WBS, do not forget required tasks such as reports, reviews, and coordinating activities. In fact, displaying them on a WBS is a good way to highlight that they are necessary and that resources must be devoted to them.

Fortunately, when a WBS is prepared, it tends to stress integration activities. That is, junctions on the WBS frequently imply a consistency check or a test activity that must occur when these heretofore separate activities are joined. Thus, a WBS again is useful for identifying an activity to which resources must be devoted.

There is also a slightly different way to create a WBS. It is a "costed WBS," and the dollar volume attached to each branch of the total project is also included at the major headings. This kind of additional information, assuming large amounts of money are associated with large amounts of activity, will direct the manager's attention to those portions of the project that represent the most activity. On a project with rigid cost limits, it is often helpful to start with a costed WBS. A trial allocation of the rigid budget is then made to see how well each work package can be performed at that level of funding. Then adjustments are made to the funding allocations to provide the best overall balance of achievable performance within the budget limit.

Others can help assure your WBS is complete.

If you can afford the time, it is desirable to have another person make a WBS for your project, independent of yours, at least down to the third or fourth level. This will take only an hour or so and will highlight any discrepancies or oversights. You will have to repay the favor on later projects, but that should help your organization by reducing problems on projects. In fact, some organizations require that two or more people independently prepare a WBS for a given project before it can be approved.

After the initial WBS has been made, schedule planning can commence. In some cases, it may be desirable to simulate the performance of a computer system at this point. The schedule planning may identify further items to add to the WBS. Although less likely, the same may occur as cost planning is done.

TYPICAL PROBLEMS

Vagueness in the SOW is a crucial problem in planning the performance dimension. For instance, the SOW may state that "appropriate tests will be performed." Who decides, and when, what is appropriate? The solution is to write a specific and detailed SOW.

We thus recommend omitting maintenance from the project definition. As we said before, consider and estimate maintenance in deciding whether the project is justified, but only plan and authorize it (as a separate project) when it can be precisely defined.

Data processing groups seem to be much more open to the idea of a systems development methodology than to a WBS, probably because these products tend to address more than just a comprehensive list of tasks to be performed. Typically, systems development methodologies address missing procedures and administrative practices as well as very detailed techniques for estimating levels of effort for every task. Indeed, if these systems development methodologies work better than a WBS for planning the performance dimension on your project, you should consider substituting one of them. The key point is that you must plan the performance dimension, and the WBS should be used unless you have a better tool.

Another problem is the blind copying of a prior project's WBS for a new project. When this occurs, we have not a WBS, but a waste of everybody's time—the people who prepare the WBS and the people who must read it. However, don't discard the effort of prior

continued

Consider using a systems development methodology.

> WBSs; you can compile a master checklist from tasks you identified and check the current project WBS against it for completeness. The issue here is that a project's WBS should be prepared thoughtfully, not by rote, to increase the odds of project success.
>
> The importance of establishing user requirements specifically and unambiguously during the definition phase cannot be overstressed. Without firm requirements, the SOW will be ambiguous, and subsequent efforts will be wasteful. Firm and clear requirements enable proper testing, user evaluation and participation, and delivery of the product contracted for, and facilitate your task as manager.

HIGHLIGHTS   *A work breakdown structure identifies all work required on a project.*

A co-worker's independently produced WBS for your project may point out omissions on your WBS.

The statement of work specifies what the customer will receive and when delivery will occur.

FURTHER READING

B. N. Abramson and R. D. Kennedy. *Managing Small Projects.* Redondo Beach, CA: TRW Systems Group, 1975.
   Pages 12–17 of this breezy, short booklet give a graphic treatment of a WBS.

R. D. Archibald. *Managing High-Technology Programs and Projects.* New York: Wiley-Interscience, 1976.
   Chapter 7, section 5, is a good treatment of a WBS, which Archibald calls the project breakdown structure.

"Bugs Can Chew Up Half the Harvest." *Electronic Design* (July 22, 1982), pp. 88–89.
   This is a discussion of the time and cost problems caused by bugs, indicating that lots of early testing should be included in the project to reduce this problem.

S. Evanchuk. "Program Simulates Computer Systems." *Electronics* (April 21, 1983), pp. 167–168.
This short article describes one tool for simulating the performance of a computer system before it is built.

J. A. Maciariello. *Program-Management Control Systems.* New York: Wiley-Interscience, 1978.
Chapters 4 and 7 provide a good treatment of the WBS, including the costed WBS.

G. J. Meyers. *The Art of Software Testing.* New York: Wiley, 1979.
This really outstanding book describes the work you must expect to do in testing your software.

R. C. Tausworthe. "The Work Breakdown Structure in Software Project Management." *The Journal of Systems and Software* (1980), pp. 181–186.
This discussion of the use of the WBS in software implementation projects presents a checklist for items to include in the WBS.

7

Planning the Schedule

This chapter deals with the second dimension of the Triple Constraint. The plan for the schedule dimension orders activities so you can identify the logical relationship between them. In general, there are three approaches to scheduling: bar charts, milestones, and network diagrams. We discuss each but stress network diagram usage based on milestones.

BAR CHARTS

Bar charts, often called Gantt charts after H. L. Gantt, an industrial engineer who popularized them during World War I, are frequently used for scheduling. Figure 7-1 is a bar chart. The project is divided into five activities with a planned duration of twelve months. When the bar chart was constructed, five open bars were drawn to represent the planned time span for each activity. The figure also shows project status at the end of the sixth month. The shaded bars represent the forecasted span of the activities as of the end of the sixth month. Activity A was completed early. Activity B is forecast to be finished half a month late. Activity C is forecast to end approximately a month and a half early. The percentage of completion for each activity in process is also illustrated. Activity A has been completed; B is 80 percent complete; and C is 30 percent complete.

Bar charts are simple to construct and easy to understand and change. They show graphically which activities are ahead of or behind schedule.

Offsetting these favorable features are some weaknesses, the most serious of which is that bar charts are essentially useless. Knowing the status of project activities gives no information at all about overall project status because one activity's dependence on another and the entire project's dependence upon any particular activity are not apparent. Bar charts are much more useful as an indication of what has happened than as a planning tool to aid the project manager in making things happen properly in the future.

In addition, the notion of a percentage completion is difficult and is most commonly associated with the use of bar charts for measuring progress (which we discuss further in Part 4). Does the percentage completion refer to the performance dimension, the schedule dimension, or the cost dimension of the job? Unless an activity is linearly measurable, for instance drilling a hundred holes in a steel plate, it is impossible to judge what percentage of it is complete. (Even in this simple case, the steel plate may have an internal defect, and the last drill hole might be through that defect, causing the plate to crack, at which point what was 99 percent complete now has to be done all over again.) Therefore, percentage completion becomes highly subjective or is frequently taken merely as the percentage of cost expended compared to

A schedule that does not show task or activity interdependencies is useless by itself for planning.

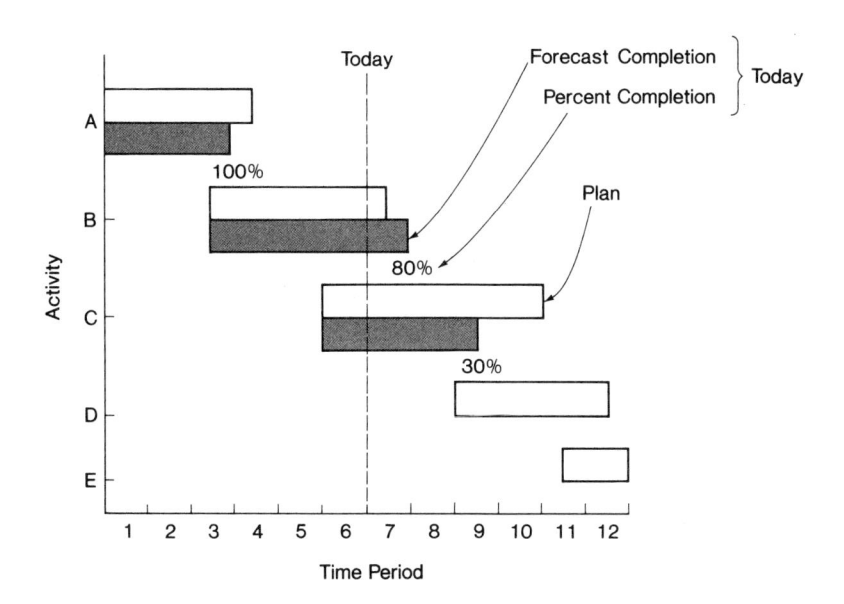

Figure 7-1. Typical bar chart, illustrating a project with five activities at the six-month review.

total projected cost. In neither situation is percentage completion a useful number. As anyone who has been told a program is 99 percent completed knows, percentages are extremely dangerous in software development reports.

MILESTONES

Define milestones early in a project.

A milestone schedule notes a few key events, called milestones, on a calendar bar chart. Milestones have been defined in various ways and are generally identified in the contract, but they probably are best defined as events clearly verifiable by other people or requiring approval before proceeding further. If milestones are so defined, projects will not have so many that the conclusion of each activity itself becomes a milestone. Usually they represent interface events between phases or parties to a project: documents, reviews, tests.

The output of each phase of the project life cycle (Figure 1-4) is a set of milestones. Milestones should be defined as early as possible in a project, and they should be meaningful deliverables. Their purpose is not only to serve as checkpoints for the anticipated progress made up to that point, but also to encourage feedback from the involved parties (users, for example, on the statement of requirements); to provide that ever-so-critical project visibility that is a nontrivial problem in software projects, especially during the feasibility and design stages; and to ensure that miscommunications have not occurred.

When milestones have been defined, for instance, in the customer's request for a proposal or in your proposal document, listing them often helps in preparing your project plan. Having such milestones with attendant schedule and budget measures also adds extra emphasis to a few key points of a project. But, in common with bar charts, milestone schedules alone do not clarify activity or task interdependencies. Thus, they must be used with other tools, if they are used at all. Milestone schedules are exceptionally useful in computer software management when combined with network diagrams.

NETWORK DIAGRAMS

There are many forms of network diagrams, but the Program Evaluation and Review Technique (PERT) and the Critical Path Method (CPM) are the most common. "Network diagram" is a generic term for PERT and CPM diagrams, arrow diagrams, bubble diagrams, precedence networks, and many others. (It is not uncommon to have any network diagram designated a PERT chart, whether or not it truly is.) Network diagrams are the recommended approaches to planning the schedule dimension. They identify the precedence conditions and the sequential constraints for each activity.

Network diagrams indicate crucial interdependencies.

PERT and CPM

PERT and CPM emerged in different ways in the late 1950s. PERT is event oriented (that is, the event labels go in the nodes of the diagram) and has typically been used for aerospace and research and development (R and D) projects for which the time for each activity is uncertain. CPM is activity oriented (that is, the activity labels are placed on the arrows) and has been applied to the construction industry, in which there is typically a controllable time for each activity. There are now many hybrid forms of network diagrams that provide the best features of PERT and CPM. The network purist undoubtedly cares about the distinctions between these two, but in reality they are not very important. For simplicity in this chapter, we will assume PERT is always event oriented and CPM is always activity oriented.

Conventions

Figure 7-2 shows how a programming task would be illustrated in PERT and CPM diagrams, and Figure 7-3 provides the symbolic conventions common to both. Activities are always shown as arrows, with the start being the tail of the arrow and the completion being the barb. Events are shown as circles (or squares, ovals, or any other convenient closed figure). The event number may be placed inside the closed figure. Event numbers are required in computer programs, which are sometimes used to facilitate network information manipulation. In such cases, a higher number activity always follows a lower number activity. In computer programs, activities are not labeled by their name (that is, "program module A" is not called "program module A") but rather by the start and end numbers (that is, 5–10 is program module A if 5 is the number of the start node and 10 is the number of the finish node). It is also conventional to place early and late date numbers or other information such as slack time within the nodes. Whenever node numbers are used, there should be a legend explaining which number is which. Using these

Arrows designate activities or tasks.

88   Planning the Schedule

PERT (Events Labeled)

```
  ( START TO   )          ( FINISH       )
  ( PROGRAM    ) ──────►   ( PROGRAMMING  )
  ( MODULE A   )           ( MODULE A     )
```

CPM (Activities Labeled)

```
  (     )    PROGRAM      (     )
  (     ) ── MODULE A ──► (     )
```

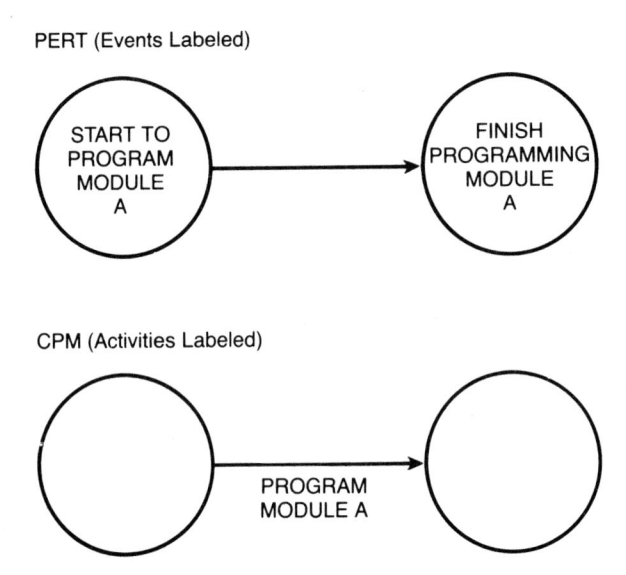

Figure 7-2.   Examples of PERT and CPM.

Activities

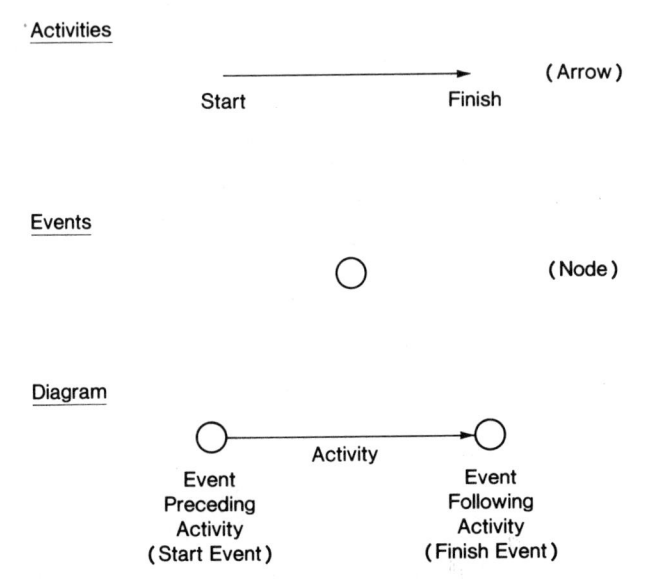

```
           ──────────►                (Arrow)
         Start        Finish
```

Events

```
              ○                       (Node)
```

Diagram

```
         ○ ──── Activity ────► ○
       Event                  Event
     Preceding              Following
     Activity                Activity
    (Start Event)          (Finish Event)
```

Figure 7-3.   Basic network diagram conventions.

conventions, a network diagram consists of a series of nodes and arrows connected to show the order of activities.

The upper drawing of Figure 7-4 depicts a schedule plan in which activity R must be complete before activity S can commence and in which activity T must be complete before activity U can commence. The middle drawing shows a schedule plan in which both activities R and T must be complete before either S or U can commence. The bottom drawing introduces the concept of a dummy activity, which is an activity requiring no work, that is, a precedence condition. It thus depicts a plan in which both activities R and T must be complete before activity S can commence and in which activity T must be complete before activity U can commence. Activity U does not depend on activity R because the dummy arrow points in the other direction.

A dummy activity is a precedence condition.

Network Terms

Figure 7-5 illustrates three terms in network diagram usage. A burst node is a node or an event at which two or more

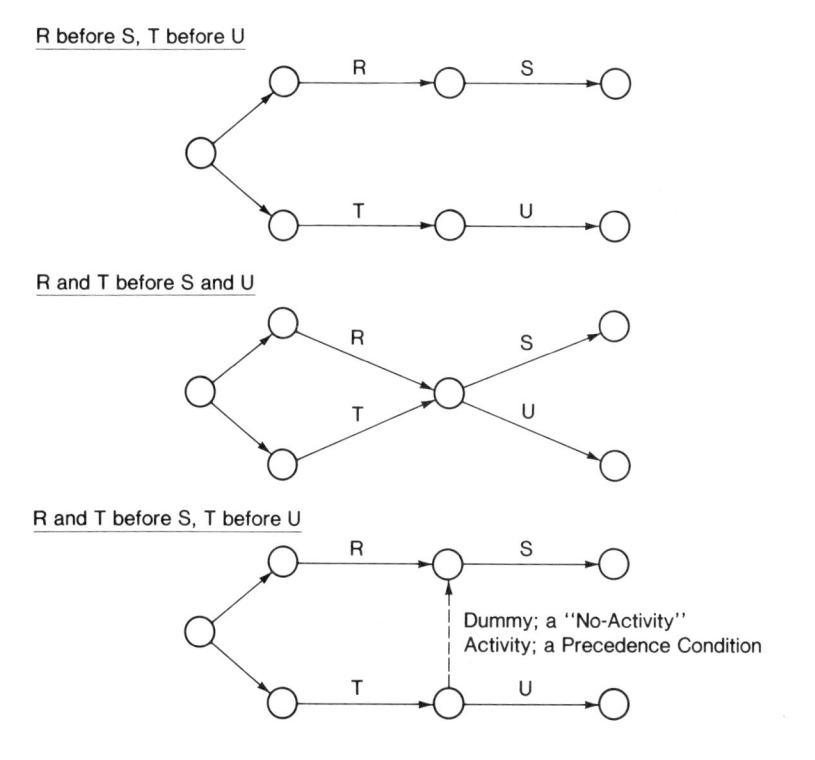

R before S, T before U

R and T before S and U

R and T before S, T before U

Dummy; a "No-Activity" Activity; a Precedence Condition

Figure 7-4. Precedence requirements.

activities can be initiated after completion of a preceding activity. A merge node or event is one in which two or more activities must be completed prior to initiation of the subsequent activity.

A dummy activity represents a dependency between two activities for which no work is specifically required. Dummies are also used to deal with an ambiguity that arises in computer-based network diagrams, also illustrated in Figure 7-5. As mentioned, in computer-based network diagram programs, the activity label is not the activity name but rather the number of the two nodes preceding and following it. Thus, is 6–7 G or H in the lower left of Figure 7-5? Using a dummy task, one can make 6–7 activity G and 6–8 activity H, as shown in the lower right of Figure 7-5. There is thus a dummy activity, 7–8, also required to remove the previous ambiguity.

Illustrative Relationships

Consider the situation illustrated in Figure 7-6. You are the project manager for a software development project with eight programming activities or tasks. At the end of four

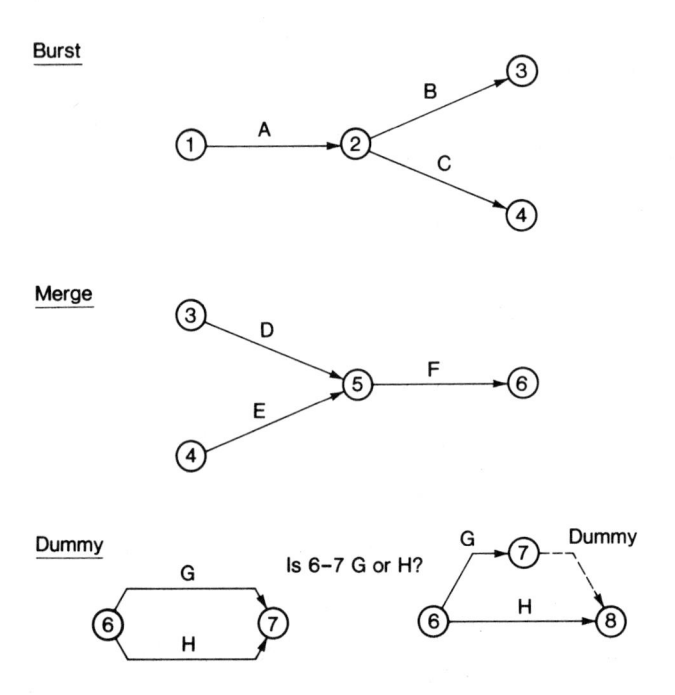

Figure 7-5. Common network terms.

months, you are conducting a project review (denoted by the solid triangle). Task managers provide status reports showing tasks B and C are two months late, A and D are one month late (denoted by the shading), and E is on schedule. The impact of these delays on the entire project's completion is not clear. (For simplicity in this example, assume task status is precisely measurable—for instance, by counting the number of lines of code or nodules completed.) Your chief concern at this point is whether the entire project is late.

First you might break the tasks into their subtasks or subactivities, as in Figure 7-7. This provides additional information but still does not tell us whether the project will be late.

At this point, a network diagram for the project can be examined (Figure 7-8). This contains more information than the bar charts because it shows the interrelationship (precedence) between different tasks. We have labeled each event in its node with the completion of the designated subtask. Thus, at the top of the diagram, you can see activity D must be completed before activity G.

Figure 7-8 also shows the problem with a PERT network: The activities per se are not illustrated, that is, there is no arrow uniquely associated with activity G, H, or C_3. This will

Networks have more information than bar charts.

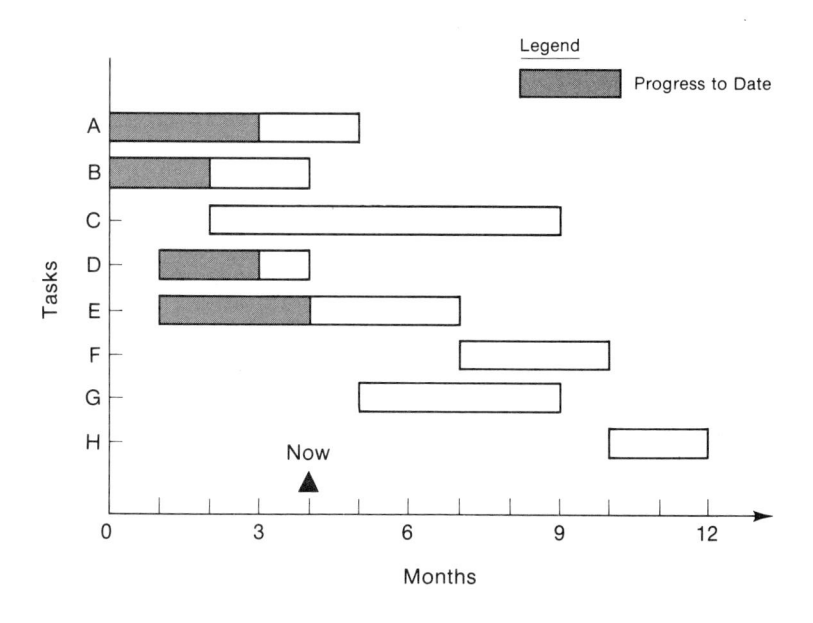

Figure 7-6. Bar chart showing tasks A, B, C, and D to be late at four-month project review.

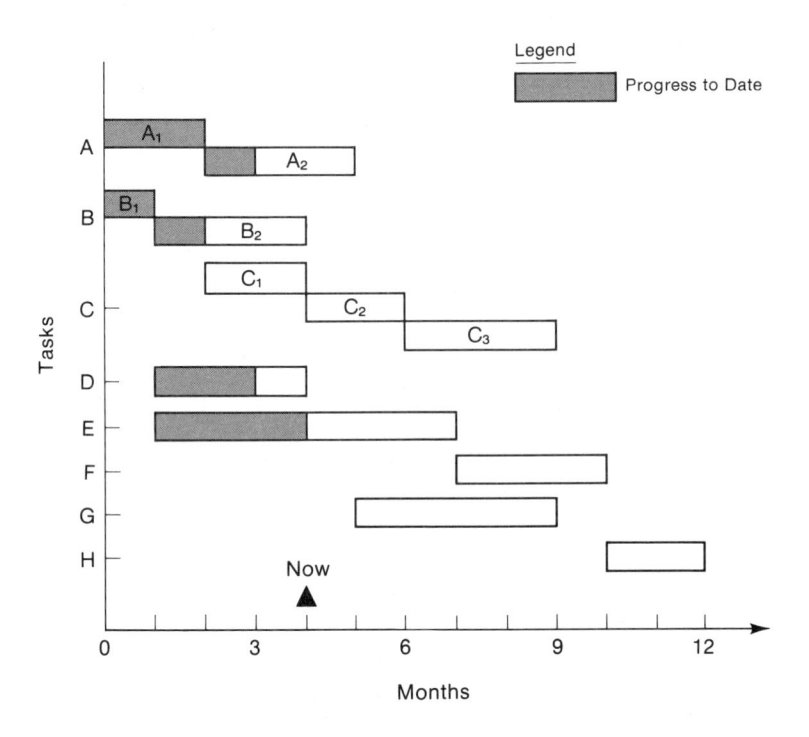

Figure 7-7. Bar chart (from Figure 7-6) with subtask breakdown.

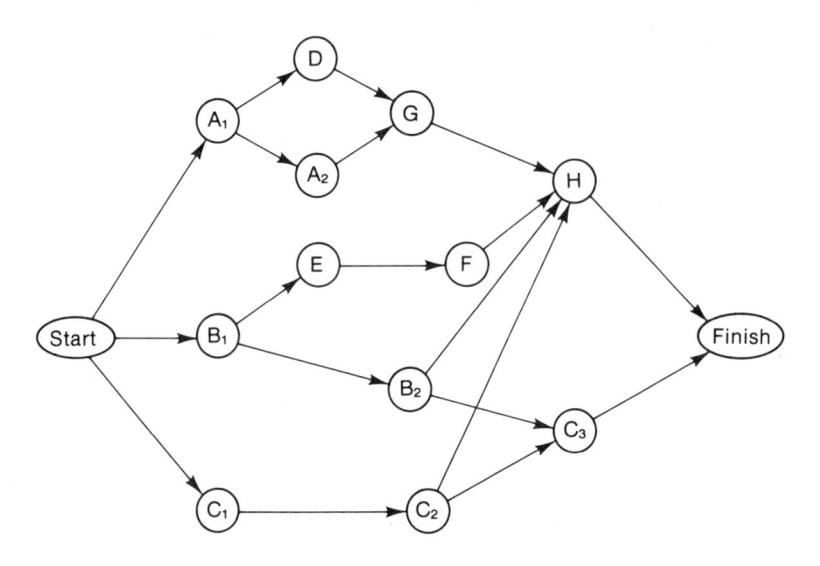

Figure 7-8. PERT network diagram for project of Figure 7-6. Each node designates the completion of the indicated task or subtask.

always be the case where two or more arrows come to a single node, that is, at all merge nodes. This is not a problem for a skilled PERT practitioner, but it does seem to present an unnecessary conceptual difficulty. When the activities are not explicitly shown on a diagram, it is more difficult for the project manager and others to visualize them and their relationship.

A project manager's ability to influence the course of his or her project depends on his or her ability to influence the work on a given activity. One of the few things a project manager can do is change the allocation of resources devoted to a particular activity. Thus, the lack of each activity's explicit visibility in a PERT diagram may be troubling.

This problem can be eliminated if you use a CPM network (Figure 7-9), which shows all activities by labels on the arrows. It clearly indicates the precedences. The requirement of dummy activity, a "no-activity" activity, is to indicate that the completion of activities B_2 and C_2 (as well as activities F and G) must precede the start of activity H. But in this CPM representation, the merge nodes are not single activity completion events. For instance, the node to which D and A_2 arrows come would now have to be designated the completion of both D and A_2. Frankly, this CPM duality does not trouble us as much as PERT's lack of activity emphasis. In

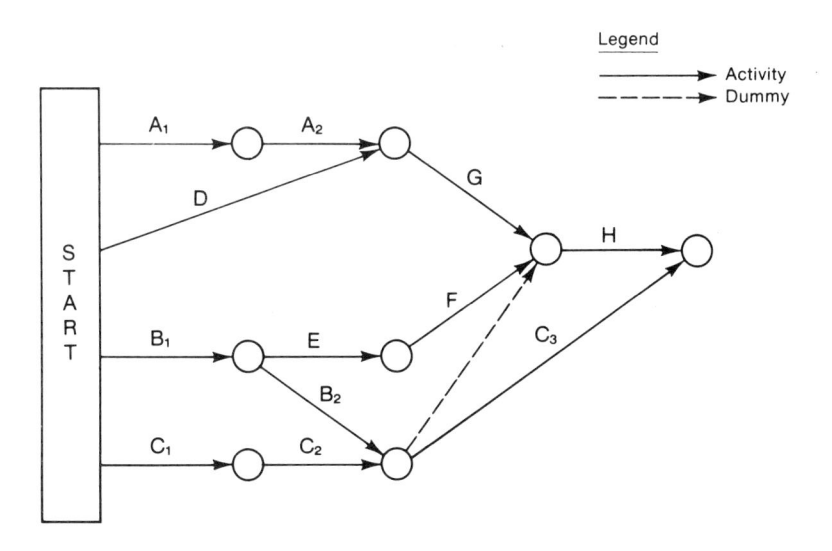

Figure 7-9. CPM diagram with each subtask activity and one precedence condition (or dummy).

The critical path indicates the shortest time in which the project can be completed, and the critical path is a path without any slack.

fact, the duality may actually help by emphasizing that both D and A_2 must be completed before G can commence.

Figure 7-10 illustrates the next step in using the CPM diagram: redrawing it to a time scale in which the horizontal projection of each arrow is proportional to the amount of time required for its activity. Doing this reveals that one path (B_1, E, F, H) is longer than any other. This is called the critical path. It may also be identified as the path that contains no slack or float time. Slack is the amount of time available on a path that is the difference between time required on the critical path and time required on the particular activity path with slack.

Figure 7-10 is drawn with each activity shown starting at the time it was scheduled in Figure 7-7. Noting the task progress status and current date, Figure 7-11 begins to provide direct information as to the implications of the delay on activities A, B, C, and D. Figure 7-12 is a redrawn version of Figure 7-11 in which the project manager has taken advantage of the slack time. That is, all late (delayed) activities are drawn to show the work remaining to be done, and subsequent tasks are thus rescheduled in several cases.

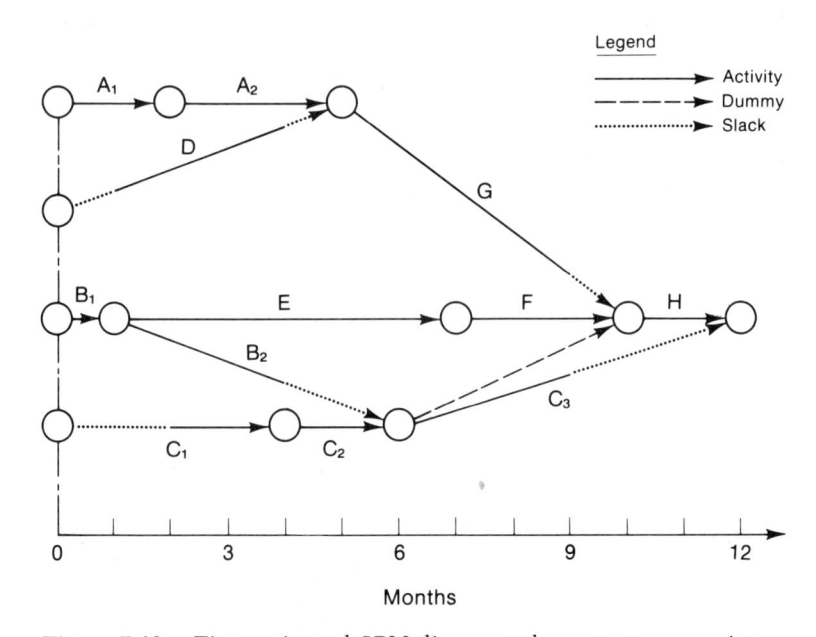

Figure 7-10. Time-oriented CPM diagram, drawn on assumption of task schedules shown in Figure 7-7. (Note start node representation alternative to that used in Figure 7-9.)

Network Diagrams   95

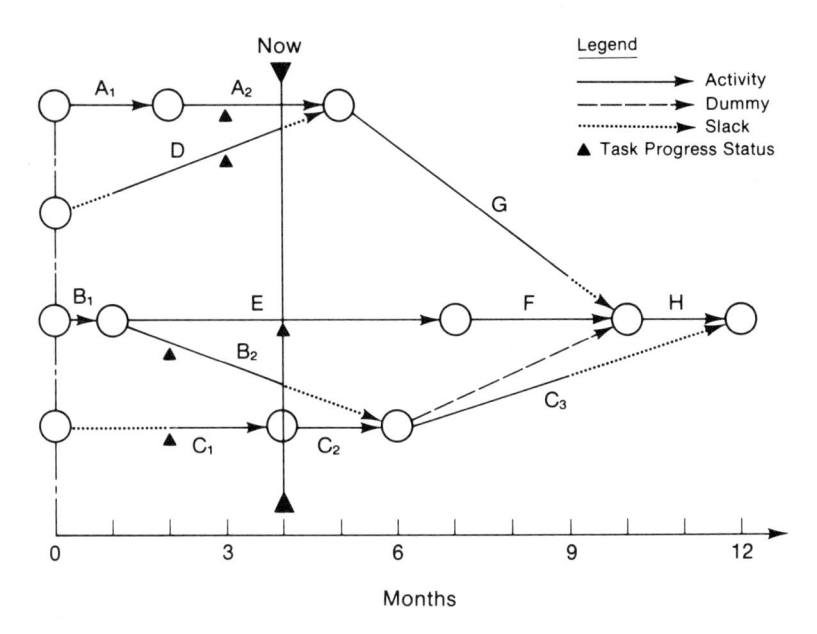

Figure 7-11. Figure 7-10 with task progress status from Figure 7-7 denoted by solid triangles.

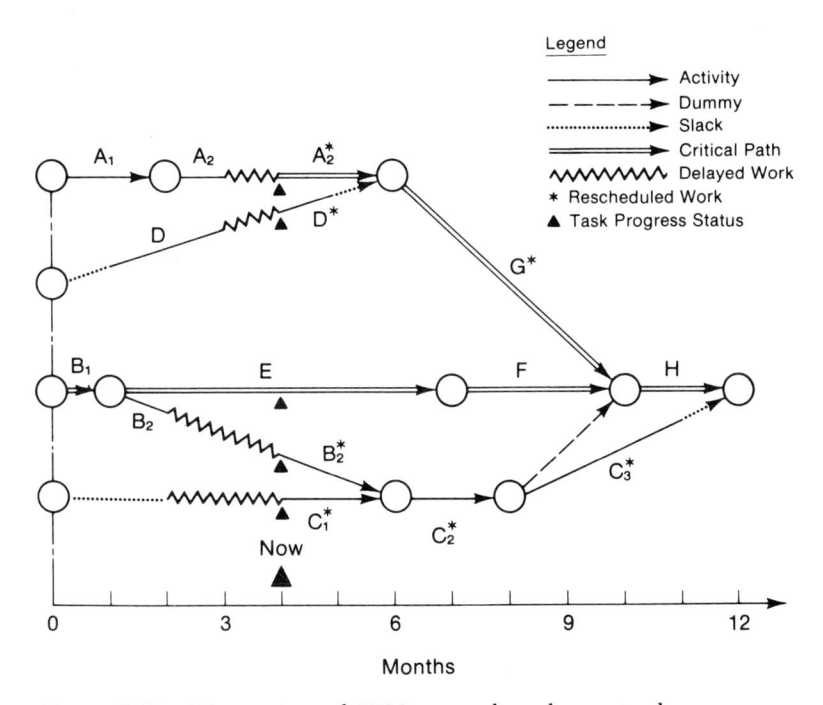

Figure 7-12. Time-oriented CPM network, redrawn to show delayed work and rescheduled activities, permitting project to be completed in accordance with original twelve-month schedule.

Thus, although activities A, B, C, and D are in fact later than planned, the project has not yet suffered any irretrievable schedule slippage. But the project now has two critical paths; whereas it previously had only one. That is, there is no longer any slack in the upper branch (A_2 and G). Because there is still one month of slack on the lower path (task C), perhaps some of the resources allocated to it might be redeployed to one of the other critical path activities. It is vastly more difficult to complete a project with more than one critical path on time, and it is unlikely this project will be completed on schedule, although it is not yet irretrievably lost.

Example
Figures 7-13 and 7-14 are a CPM diagram and bar chart for a system implementation. The network diagram clearly contains far more information than the bar chart.

Helpful Hints
One frequently asked question is, "How do I start a network diagram?" One answer is, "With lots of scrap paper." But the best way to start is with the work breakdown structure. From the WBS, you can start the network diagram from either the beginning or the end of the project. There are frequently somewhat obvious large subnets you can quickly put down on a piece of scrap paper. As a general rule, it is probably best to start from each end with scrap paper and sort out the connectedness in the diagram where there are activities in progress simultaneously. You can then transfer the entire diagram to a clean piece of paper. It is probably helpful to do this with a time base and with the presumption that each activity starts at the earliest possible time.

Include every element in the WBS in the network diagram.

This raises the question of how much time is required for each scheduled activity. Later in this chapter we describe PERT time estimating in more detail. Here we recommend you get the people who will be responsible for each activity to estimate how long it will take to carry it out on a normal work basis. When you put these time estimates onto the network diagram, it may become apparent that the entire project will take too long. At this point, you can identify particular activities for time compression, that is, planning to do them faster than is ideal.

An alternative to time compression is the parallel scheduling of activities—for instance, simultaneous rather than sequential development of two programs. Clearly, there may be increased risk in such a schedule, but that may be the lesser evil.

As shown in Figure 7-15, network diagrams may require crossovers of lines. This is to be expected. Although some diagram rearrangement may get rid of crossovers, it may also distort the logical relationship of groups of activities, for instance, all those being carried out by one department being within a general band of the diagram. If activities A, B, C, D, E, F, and G in Figure 7-15 are performed by one section, the upper diagram, which has two crossover intersections, would be preferable to the lower one. Thus, there are cases in which increased use of crossovers will be clearer.

The project manager should construct a network diagram of perhaps three dozen activities or up to five dozen if required. Such a diagram can normally be drawn in less than two hours and will fit onto a standard seventeen-by-twenty-two-inch sheet of paper. If some activity in this network is very large, its activity manager can make a network diagram for it. In this way, with a few hand-drawn networks of a few

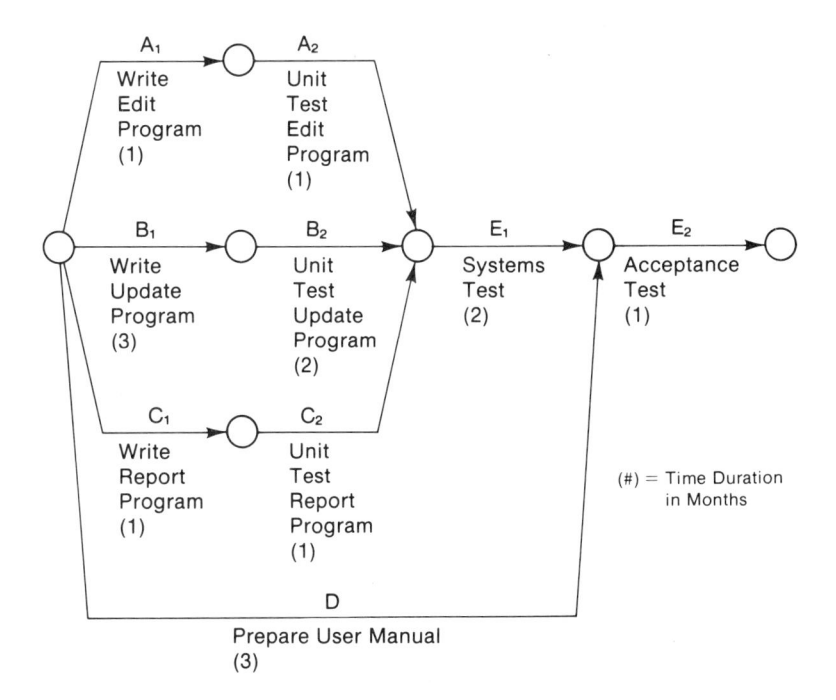

Figure 7-13. CPM network for system implementation, with activity duration in weeks.

If you can't make a network diagram, you can't run the project.

dozen activities each, large projects can be handled without the use of a computer-based network system.

Some project (and other) managers resist the use of network diagrams because they consider them complex or because they lack a computer-based project planning network program. This is a serious mistake because it is not the network diagram that is complex; it is the project itself that is complex. In fact, if you can't draw a network diagram for your project, that should be a clear danger signal that you do not understand your project.

We are not opposed to the use of a computer-based planning network program to assist with the mechanics of network usage. In fact, computer programs have great value in determining resource requirements quickly. But a computer-based network diagram program is not required to manage most projects, and the lack of such computer assistance is no excuse for not using a network diagram.

Very large projects, however, will normally require a computer-based system, and many are available. But you usually lose the "hands on" feel you can get by drawing your

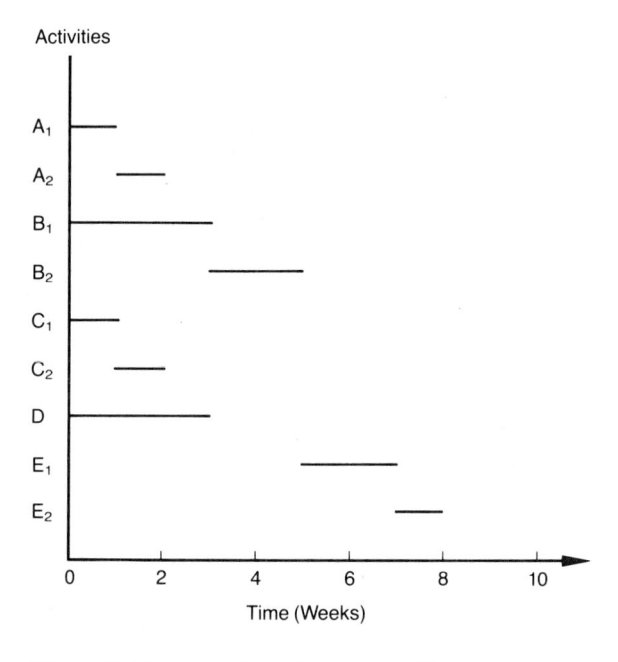

Figure 7-14. Bar chart for project illustrated in Figure 7-15, revealing lack of task interdependency information.

own network diagram. In general, avoid the computer until you are forced to use it. The time required to redraw a network periodically to keep it current is usually less than what you would spend correcting incorrect data entered into the computer.

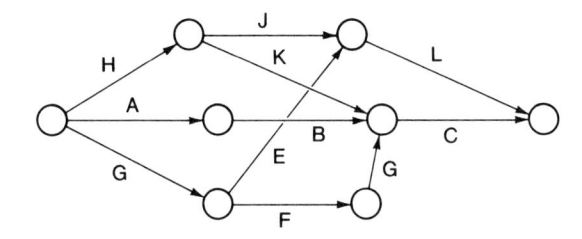

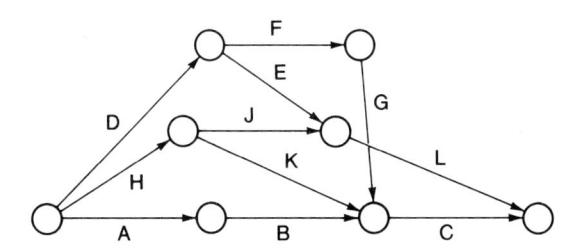

Figure 7-15. CPM network diagram with crossovers.

The critical issue in using networks, whether sketched out by hand or ornately printed by computer, is the granularity— the level of detail being reported. The level of granularity should be appropriate to the level of management that will be receiving the report. Although accuracy and presentation are likewise important, if a schedule is too detailed, its purpose as a control device will be greatly obscured. Additionally, the effort that is put into the management of the schedule (and other aspects of the software project, for that matter) should be proportional to the size of the project being managed. Techniques that are top-heavy in form will probably not be usable enough to manage in a responsive manner. If the methods to change the reporting system are so cumbersome that they cannot be done as the changes occur, then the

Always use a network diagram to plan the schedule dimension, even if you do not show it to your management or customer.

Earliest and Latest Start and Finish Times

The difference between earliest and latest times at a node indicates the amount of slack.

Figure 7-16 is a PERT version of a network diagram, with emphasis on the nodes. It is conventional to assume that projects start at time equal to zero. The earliest time (T_E) we can emerge from the start node is zero. On the critical path, adding the activity time (in this case, 10), we see that the earliest time we can get to the finish node is 10. Latest and earliest are always the same on nodes for the critical path, hence $T_L = 10$ at the finish node and $T_L = 0$ at the start node. Off the critical path, we see that the earliest we can reach the upper node is the earliest we can leave the start node plus the activity time on that path (in this case, 2). Latest times are calculated by working backward. Thus, T_L at the finish node (10) less the activity time (6) tells us that the latest we can leave the upper node, without delaying completion, is $T_L = 4$. The difference between $T_E = 2$ and $T_L = 4$ at this node (2) is the slack, or float, on this upper path.

Now consider a CPM activity-oriented network diagram, which we prefer. The entire project is always assumed to start at time zero. Thus, the start of each activity that emerges

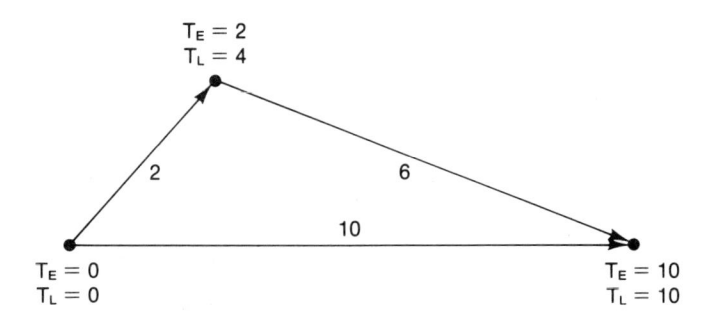

Figure 7-16. Earliest and latest start.

Source: "Project Management." Lecture notes by Milton D. Rosenau, Jr. Copyright © 1981 by the Association for Media-based Continuing Education for Engineers, Inc. (AMCEE). Reprinted by permission.

from the start node has zero as its earliest start time (E_S). The earliest finish time (E_F) for each of these initial activities is the duration of the activity itself (Figure 7-17). Earliest start and finish times are calculated by proceeding from the start node to the finish node. In Figure 7-17A, activity duration is shown by the number above the middle of the activity arrows. The earliest finish of an activity is equal to the activity duration plus the earliest start. At the merge node, the earliest start of the following activity is the higher of the earliest finishes for the preceding activities. On the critical path, the earliest finish at the finish node is both the minimum project duration and the latest finish for that activity.

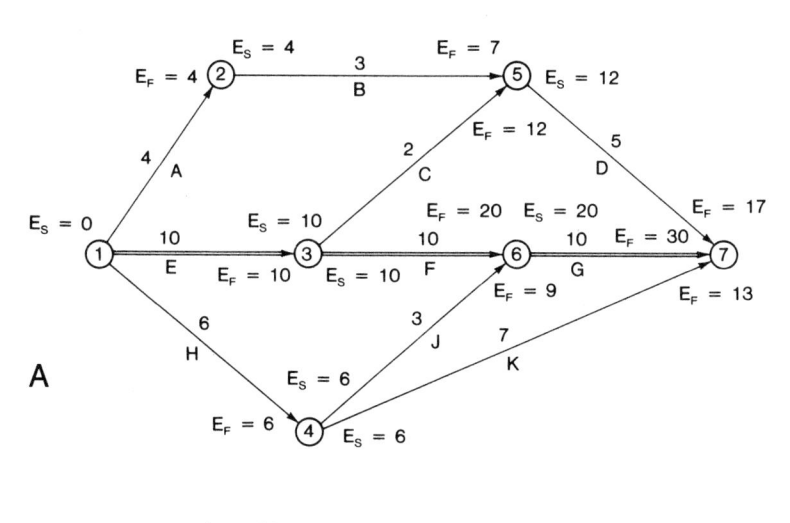

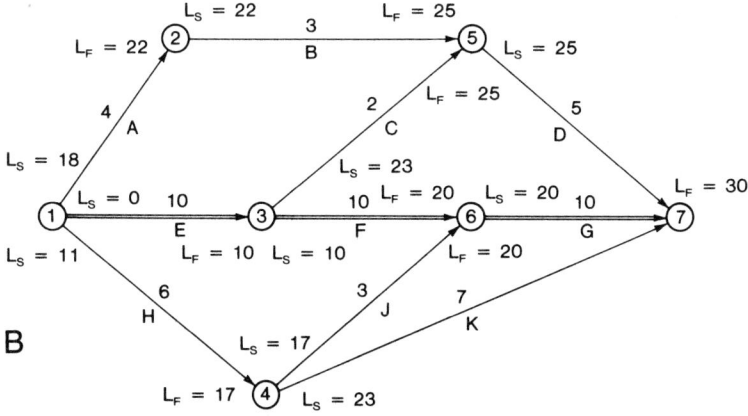

Figure 7-17. Earliest start (E_S) and earliest finish (E_F) and latest start (L_S) and latest finish (L_F) calculations.

Figure 7-17B shows how to calculate latest finish (L_F) and latest start (L_S) times for each activity. Calculation commences at the finish node and proceeds backward to the start node. In Figure 7-17B, on the critical path, the latest and earliest times are equal. The latest start of an activity equals the latest finish of that activity minus the activity duration. At the burst nodes, the latest finish of the preceding activity is the lower of the latest starts for the following activities.

Table 7-1 shows the kinds of data provided by a typical computer printout for the project illustrated in Figure 7-17. Although less graphic, these data reveal the same information. Normally, all the earliest and latest information would be on one diagram. This is illustrated in Figure 7-18. Note that the use of vertical dashed lines, without any dependency arrow indication, permits a node to be drawn in more than one location. This permits spatial separation of activities, thus providing additional open space on the network diagram.

PERT Time Estimating

PERT networks originated in projects characterized by uncertain times for activities. This problem was dealt with by requiring three time estimates for each activity:

TABLE 7-1. Typical Data Provided In a Computer Printout for Computer-Based Network Reporting. (Use with Figure 7-17.)

Event Start	Event Finish	Description	Duration	Start E	Start L	Finish E	Finish L	Slack
1	2	Activity A	4	0	18	4	22	18
1	3	Activity E	10	0	0	10	10	0
1	4	Activity H	6	0	11	6	17	11
2	5	Activity B	3	4	22	7	25	18
3	5	Activity C	2	10	23	12	25	13
3	6	Activity F	10	10	10	20	20	0
4	6	Activity J	3	6	17	9	20	11
4	7	Activity K	7	6	23	13	30	17
5	7	Activity D	5	12	25	17	30	13
6	7	Activity G	10	20	20	30	30	0

1. The most probable activity time (T_m)
2. The optimistic activity time, namely, the shortest time that might be achieved 1 percent of the time such an activity was carried out (T_o)
3. The pessimistic activity time, namely, the time that would be exceeded only 1 percent of the time such an activity was carried out (T_p)

As Figure 7-19 shows, this permits calculation of the expected time for the activity (T_e). The basis for this calculation, unproven and unprovable, is the rule applied in PERT networks

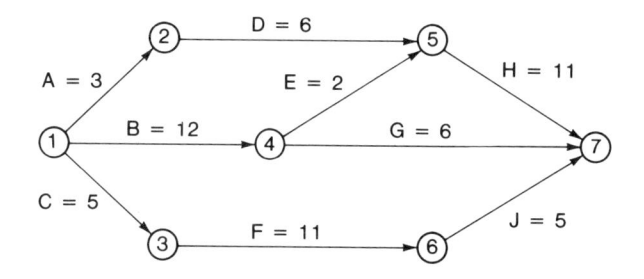

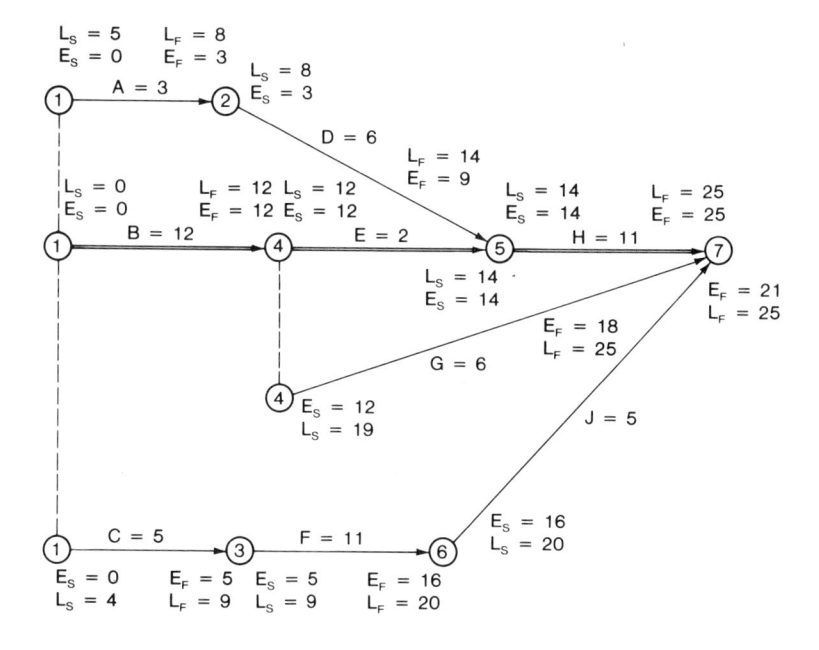

Figure 7-18. CPM earliest and latest start and finish.

and is, in fact, a reasonable way to estimate. You can also calculate the uncertainty of that time, which is called the standard deviation (σ). The calculation is illustrated in Figure 7-20.

Figure 7-21 shows how to calculate the expected time for a path and the standard deviation of the path's expected time. The significance of the calculated standard deviation is the same as with the normal (Gaussian) probability distribution:

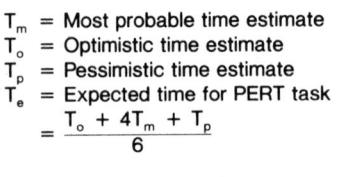

T_m = Most probable time estimate
T_o = Optimistic time estimate
T_p = Pessimistic time estimate
T_e = Expected time for PERT task
$= \dfrac{T_o + 4T_m + T_p}{6}$

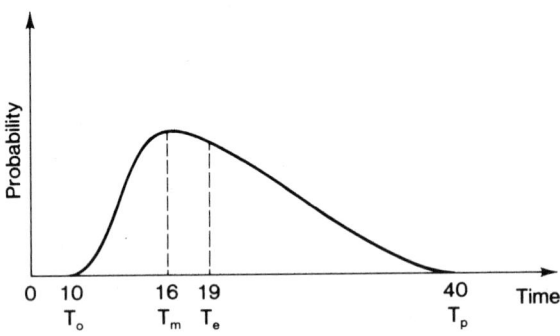

$$T_e = \frac{10 + 4 \times 16 + 40}{6} = 19$$

Figure 7-19. PERT time estimating.

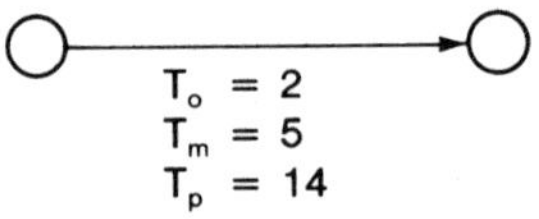

$T_o = 2$
$T_m = 5$
$T_p = 14$

$$T_e = \frac{(1 \times 2) + (4 \times 5) + (1 \times 14)}{6} = 6$$

$$\sigma = \frac{1}{6}(T_p - T_o) = 2$$

Figure 7-20. PERT time uncertainty (σ-standard deviation) for a single event.

Two-thirds of the time, the work will be completed within plus or minus one standard deviation of the expected time; 95 percent of the time, it will be completed within two standard deviations; and 99 percent of the time, it will be completed within three standard deviations. This kind of calculation can be important and helpful if there will be a cost penalty for lateness because you can estimate the likelihood of being late.

Figure 7-22 illustrates the three time estimates for a particular path containing three activities. Completion of the calculations for this case would show that the expected time is twenty-nine days and the standard deviation is six days. Thus, the project's completion would be between the twenty-third and thirty-fifth day two-thirds of the time.

Because it requires a lot of effort to make three time estimates and even more to calculate the expected time and standard deviations, you would normally do this only with a PERT network that was being put on a computer. Nevertheless, it is important to appreciate the technique and apply it where warranted.

PERT time estimating is useful when time schedule is critical.

Pragmatic Time Estimating

We recommend pooled judgment for time estimating. The task leader, project manager, and one to three others should discuss the task and arrive at a judgment as to what the schedule should be. The task leader is there because of the Golden Rule. The project manager is there to provide balance with the other project time estimates. The others are there to bring expertise and experience to bear.

Factors to be considered in making time estimates for a programmer's performance on a task include the following:

- Computer hardware characteristics, such as memory size and storage devices

$$T_{e,path} = T_{e,1} + T_{e,2} + T_{e,3}$$

$$\sigma_{path} = \sqrt{\sigma_1^2 + \sigma_2^2 + \sigma_3^2}$$

Figure 7-21. PERT expected time and uncertainty for a path.

- Operating system characteristics, such as number of users supported and memory utilization schemes
- Source language software characteristics, such as the instruction set and self-documentation
- Programming mode characteristics, such as the amount of off-line or on-line code entry
- Organizational operations standards, such as programming standards and system documentation standards
- Programming problem characteristics, such as input edits and report formats.
- Programmer characteristics, such as overall experience and source language experience

The simple rule of thumb about lines of code per person-month is a useful guide only if the new software is similar to software to which the old rule applied. For instance, twenty thousand lines of code per person-month (*Business Week*, April 18, 1983, p. 82) is remarkably high productivity, likely to be realized only in a unique case. One hundred twenty-five to fifteen hundred lines of code per person-month, which various authors report, is a more normal range, but even this range is so large as to render simple productivity rules of thumb almost worthless.

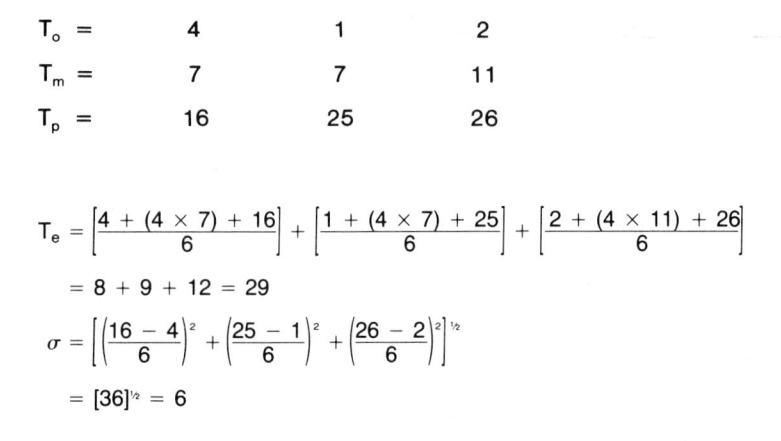

$$T_o = \quad 4 \quad\quad 1 \quad\quad 2$$
$$T_m = \quad 7 \quad\quad 7 \quad\quad 11$$
$$T_p = \quad 16 \quad\quad 25 \quad\quad 26$$

$$T_e = \left[\frac{4 + (4 \times 7) + 16}{6}\right] + \left[\frac{1 + (4 \times 7) + 25}{6}\right] + \left[\frac{2 + (4 \times 11) + 26}{6}\right]$$

$$= 8 + 9 + 12 = 29$$

$$\sigma = \left[\left(\frac{16 - 4}{6}\right)^2 + \left(\frac{25 - 1}{6}\right)^2 + \left(\frac{26 - 2}{6}\right)^2\right]^{1/2}$$

$$= [36]^{1/2} = 6$$

Figure 7-22. Path with three time estimates for each activity.

BAR CHART FORMATS OF CPM DIAGRAMS

Although it is often said that CPM diagrams are difficult to use during project reviews and management briefings because of their apparent complexity, many organizations insist they be used for these purposes. There are at least two ways to make management personnel attending such reviews comfortable with CPM presentations. First, activities can be displayed in a bar chart, indicating their planned time, the earliest start and latest finish, and slack, as shown in Figure 7-23. A second approach is to use vertical connections between activities that are dependent on one another to illustrate that dependency (Figure 7-24). However, to use the bar chart representation of a CPM diagram, you must start with the CPM diagram, not with a bar chart. Figure 7-24 is really a time-phased CPM diagram with all the activity arrows drawn horizontally.

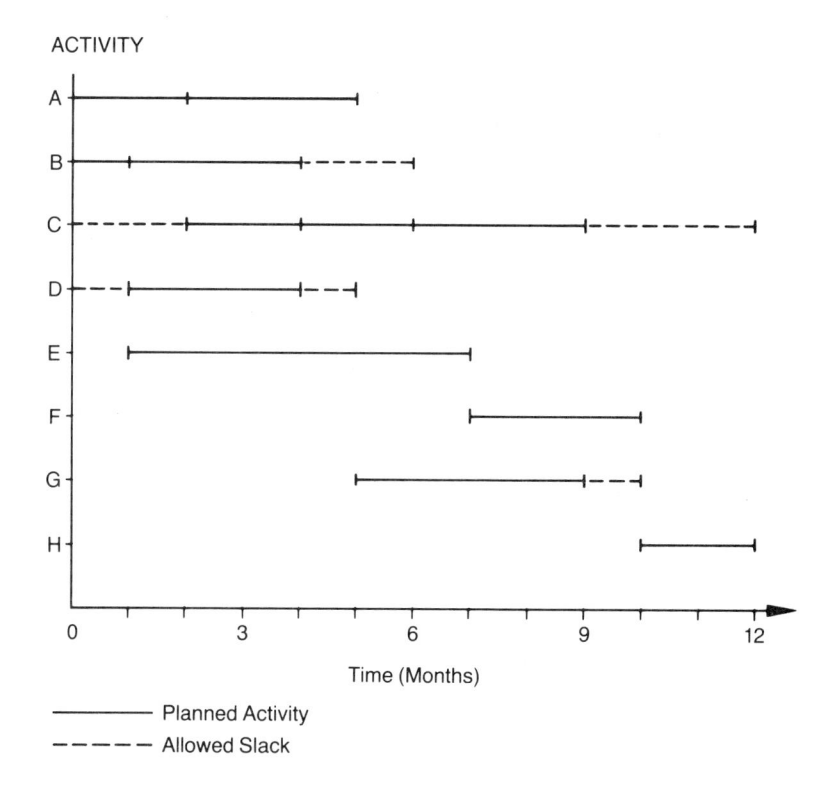

Figure 7-23. Bar chart representation of network diagram from Figure 7-11.

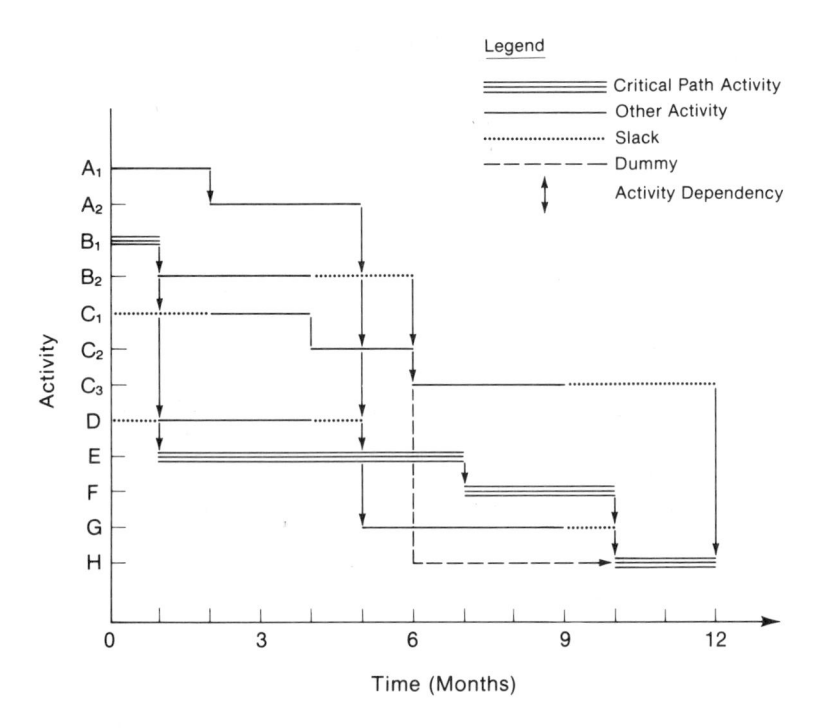

Figure 7-24. Bar chart representation of network diagram from Figure 7-11 with task dependency illustrated.

TYPICAL PROBLEMS

> In many ways, the worst schedule dimension planning problem is to avoid the indicated scheduling problems. For instance, the completed network diagram may show that required hardware will not arrive early enough. This conflict is often avoided or dismissed by saying this can be adjusted later. Maybe it can, but that is hoping for luck to save your project schedule. The solution is to admit that the problem exists and revise the schedule to overcome it—now, not when there is no longer time to correct the problem and maintain your schedule.
>
> It is difficult to obtain accurate time estimates for hardware and new firmware or when applying new
> *continued*

software techniques (for example, relational data bases) to existing problems. As suggested earlier, getting a few people together, including especially those who will be responsible for the activity, and pooling judgments is the best solution to this problem.

Remember also that there is an interaction of schedule with resources applied. A good programmer is usually fast and accurate, and the later walkthroughs or integration activities may thus be fairly quick. Conversely, a poor or junior programmer may be slower and less accurate, and subsequent activities may take longer. The plan reflects what you intend to do, but is not necessarily what you will do. Another aspect of this resource interaction is that two people on one task are not necessarily as productive as one person taking twice as long because the two people must spend time communicating with each other.

Another problem that seriously impacts schedule is when additional resources can be added to the project and indeed have an effect (positive, it is hoped) on it. Adding additional designers during the feasibility and design stage usually will cause the project to fall even further behind, unless a new design is incorporated, because of the great need for educating the new member(s) of the team. Occasionally, additional programmers can be added during implementation, especially if the specifications are complete and the programmers' talents are known to the manager. However, changing design during the implementation stage will clearly require the addition of new milestones and rescheduling of the project, as the impact of such changes percolates throughout. Such perturbations should be minimized whenever possible.

Pool the judgments of those involved to estimate the required time for new activities.

HIGHLIGHTS

Although easy to make and understand, bar charts and milestones alone are inadequate for schedule planning because they do not show how one activity depends on another.

Network diagrams show activity interdependencies.

The most common network diagram forms are PERT and CPM.

Always use a network diagram, which must include every element in the WBS, to plan the schedule dimension of the Triple Constraint.

FURTHER READING

J. Gido. *An Introduction to Project Planning.* Schenectady, NY: General Electric, 1974.
   This is a simple, concise treatment of network diagrams.

L. L. Gremillion and P. Pyburn. "Breaking the Systems Development Bottleneck." *Harvard Business Review* (March-April 1983), pp. 130–137.
   This article describes some ways to save time in systems development.

D. W. Lang. *Critical Path Analysis,* 2nd ed. London: Hodder and Stoughton Paperbacks, 1977.
   This is a good book on networks.

J. Mulvaney. *Analysis Bar Charting—A Simplified Critical Path Analysis Technique,* U.S. ed. Washington, DC: Management Planning Systems, 1977.
   This is a simple, concise treatment of precedence diagrams.

J. D. Wiest and F. K. Levy. *A Management Guide to PERT/CPM,* 2nd ed. Englewood Cliffs, NJ: Prentice-Hall, 1977.
   This is the best book on PERT and CPM. It is clear and complete.

8

Planning the Cost Dimension

Having a cost plan can help you avoid a situation where actual project cost overruns the estimate or you fail to get the job because you overestimated costs during the proposal and negotiation phase. This chapter tells you how to estimate costs and describes several of the most commonly used cost systems.

COST ESTIMATING

Costs may be stated only in terms of the number of labor hours required, a situation not uncommon in a programming group in which a certain number of programmer hours have been allocated to a particular project. Cost is more commonly stated in dollars (or yen or marks), however, which entails converting labor hours into dollars. Different hourly rates typically prevail for different seniority levels, and the cost of nonlabor elements (computer time, purchases, or travel, for instance) is also included. Figure 8-1 shows one way to summarize and total time-phased labor and nonlabor estimates for a task. This figure illustrates the main elements of any successful cost estimating system: Estimate *labor hours* (preferably by category) and *nonlabor dollars* for each task in each involved department or group.

Cost is, of course, necessary for planning, both to sell and manage the job. In general, do not plan costs in detail greater than what you will receive in accounting cost reports. There

Plan costs to the level of detail to which they will be reported to you.

112 Planning the Cost Dimension

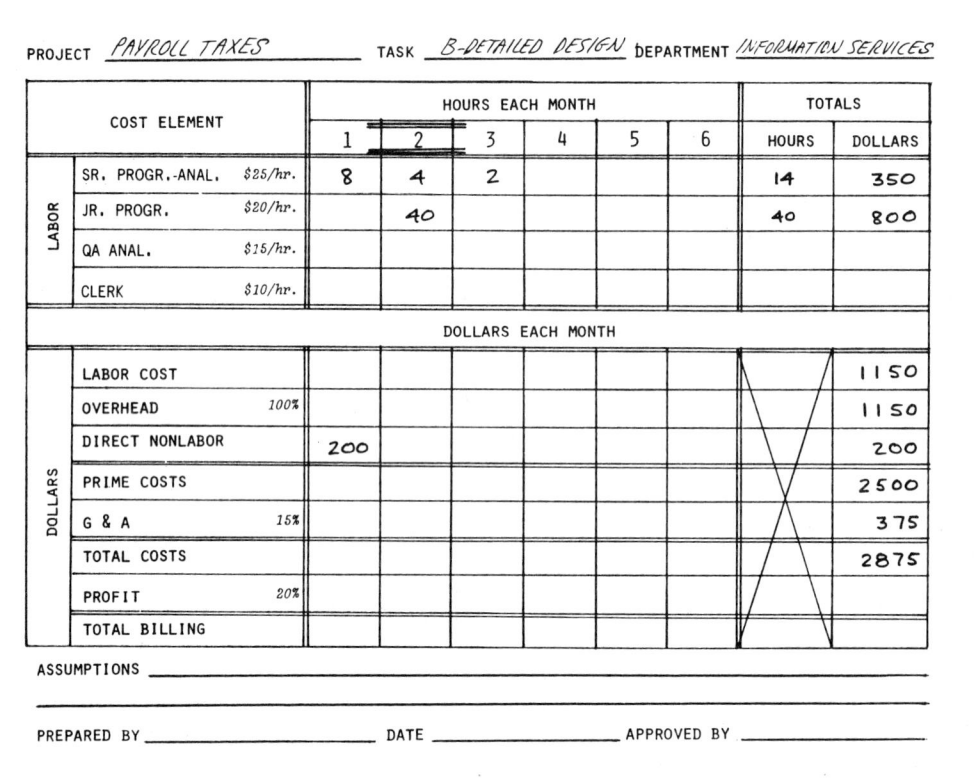

PROJECT PAYROLL TAXES   TASK B-DETAILED DESIGN   DEPARTMENT INFORMATION SERVICES

	COST ELEMENT		HOURS EACH MONTH						TOTALS	
			1	2	3	4	5	6	HOURS	DOLLARS
LABOR	SR. PROGR.-ANAL.	$25/hr.	8	4	2				14	350
	JR. PROGR.	$20/hr.		40					40	800
	QA ANAL.	$15/hr.								
	CLERK	$10/hr.								
			DOLLARS EACH MONTH								
DOLLARS	LABOR COST									1150
	OVERHEAD	100%								1150
	DIRECT NONLABOR		200							200
	PRIME COSTS									2500
	G & A	15%								375
	TOTAL COSTS									2875
	PROFIT	20%								
	TOTAL BILLING									

ASSUMPTIONS _____

PREPARED BY _____ DATE _____ APPROVED BY _____

Figure 8-1. Typical task cost estimate.

is no point making cost plans out on a daily basis if the organization's cost reports are furnished biweekly or monthly. Cost plans, regardless of how they are arrived at, should typically be summarized in monthly periods corresponding to expense reporting. In counting such things as travel cost or computing hours, however, work with hours or days of travel in estimating and sort these into monthly periods.

Just as with the schedule dimension plans, there are inaccuracies inherent in cost estimates, and these must be expected and tolerated. But tolerating such inaccuracies does not mean encouraging them. The goal is to be as accurate as possible and to recognize that perfection is impossible.

Techniques

"Forecasting" and "estimating" are frequently used interchangeably to refer to preparing a plan for the cost dimension. Actually, the dictionary definitions of these words are somewhat different. In project management, we are talking about the amount of money required to complete a piece of work.

If you were asked to estimate *pi,* you could do so as accurately as you wish because *pi* is a known quantity (3.14159 . . .). If, however, you were asked how long an untelevised football game will take, you would probably reply two and a half hours. You are now estimating a future event's duration based on similar previous events. You might have made this estimate by looking up the time for the longest and shortest football games ever played and by noting the times of all other football games for which durations were recorded. You would have learned that the vast majority of football games took between two and a quarter and two and three-quarter hours; therefore, two and a half hours is a reasonable estimate.

Actually, the football game you will see will not take two and a half hours. The probability of your estimate being correct is essentially nil. The only way to *guarantee* that actual costs do not exceed your estimate is to make the estimate very, very high—in which case there is little likelihood of getting the project authorized. The fact that you are not going to be right means you should become accustomed to being wrong and should not be afraid of it. But it does not imply that you should not try to be accurate. Despite these hazards, the goal in estimating is to have a meaningful plan for your project, one you can use to sell the project proposal to your customer, explain your actions to your boss, and provide enough resources to do the job successfully.

There is no point in attempting to estimate a budget for an activity until you have established its duration. In addition, you should understand the preceding and following activities in order to define better the activity you are estimating. Such understanding may clarify that a following activity is farther downstream than it first appears. If so, the activity you are estimating probably is longer, and therefore costs more, than you first thought.

Schedule first; estimate second.

You do the estimating by breaking the project into tasks and activities, using the WBS and network diagrams. The budget of any large activity is the sum of the smaller tasks that compose it, as shown in Figure 8-2. In general, use as much detail as possible. Every task in the WBS should probably have an individual task estimate (such as Figure 8-1) prepared by the responsible task manager.

Estimate the cost of each task.

114   Planning the Cost Dimension

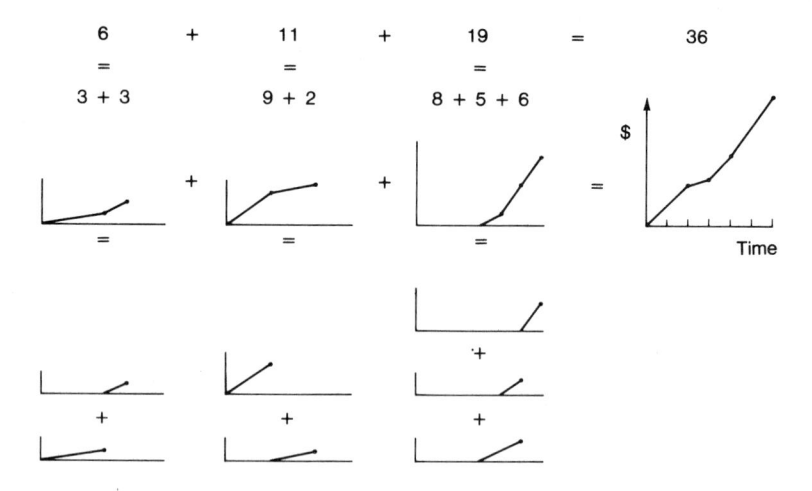

Figure 8-2. A project's cost is the summation of costs for all project tasks.

Shortcuts

There is a variety of means to prepare cost estimates. Using as much detail as possible is commonly called the "bottom up" method. The major project is divided into work packages small enough to allow accurate estimation. The project estimate is the sum of the estimates for all the individual work packages.

There are shortcuts to estimating some of the small work packages. You can use similarities to and differences from other tasks to shortcut a complete level of detail for a second task. Or you can use ratios or standards to relate one small task to another.

To make a project cost estimate, add detailed task estimates for each work department and adjust them if the overall summation seems unreasonable.

Whenever you use the bottom up technique, judge it against a "top down" estimate. The top down estimate is done first, quickly and judgmentally, and then it is set aside. For instance, assume the bottom up estimate comes to $10 million. Your top down estimate, which you now retrieve, is $5 million. Go back and look at each individual work package in the bottom up estimate to find out where the excess costs arise. Examine each package to discover to what extent there has been an incorrect assumption as to the amount of work called for. Or your top down estimate may indicate that the total job should cost $20 million. Explore the details to find out what has been overlooked or what unwarranted simplifying assumptions were made. The role of the top down estimate is to provide a point of view from which to scrutinize the bottom up estimate. Note, however, that the bottom up estimate is probably more accurate than the top down estimate.

Parametric Cost Estimating

Figure 8-3 illustrates a relationship between project cost and program lines of code that we might discover if we examined a large number of previous projects. The shaded area in the figure would surround a cloud of points, each of which represents a particular project outcome.

If we examine these projects in more detail, we could ask how many separate modules were involved. Then the data points could be separated, and we might find a trend as in Figure 8-4, where the lines are the centroids of smaller clouds of data points.

Use historical data in parametric cost estimating.

This is the underlying notion of parametric cost estimating. Historical data for many factors are used:

- Project magnitude—How big is it?
- Program application—What is its character?
- Level of new design and code—How much new work is needed?
- Resources—Who will do the work?

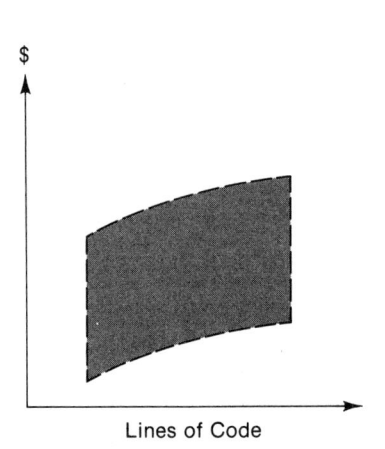

Figure 8-3. Relationship between project cost and lines of program code for a large number of computer software projects.

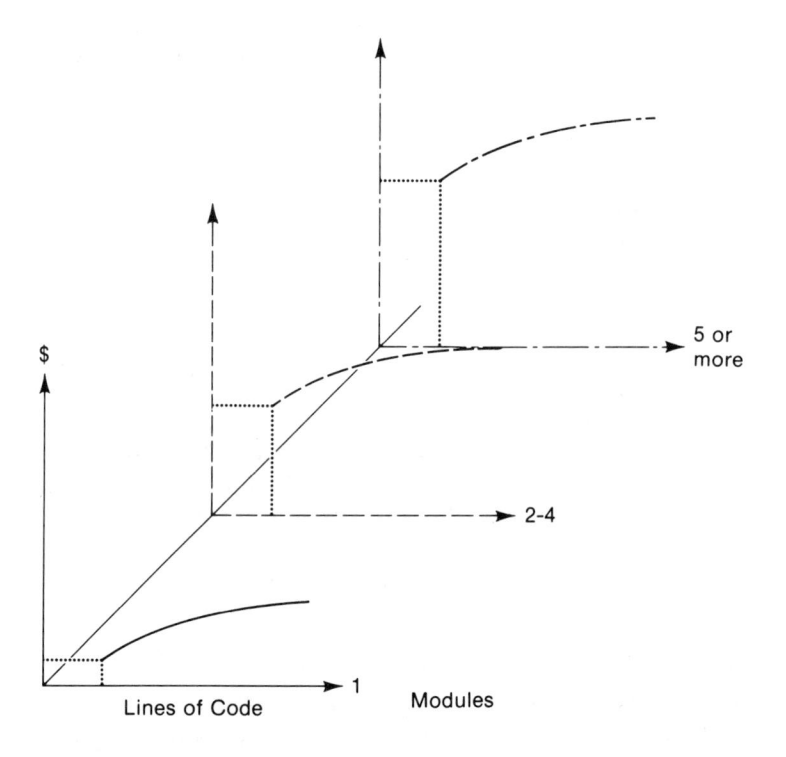

Figure 8-4. Trends of Figure 8-3 data when number of program modules is considered.

- Utilization—What are the hardware constraints?
- Customer specifications and reliability requirements—Where and how are these used?
- Development environment—What complicating factors exist?
- Complexity of effort—How difficult are the various modules?

Then, if your project falls within the range of these historical data, you merely insert your project's parameters into the multidimensional regression model to estimate your project's cost.

There are many such parametric cost estimating models. RCA's PRICE S, primarily applicable to government software projects, is accessible for interactive on-line use. The estimate you get from using such a parametric model is only an estimate and will be inaccurate if your input data (for instance, the number of lines of code) are poor estimates.

Basing Cost Estimates on Experience

One of the chief reasons cost estimating is so difficult in software development projects is that writing and implementing computer software is a creative process. Artists would be hard put to quantify the cost of what they have yet to execute! However, although it is difficult, it is not impossible, as long as you give up hopes of being 100 percent precise. You can estimate costs if you use your own experience as a guideline.

You cannot make a 100 percent accurate estimate.

Costs will be affected by at least five factors. One is the newness of the effort. If it has not been done before, then it will be much harder to determine just what tasks are required to get you to completion.

A second factor is the people working on the project. New personnel need time to become familiar with others on the project as well as with the project itself. The existing team also needs additional time to absorb newcomers. These factors tend to increase your costs. You know your people—and their capabilities—and when you have the same people on a new project, you should be able to estimate the cost dimension more accurately than when you have unknowns coming on board. Especially in the implementation of computer software, the task performer's familiarity with language and machines should not be ignored by managerial dictates.

The facilities will also affect costs. If you have been working with the equipment and operations personnel, you will have a good idea of issues such as reliability and performance to help in estimating your project costs more accurately. If a new development center is going to be required for your project, you can assume your costs will be higher because you will in effect be debugging the development center as well!

Time is a fourth factor. Again, based upon your experience in working within your organization, you can get a pretty good idea as to the effects an intense deadline will have on your project. For example, if your company is always issuing unrealistic due dates and programmers tend to spend months with odd schedules because of limited computer time availability, you have probably already observed a decline in programmer productivity as burnout occurs. In estimating, you can assume greater costs because productivity is down, or perhaps you might even plan for outside computer access during the critical implementation phase. Another issue related to time concerns the time estimates as they relate to the project life cycle phases. Again, based on your experience in your organization, you may observe that very little time is allocated for feasibility determination, but much time is spent in detailed design. As long as you incorporate this experience into your cost estimates, your figures will be more accurate for each phase of your project.

A fifth factor affecting cost is complexity. The larger the project—number of people, number of modules, number of installations, length of time—the greater the cost. Within your organization, there will be a critical size within which efficiency is the hallmark. Above that there is a degradation in performance of all resources. When you have identified your company's critical size, you can better estimate your project costs.

Experience-based estimates work the best.

The better you know what and who your resources are, the more accurate will be your estimate. Never suspend common sense in the estimating process!

Cautions

Cost estimates are frequently made prematurely, before the work performance and time schedule are fully understood and defined. Such cost estimates must then be redone or adjusted when the performance and schedule are set. It is clearly more efficient to do the cost estimating after the other two dimensions are defined.

There is a danger signal to which project managers must be alert when receiving cost estimates: the person-month dimension to describe the labor requirement (or, to use Brooks's more sexist term, "the mythical man-month"). This is a danger signal because it frequently indicates a snap judgment on the part of the estimator (and not because it is an inappropriate measure, although hours seem preferable). The person who can do the task in two months may not be available when he or she is needed. Or a task that can be done by one person in three months (three person-months) may require four people if it must be completed in one month (four person-months). And, because technical skill levels differ and also because adding additional personnel to subdivide a task requires time for intercommunication (thus reducing efficiency), months are not distributed over just any people.

On lengthy projects, have an inflation hedge.

A pertinent issue today is how to plan for inflation. Such planning can be done only with great difficulty and caution. Unfortunately, there are no guarantees in dealing with the future; so some method of coping must be adopted. Make the best estimate of labor hours regardless of when the activity will occur. Then estimate the rates for these labor hours and the dollar amounts for nonlabor ingredients in current dollars. You can then apply inflation factors for future years to these numbers by consulting with your organization's financial planners.

PREDEFINED COST

In some situations, you may be asked what (or how much) can be done for a specified amount of money (or in a specified time). In such a case, you have to work backwards. The best approach is to start with a two-level WBS. Put the specified cost target in the top-level box. Then allocate this into the second-level boxes in a trial assignment.

Next add further WBS levels and continue trial cost allocations. When you encounter a WBS box for which the trial cost allocation is inadequate, try to adjust all boxes to allow more cost for the one you feel is inadequately funded. At this point, you will be able to provide a rough or preliminary estimate of what can be accomplished for the specified funding.

It is now wise to ask the customer (or requester) for an informal reaction. If it is favorable, start the planning and cost estimating work as previously described in this book. If the reaction is unfavorable, it is usually best to reiterate that you believe you can only accomplish what was previously stated, and ask the customer (or requester) to help you reallocate the specified cost. If the customer chooses to join you in this cost allocation work, you are both more likely to arrive at a harmonious outcome.

PROJECT COST SYSTEM

To use project cost reports, you must have a project cost accounting system, which is a means to accumulate costs by project and project activity or task detail. There are four elements to such a system:

1. Labor
    Own people
    Other people in company
2. Overhead burden

3. Nonlabor
    Purchases
    Subcontracts
    Travel
    Computer charges
4. General and administrative burden

There are many variations in detail for project cost systems, some of which are shown in Table 8-1. We are making the simplifying assumption that the organization has three projects (A, B, and C), which all start at the beginning and will end at the close of the fiscal year. It does not matter whether the work is for the company or an outside client or whether it is to be paid for by the sale of goods or contract billing. The point is there has to be some way of allocating the cost of these three projects to different customers or product lines. The table illustrates four methods of allocating these costs to the three projects. In method 1, the direct labor and direct nonlabor are allocated to the project, and these are summed to provide a direct total. All the burden and overhead accounts are then lumped and apportioned to each project in proportion to the direct total expenses. In method 1, these are equal and the billings to each of the three projects would be equal.

In method 2, the direct labor and direct nonlabor are treated as before, but the overhead portion is allocated to each project in accordance with the amount of direct labor it requires. Nevertheless, the general and administrative (G and A) expenses are allocated to the projects in accordance with the direct total, as in method 1. In this case, the billings to the projects are not equal. Project A is more than B, which is more than C.

Method 3 and its variants are the most common project cost systems.

In method 3, the overhead is treated as in method 2, and the direct nonlabor is treated as in both methods 1 and 2. But in this case, all these items and direct labor are joined to come up with a prime cost, and the G and A burden is allocated in proportion to that. In this case, we arrive at a still higher amount of billing for project A.

Method 4 is one of many common variations of method 3. Direct labor and overhead are treated as in method 3, but purchases are subject to a material handling charge. (In method 3, this material handling charge is included in G and A; in method 4, it is pulled out of G and A and assigned to the projects in proportion to their required purchases.) But other direct nonlabor, in this case, travel, is not allocated a handling fee, as illustrated in project C. This results in a still different prime cost. Finally, the G and A expenses are again distributed, and a still different billing arrangement is arrived at.

All these methods, and others as well, are used. The project manager must understand his or her company's method in order to know when to use subcontract help and when to use in-house, direct labor.

It is also important to understand any subcontractor's cost accounting system. If you are placing a labor intensive contract with a subcontractor, you should not use a subcontractor who practices method 3 as opposed to method 1.

In addition to understanding project budgets, you should understand the relationship between project budgets and administrative budgets, as illustrated in Figure 8-5. The

Understand the relationship between project budgets and administrative budgets.

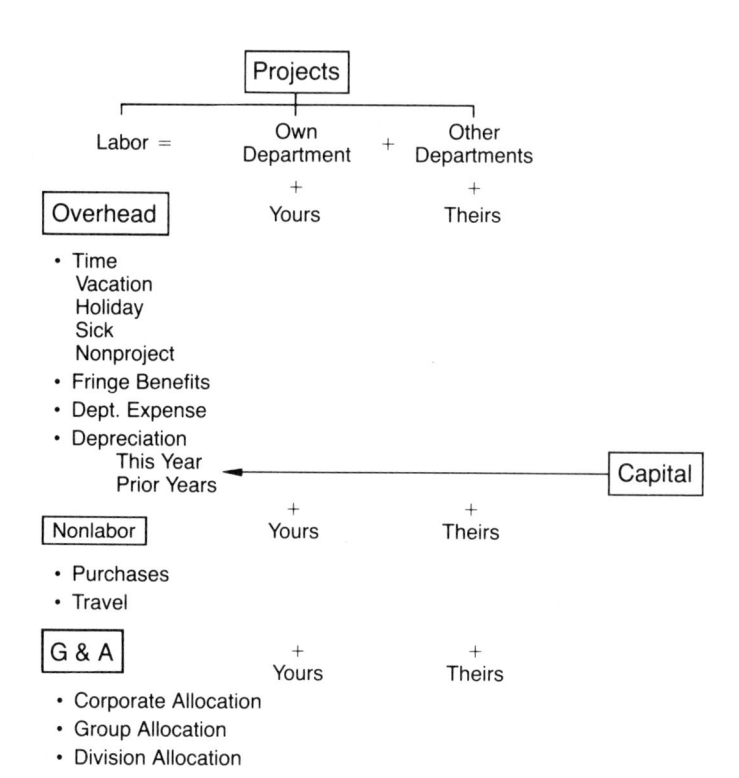

```
                        ┌──────────┐
                        │ Projects │
                        └──────────┘
           ┌─────────────────┬─────────────────┐
 Labor =         Own            +    Other
              Department           Departments
                  +                    +
                Yours                Theirs
┌──────────┐
│ Overhead │
└──────────┘
 • Time
   Vacation
   Holiday
   Sick
   Nonproject
 • Fringe Benefits
 • Dept. Expense
 • Depreciation
     This Year                              ┌─────────┐
     Prior Years  ◄────────────────────────│ Capital │
                                            └─────────┘
                  +                    +
                Yours                Theirs
┌──────────┐
│ Nonlabor │
└──────────┘
 • Purchases
 • Travel
┌──────┐
│ G & A│
└──────┘         +                    +
                Yours                Theirs
 • Corporate Allocation
 • Group Allocation
 • Division Allocation
```

Figure 8-5. Budget relationships.
Source: "Basic Management Skills for Engineers and Scientists." Lecture notes by Milton D. Rosenau, Jr. Copyright © 1982 by the University of Southern California. Reprinted by permission.

TABLE 8-1. Four Common Project Cost Systems, Illustrated for Three Projects ($000 omitted).

	Project A	Project B	Project C	Indirect		Total
Direct Labor	50	30	10	90	⎫ = 150 ⎧ Labor ⎭ ⎨ Purchases ⎩ Travel	
Direct Nonlabor	0	20	40	30		
Overhead on Direct Labor					⎫ = 120 ⎧ Fringe Benefits	= 270
General & Administrative					⎭ ⎨ Indirect time of direct labor personnel	
Burden					⎧ Indirect labor personnel	
					⎨ Facility costs	
					⎩ General supplies	
					⎩ Publications	
Method 1						
Direct Labor	50	30	10			
Direct Nonlabor	0	20	40			
Direct Total	50	50	50		= 150	
Burdens on Direct Total	40	40	40		= 120	
Total Costs	90	90	90		270	
Method 2						
Direct Labor	50	30	10			
Direct Nonlabor	0	20	40			
Direct Total	50	50	50		⎫ = 150	
Overhead on Direct Labor	50	30	10		⎬ = 90	
General & Administrative					⎭ = 120	
Burden on Direct Total	10	10	10		= 30	
Total Costs	110	90	70		= 270	

TABLE 8-1. Four Common Project Cost Systems, Illustrated for Three Projects ($000 omitted).

	Project A	Project B	Project C	Indirect	Total
Method 3					
Direct Labor	50	30	10		
Overhead on Direct Labor	50	30	10	$\Big\}=90$	
Direct Nonlabor	0	20	40		
"Prime" Costs	100	80	60		= 120
General & Administrative					
Burden on "Prime" Costs	12.5	10.	7.5	$\Big\}=30$	
Total Costs	112.5	90	67.5		= 270
Method 4					
Direct Labor	50	30	10		
Overhead on Direct Labor	50	30	10	$\Big\}=90$	
Direct Nonlabor–Purchases	0	20	20		
Material Handling Burden	0	5	5	=10	=120
Direct Nonlabor–Other	0	0	20		
"Prime" Costs	100	85	65		
General & Administrative					
Burden on "Prime" Costs	8	6.8	5.2	=20	=30
Total Costs	108	91.8	70.8		=270

Project Cost System 123

administrative budgets are overhead, general and administrative, and capital. As we saw in Table 8-1, overhead and G and A may be combined into a single burden pool. Capital expenditures enter into the overhead (or G and A) budgets by requiring inclusion of depreciation. Thus, the direct cost of a project, its own direct labor and nonlabor expenses, is not really a measure of its cost to the organization. The project must, in common with all other organizational activities, carry burdens that depend on other organizational activities and budgets.

TYPICAL PROBLEMS

There are four important problems in planning the cost dimension of the Triple Constraint. First, many project groups or project managers have a deplorable tendency to make cost estimates for support group work. This forecloses the possibility of benefiting from support group expertise and violates the Golden Rule. This is easily solved by requiring every department to approve the estimate for the work it will do.

A second problem is dealing with inflated estimates by support groups. Here the project manager can first try discussion and negotiation. If that does not produce a satisfactory agreement, the project manager could alter the nature of the requested support work. Two other possible solutions are to subcontract the support work to another company or appeal to higher management.

Higher management, if they decide to "buy in," often cause a third problem. "Buying in" is bidding a lower price than truly estimated, hoping for later contract changes that will justify price increases. If you are convinced that buying in is disaster, you can request someone else assume project management. Or you can record your objections in a memo and try to accomplish the promised work within the budget. Finally, you can undertake the job and work actively to sell your customer on changes of scope that provide an opportunity for more funding.

continued

> Another problem concerns project cost systems that do not give you enough information. If you cannot get the cost data broken out as you need it, then you will not be able to report against plans throughout the life of the project. Resolve this with the accounting department before you agree to manage the project.

HIGHLIGHTS

Cost estimates are usually made in dollars.

Cost estimates can be made top down or bottom up, but a better method is to do both, in that order.

A parametric cost estimate may be useful and simple, especially if your project is reasonably similar to others for which historical data are available. But there is nothing better than your own personal experience within your organization and a knowledge of its resources.

The elements of a project cost accounting system, a means to tally costs by project and project task, are labor, overhead burden, nonlabor, and general and administrative burden.

FURTHER READING

F. P. Brooks, Jr. *The Mythical Man-Month: Essays on Software Engineering.* Reading, MA: Addison-Wesley, 1975; portions of this are abstracted in *PC Magazine* (September 1983), p. 211.
 This is the source of Brooks's Law: Adding personnel to a software project will only make it later.

J. Celko. "The Software Manager's Guide to Guesstimating." *Information Systems News* (August 22, 1983), pp. 35–36.
 This short article contains practical advice on estimating, stressing the need to reestimate as more is known.

R. H. Clough and G. A. Sears. *Construction Project Management*, 2nd ed. New York: Wiley-Interscience, 1979.
 Chapter 3, although specific to the construction industry, is a thorough treatment of estimating.

T. DeMarco. *Controlling Software Projects.* New York: Yourdon, 1982.
> *Chapters 1–5, pages 1–38, are a folksy discussion that provides a very practical treatment of the special problems in estimating software project cost. (However, the author recommends that there should be a separate cost estimating group, with which we disagree because it violates the Golden Rule.)*

L. Fried. *Practical Data Processing Management.* Reston, VA: Prentice-Hall/Reston, 1979.
> *Chapter 3, pages 70–146, provides a discussion of the basis of parametric cost estimating, although the treatment is a bit too mathematical.*

V. G. Hajek. *Management of Engineering Projects.* New York: McGraw-Hill, 1977.
> *Chapter 6 has a brief discussion of cost estimating pitfalls.*

J. A. Maciariello. *Program-Management Control Systems.* New York: Wiley-Interscience, 1978.
> *Chapter 7 is a brief treatment of project cost accounting systems.*

F. W. McFarlan. "Portfolio Approach to Information Systems." *Harvard Business Review* (September-October 1981), pp. 142–150.
> *This article discusses project risk and enumerates some of the factors to be weighted in parametric cost estimating.*

"PRICE Parametric Price Models." Cherry Hill, NJ: RCA PRICE Systems.
> *Descriptive brochures on all the RCA PRICE models.*

9

The Impact of Limited Resources

This chapter treats several topics that typically involve two or three dimensions of the Triple Constraint. The first is resource allocation and how to resolve these resource constraints. Then we present techniques that allow analysis of schedule and budget trade-offs. Following that, we review methods to provide vitally important schedule and cost contingency and discuss the trade-off with risk. Next we cover ways to use computers to assist planning. Finally, we discuss a hybrid system, C/SCSC, used in large Department of Defense contracts.

RESOURCES

Allocation

Resources are either people or things. Human resources may include everyone in a particular unit or those with a specific skill (typing, software engineering, or computer programming, for example). Things include any kind of equipment (for instance, terminal availability or computer time) as well as floor space to house the equipment and the people. Money may also be considered a nonhuman resource.

There are three reasons to consider resource allocation in a project management environment. First, forecasted use of some key resource (for instance, systems architects) may indicate there will be surplus personnel at some future period. This information should warn the appropriate managers to obtain new business to utilize the surplus talent or to plan to

Surplus resources waste money and talent.

128   The Impact of Limited Resources

reassign the involved personnel. Due to its very nature, each phase of the project life cycle has different resource requirements. Failure to plan for effective use beyond the appropriate phase demotivates personnel and wastes costly resources.

Another reason for resource allocation is to avoid inherent inconsistencies, such as using a particular resource (Jane Programmer, for example) on two tasks at the same time. Preparing a network diagram to a time base emphasizes resource allocation and reveals latent conflicts.

Use network diagrams to show what resources are needed when.

A network diagram can show what resources are required and when, which may reveal that more of some resources will be needed than will be available at some time. When you discover this, you must adjust the network diagram to shift the overloaded resource requirement to some other time. If you fail to do this, slippage will occur. Figure 9-1 illustrates resource allocation. In this case, the resource is the personnel headcount. Tasks A and B, each of eight weeks duration, require three and five personnel, respectively. Tasks C, D, and E are not on the critical path, and examination of the earliest and latest times for them shows they can be commenced

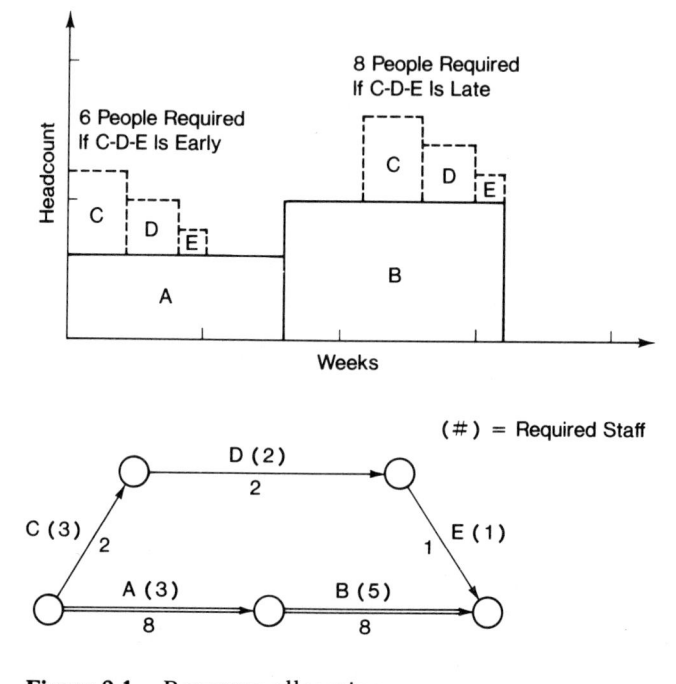

Figure 9-1.   Resource allocation.

immediately or as late as the eleventh week. If the company performing this project employs only six people, task D would have to start early enough to be completed before the end of the eighth week, when task B is scheduled to start.

A third use of this kind of analysis occurs in a large company. Imagine that tasks C, D, and E are performed by a particular support department, for instance, the quality assurance section. If the quality assurance section were provided with resource allocation information for all projects, as shown in Figure 9-1, they could identify the earliest and latest dates at which the support, in this case, C, D, and E, would have to be applied. Doing the same for all projects would allow the support group to even out its work load and to identify in each case the impact of any slippage.

Constraints

Consider the CPM network diagram in Figure 9-2. After planning the work, you arrive at a summary of labor skills required for this project (Table 9-1). Suppose that you have only nine junior programmers. What are your options? What might you do? What are the risks?

Figure 9-3 graphically summarizes the junior programmer staffing each week. There are two weeks when ten junior programmers are required, but the constraint is that only nine are available. Some of your options are to use overtime, use senior programmers to do the work, or delay task F (which has slack) by two weeks. The last option, which seems most appropriate, runs the risk of reducing slack that may be needed later. In general, the way to remove resource constraints when only one project is involved is as follows:

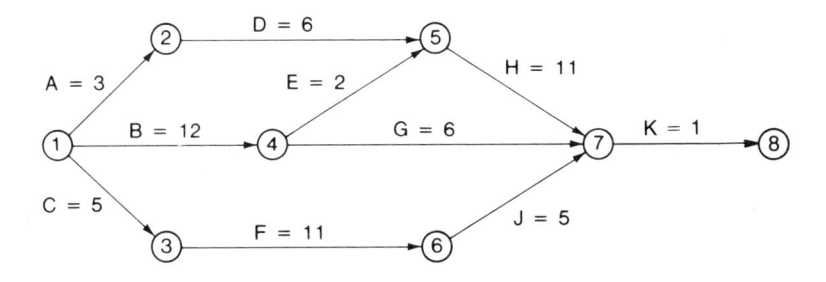

Figure 9-2. CPM diagram.

TABLE 9-1. Resource allocation, using network of Figure 9-2.

		Required Resources					
Task	Planned	Senior	Junior	System	Data Entry	Oper.	Word
	Duration	Progr.	Progr.	Analyst	Clerk		Processor
A	3	2	4	4			
B	6		2			3	
C	12*	3	4	4			
D	2*		2		5		
E	11*	2	5		2	2	
F	6		2	7			
G	6	4	1				
H	10	1	3				
J	5		2				
K	1*	2	2				3

* = Task is on critical path.

1. Identify resource requirements for tasks on the critical path.
2. Add resource requirements for other tasks, using desired start dates.
3. Compare resource requirements with resource availability.
4. Identify options to remove resource conflicts that are found, such as the following:
   - Verify that the conflict is real.
   - Adjust start dates for tasks with slack.
   - Give the schedule more attention to reduce downtime inefficiency.
   - Improve productivity, using new tools, improved match of people with tasks, or incentives.
   - Adjust resource availability temporarily by planning overtime, rescheduling vacations, obtaining temporary employees (carefully), subcontracting tasks, using more senior people on junior tasks, changing resource availability, training or promoting surplus skill to fill the need, or hiring new people.
   - Change the time schedule by accelerating the cri-

Task	Junior Programmer Required Each Week (Assuming Earliest Start on Each Task)
A	4 4 4
B	2 2 2 2 2 2
C	4 4 4 4 4 4 4 4 4 4 4 4
D	2 2
E	5 5 5 5 5 5 5 5 5 5
F	2 2 2 2 2 2
G	1 1 1 1 1 1
H	3 3 3 3 3 3 3 3 3 3
J	2 2 2 2 2
K	2

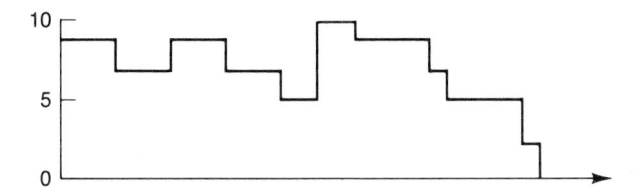

Figure 9-3. Junior programmer resource requirement on first project (network diagram of Figure 9-2).

tical path to get ahead of schedule, delaying the critical path to be late, changing the start date of new projects, or delivering in phases rather than at once.
- Change the plan specifications, task sequence, or standards.

Suppose you have a simultaneous second project (Figure 9-4). Suppose that task W requires four quality assurance analysts and you have only six. That's no problem on the second project taken alone, but it is when you try to accommodate its need for quality assurance along with the first project's need, as shown in Table 9-1. Both task W in the second project and Task K in the first project are on the critical paths, and they need a total of seven analysts at the same time. Something has to be done.

The procedure in this case is the same as removing conflicts on a single project, except that:

1. Projects must be ranked by priority.

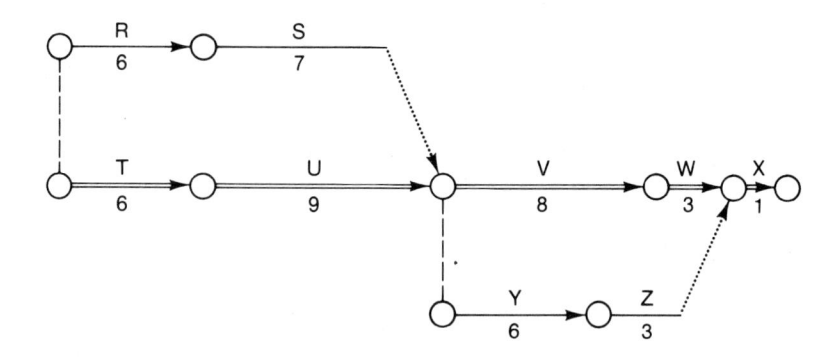

Figure 9-4. Resource allocation with second project (This project starts at the same time as the first project. The network diagram, including task durations, is shown.)

2. The highest priority project gets first claim on available resources.
3. The second priority project gets second claim, and so on.
4. Lower priority projects usually get delayed.

A network diagram is not merely a schedule dimension plan; it also clarifies resource allocation.

Sometimes it is cost-effective to accelerate a small or low priority project to get it out of the way and thus avoid a major conflict that would otherwise arise or to utilize temporarily available personnel more effectively. For example, if you were using a consultant to perform architectural design on project A and his or her design capabilities were also needed briefly on project B, a related but important project, it would be more cost-effective to have him or her work on project B as well. It would be more expensive to reeducate another architect at a later point, and the work done on project B would enable subsequent development work to start whenever those resources become available.

Work Load Forecasting and Planning

Usually, when the work load for all personnel on all projects is added up, the result indicates too much work for the existing personnel in the near term. Later on, typically three to six months down the road, the prediction is for insufficient work (Figure 9-5). In fact, there is usually too much work initially; so projects slip. This slippage, plus new projects, tends to fill up the future work load gap.

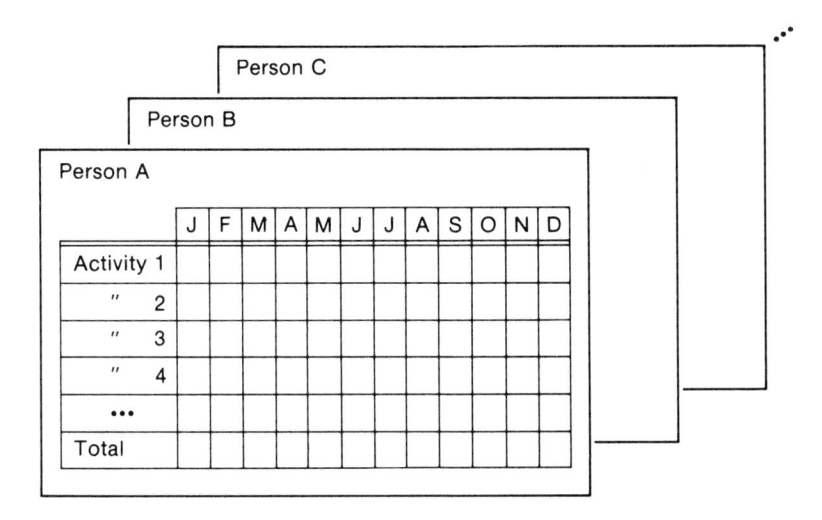

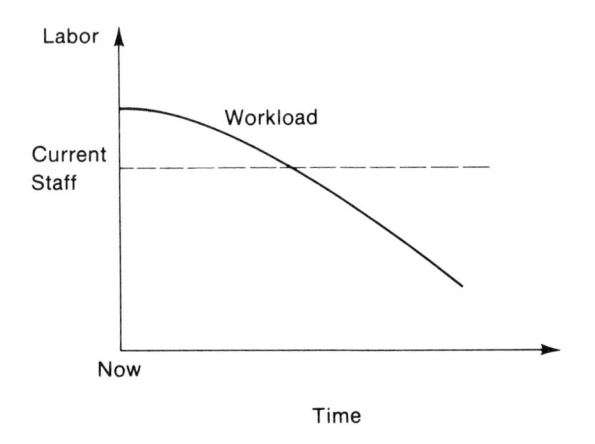

Figure 9-5. Work load forecasting and planning.
Source: "Basic Management Skills for Engineers and Scientists." Lecture notes by Milton D. Rosenau, Jr. Copyright © 1982 by the University of Southern California. Reprinted by permission.

Use of Microcomputer Spread Sheets

Resource allocation can be done by manual inspection of predicted resource use. Computers can also do resource leveling and work load prediction and are not prone to making arithmetical mistakes (assuming, of course, they have been programmed correctly and the data have been loaded accurately). Microcomputers can also be used. Figures 9-6 and 9-7, prepared easily using a spread sheet program, show how microcomputers can easily assist with work load forecasting.

TIME VERSUS COST TRADE-OFF

CPM has historically been associated with network diagrams in which there is considered to be a controllable time for each activity. This implies that activities can be accelerated by devoting more resources to them. Thus, there is a time versus

FIGURE 9-6. Original Work Load for Three Projects.

	Jan	Feb	Mar	Apr
Proj A				
Sr	1	2	3	4
Int	5	6	7	8
Jr	1	2	4	8
Proj B				
Sr	4	3	2	1
Int	2	4	6	8
Jr	3	6	9	9
Proj C				
Sr	3	4	5	6
Int	3	5	7	9
Jr	1	3	5	7
Total				
Sr	8	9	10	11
Int	10	15	20	25
Jr	5	11	18	24
Available Resources				
Sr	8	8	8	9
Int	11	13	15	15
Jr	6	8	10	12
Resource Surplus (+) or Deficit (−)				
Sr	0	−1	−2	−2
Int	1	−2	−5	−10
Jr	1	−3	−8	−12

FIGURE 9-7. Revised Work Load for Three Projects When Project B is Delayed Two Months.

	Jan	Feb	Mar	Apr
Proj A				
Sr	1	2	3	4
Int	5	6	7	8
Jr	1	2	4	8
Proj B				
Sr			4	3
Int			2	4
Jr			3	6
Proj C				
Sr	3	4	5	6
Int	3	5	7	9
Jr	1	3	5	7
Total				
Sr	4	6	12	13
Int	8	11	16	21
Jr	2	5	12	21
Available Resources				
Sr	8	8	8	9
Int	11	13	15	15
Jr	6	8	10	12
Resource Surplus (+) or Deficit (−)				
Sr	4	2	−4	−4
Int	3	2	−1	−6
Jr	4	3	−2	−9

cost trade-off for each activity and consequently for a path or the entire project.

Figure 9-8 shows this kind of situation. If you are trying to accelerate a project, you should accelerate the critical path. Of all the activities on the critical path, the most economical to accelerate are those with the lowest cost per amount of time gained.

Figure 9-9 shows another aspect of this. The direct cost curve depicts those costs associated with carrying out the project that are time dependent and for which there is a cost premium associated with shortening the program. In addi-

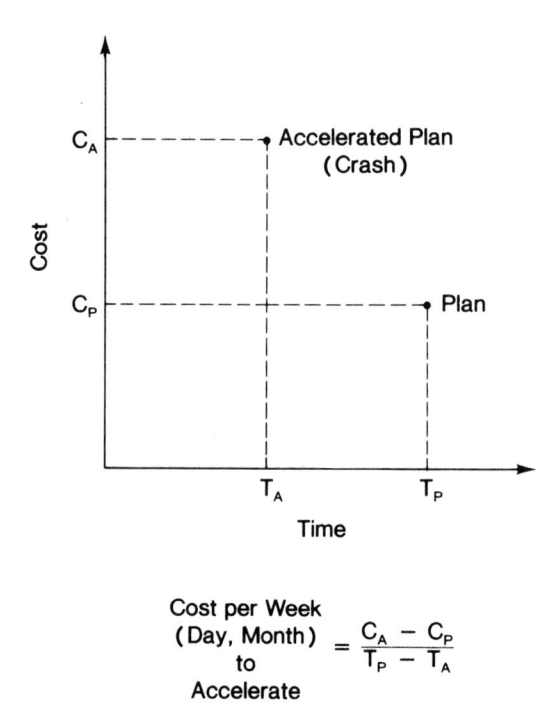

Figure 9-8. CPM time versus cost trade-off.

Cost per Week (Day, Month) to Accelerate $= \dfrac{C_A - C_P}{T_P - T_A}$

tion, there might very well be continuing costs associated with the program, for instance, the rental of standby power generators or other such facilities. In this kind of situation, there will be a time that leads to the lowest cost for the project.

CONTINGENCY

All project plans must contain contingency.

Plans represent the future. Because nobody has a crystal ball, plans must include contingency. In fact, this contingency should be placed on each of the three-dimension plans of the Triple Constraint.

On the performance dimension, it is important that the contingency not take the form of gold plating. Where appropriate, include a small design margin. For instance, if the goal is to have a new program's running time be less than one minute, it might be appropriate to try to design the program to run in fifty-five seconds. However, never carry this

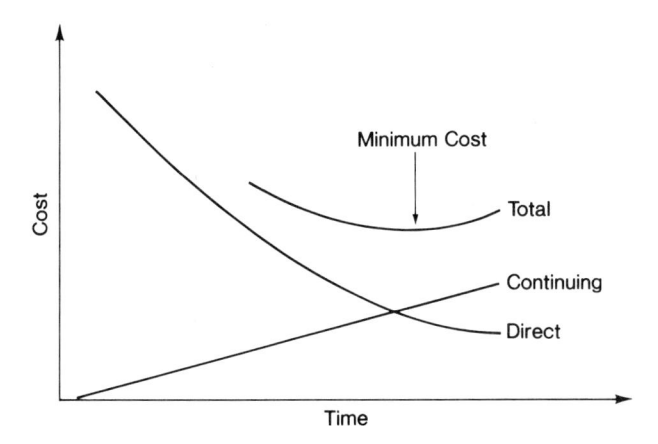

Figure 9-9. Finding the lowest cost.

to an extreme (targeting the running time to thirty seconds, for example).

Contingency is most often associated with the schedule and cost dimensions because projects will inevitably encounter difficulties there. Many things that occur simply require more time and money than planners think. For instance, whenever you must interact with other people, obtaining your boss' approval, perhaps, their schedules constrain you. You will not have instant access, and a delay will occur. Customer furnished items, such as test data, frequently do not arrive when expected or in the condition promised. Work done at remote locations often takes longer than work done in your own organization's facilities because things like copying machines or other support resources are simply not as conveniently available. If your project involves hiring people, it takes time to train them and make them effective workers on the job. Similarly, there will be illnesses and vacations pulling people away from the job. These and other tasks, some of which are included in the following list, make it important to build in schedule and cost contingency.

Build in both schedule and cost contingency.

Resource conflicts.
Interface with others.
Get approvals.
Get support from other groups.
Place major subcontracts and purchase orders.
Make mistakes.
Train people.

Replace sick and vacationing personnel.
Obtain security clearances.
Obtain customer furnished equipment.
Work at remote locations.
Cope with travel delays.
Handle customs duty clearance.
Adjust for labor strikes.
Comply with customer procedures.
Advance the state of the art.
Handle system failure.
Handle misunderstandings.
Replace key personnel who leave.
Cope with employee burnout.
Deal with legal changes.

There are several ways to build in the necessary contingencies. The first is to have everybody who provides an estimate make his or her own time and cost contingency estimates. The problem with this approach is that contingency gets applied on top of contingency, which is then applied on top of other contingencies, and so on. It does not take many multiplications of 110 or 120 percent before the price of the entire project exceeds the customer's reach, and it does not take many extra hours, days, weeks, or months before the schedule becomes unreasonable.

The second method to insert schedule and cost contingency is to put a small amount of contingency, 5 or 10 percent, on each activity in the network. This method is fine, but it misses the point that some activities can be accurately estimated and some others cannot.

A third method to add contingency is to add an unplanned, and hopefully unrequired, activity. For instance, adding a project management task (from start to finish) is really a variation of the second method but provides only cost contingency. A given level of cost contingency, the amount of the system management task, is attached to the entire project. A weakness of this method is that it does not inherently provide a time cushion as well.

A variation on this third method, which we prefer, is to add additional tasks near the end of the project, as shown in Figure 9-10. This has the effect of pushing activities forward from the project's scheduled completion, in this case, shipment, to the earliest possible point. These extra tasks thus

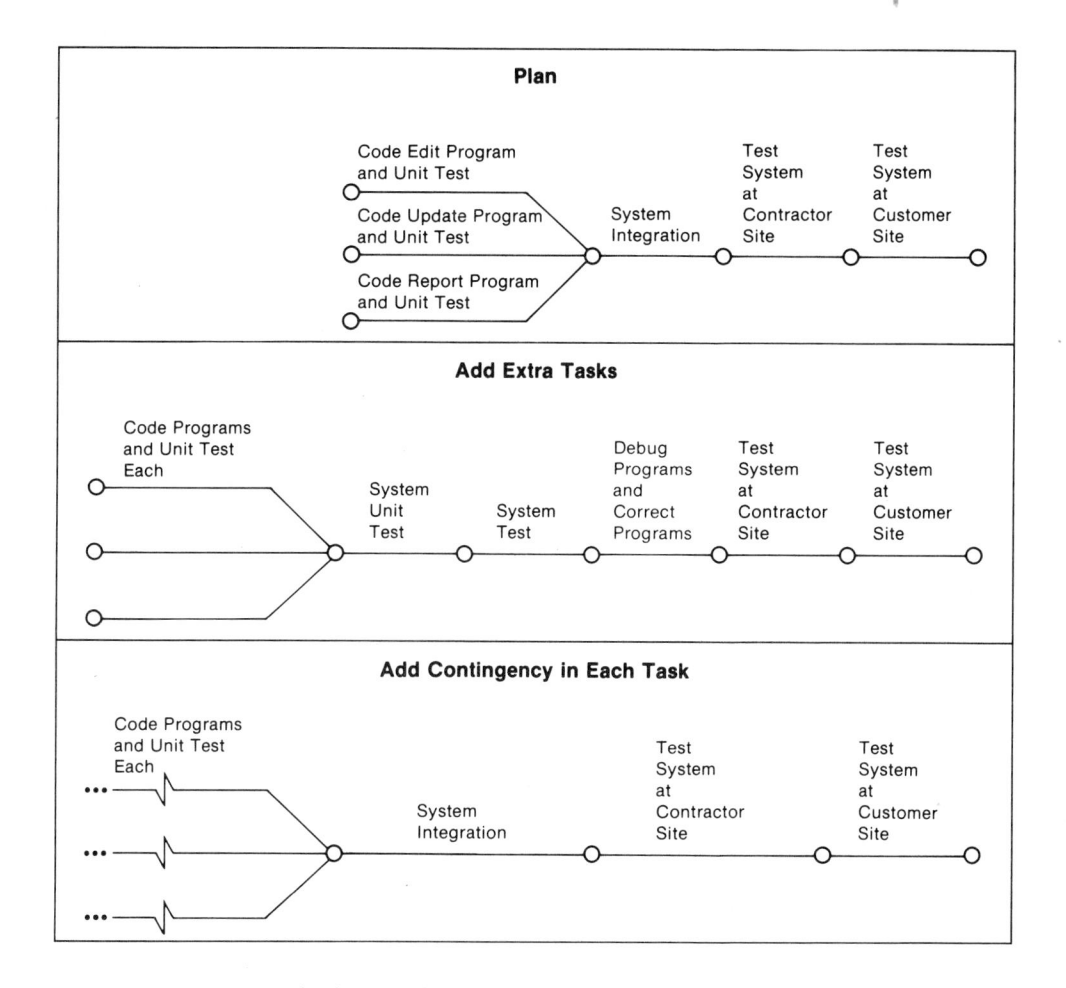

Figure 9-10. Two methods to add time and cost contingency.

have the effect of providing schedule contingency. Because money is devoted to them, they also supply a cost contingency. However, both the time and money contingencies are purely arbitrary.

A fourth method is a variation of the second method (that is, adding 5 or 10 percent). The variation, which is far better, is to explain to everyone providing estimates that they should be as accurate (or optimistic or pessimistic) as possible. Then the entire group can discuss how much schedule and cost contingency should be put on which activities. This can be done by considering the likelihood of things going wrong, the importance of such an outcome, and the maximum and minimum impacts produced by this undesired outcome. There

Risk has two components: tangible and psychological.

might be some highly uncertain activities that receive a contingency of 50 percent or more. Conversely, a final report might be assigned no or only a small percentage contingency. This fourth method is illustrated in the bottom of Figure 9-8.

In fact, multiple time (and cost) estimates can be made for each task (see Table 9-2). (Note that the critical path might be different under different assumptions.) Then the project team can decide which estimates to present when selling the project. This is always a trade-off with risk (see Figure 9-11). Risk actually has two components: tangible (for instance, financial) and psychological. Very often the latter is the more important issue because some people may have a very low tolerance for tangible risk and thus insist on padding their schedule and budget estimates.

OTHER COMPUTER USES FOR PLANNING

Some computer programs can control graphic output terminals to produce network diagrams or colored bar chart displays. Computers can digest various WBSs and integrate them to show multiple project dependencies on identical resources. Computers can also furnish summary project planning and control information for several projects and can easily provide a wide variety of other planning detail to the project manager, support group managers, and task leaders.

TABLE 9-2. Multiple Time (and Cost) Estimates, Using Network of Figure 9-2.

Task	80% Optimistic	50-50 Plan	20% Pessimistic
A	2	3	6*
B	5	6	14*
C	11*	12*	14
D	2*	2*	4
E	10*	11*	13*
F	5	6	8
G	6	6	8
H	10	10	12
J	5	5	6
K	1*	1*	2*
TOTAL	24	26	35

* = Task is on critical path.

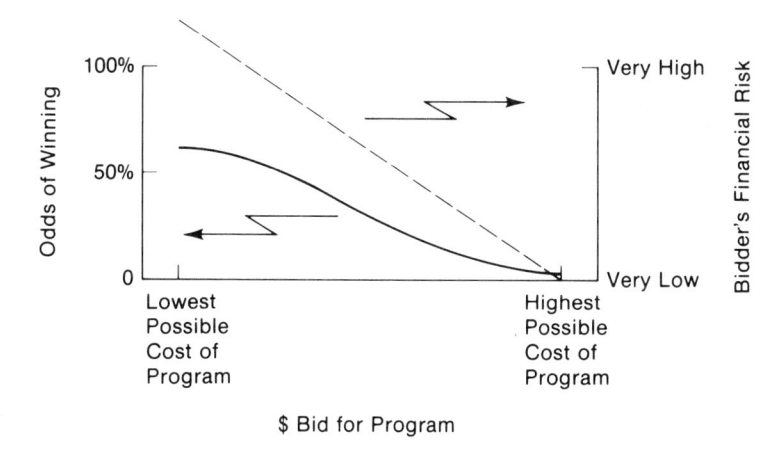

Figure 9-11. Contingency trade-off.

Project planning and control software programs for microcomputers are also becoming widely available. Compared to the software that runs on minicomputers and mainframe computers, these programs are not as flexible or fast. Nevertheless, they may be adequate in many cases.

Computers are often useful for project planning.

COST/SCHEDULE CONTROL SYSTEM CRITERIA

The Cost/Schedule Control System Criteria (C/SCSC) was devised by the U.S. Department of Defense to predict cost overruns early in major military procurement projects. On many projects, the actual cost being reported conformed closely to the initial planned cost, but this concealed the fact that actual work accomplishments were lagging behind plan. Consequently, the total project cost for the work performed exceeded planned cost for the work accomplished. Thus, when projects were far advanced and major commitments had been made to them, it became apparent there were going to be major cost overrun problems at the end.

C/SCSC is used on major military projects.

As with many things done by the military, this is a very formal, rigid system. It provides a standard terminology and approach, which clearly are helpful, but it saddles both the military and its contractors with a highly detailed system. C/SCSC must be initiated in the planning phase, but it is really more useful as a control tool than as a planning device.

To work with this system, you must deal with three quantities, shown in Figure 9-12. The budgeted cost of work per-

```
        BCWS
            \
             \
              > Schedule Variance
             /
            /
        BCWP<
            \
             \
              > Cost Variance
             /
            /
        ACWP
```

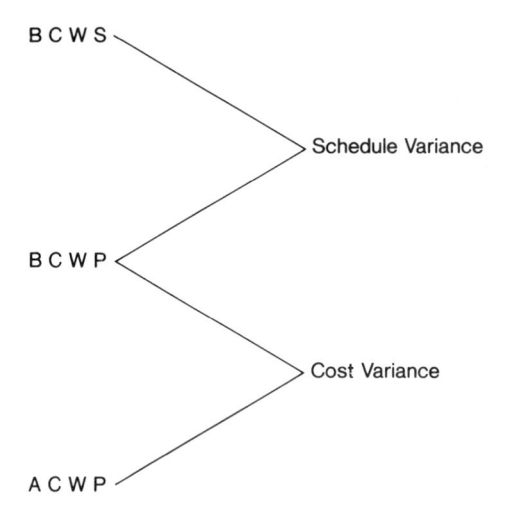

Figure 9-12. C/SCSC methodology.

formed (BCWS) is compared with the budgeted cost of work performed (BCWP) in a given period. The difference between these is a measure of schedule variance. In addition, the actual cost of work performed (ACWP) is compared to the budgeted cost of work performed, and the difference, if any, is a cost variance. The details of the C/SCSC system are far too intricate to explain here and are of only limited interest. If you must use it, seek specialized training.

TYPICAL PROBLEMS

> When computers are used to assist with planning (or anything, for that matter), there is always the danger of entering incorrect data or making programming errors. With standard project control software, the software is proven, but there can still be incorrect data entry. To avoid this kind of problem, verify data entry or run manual spot checks of output. Never blindly accept any computer output as gospel.
>
> Human resources on a computer software project are not mutually interchangeable. There are different levels of proficiency, experience, and expertise. Adding
> *continued*

additional people to a project often causes even further overruns and delays because the new people require some training and communication from critically needed existing personnel. Add people when they already know the new system so that they are immediately productive without additional training. However, take care when adding them that they also have the talent required for the task at hand—for example, a programmer analyst might help enormously to code some print modules formerly allocated to a programmer trainee but would have difficulty in doing a high level architectural design.

In general, it is easier to reallocate human technical resources when the task involved is more execution than conceptual. The problem to be solved is usually more clearly defined in the former case. Thus, switching personnel to a project in distress during the definition and feasibility phases might well create more problems than it solves.

Finally, be careful to allocate enough resources to accommodate the successive iterations that occur during the project life cycle. Although the phases are successive, changes in later phases may well alter work from prior phases. Time and money are required to review changes to preceding milestones and must be considered. Thus, during the design of a customer billing program, certain printer limitations might be discovered that change the billing report format agreed upon during the feasibility phase in the product specification. Not only must the specification be changed, but the customer must review and approve the change. Account for these eventual iterations.

Human resources on software projects are not interchangeable.

Resources, whether people or things, should be carefully allocated in a project.

A network diagram can clarify resource allocation.

Each activity, critical path, and project has a time versus cost trade-off.

All projects should contain contingency, which may be best in-

HIGHLIGHTS

serted by adding tasks near the end or by distributing it in each task.

Computers can aid project planning in several ways, although care must be taken to avoid entering incorrect data.

FURTHER READING

R. H. Clough and G. A. Sears. *Construction Project Management*, 2nd ed. New York: Wiley Interscience, 1979.
> Chapter 7 is a thorough treatment of time reduction trade-off, using construction industry examples.

Cost/Schedule Control Systems Criteria—Joint Implementation Guide. Published by Departments of the Air Force (AFSC/AFLC Pamphlet 173-5), Army (DARCOM-P 715-5), Navy (NAVMAT P5240), and Defense Supply Agency (DSAH 8315.2) (October 1, 1976).

Cost/Schedule Management of Non-Major Contracts (C/SSR Joint Guide). Published by Departments of the Army (Pamphlet DARCOM-P 715-13), Navy (NAVMAT P5244), Air Force (AFLCP 173-2 and AFSCP 173-3), and Defense Logistics Agency (DLAH 8315.3) (November 1, 1978).
> These two books provide an overview of C/SCSC.

J. A. Maciariello. *Program-Management Control Systems.* New York: Wiley-Interscience, 1978.
> Chapter 8 is a good but brief treatment of resource allocation.

Project Management Institute. *Survey of Project Management Software Packages.* Drexel Hill, PA: Project Management Institute, October 1982.
> This publication contains the most complete listing of currently available scheduling and control software. Note, however, that it omits some important existing products and that new software for microcomputers appears frequently.

M. D. Rosenau. *Successful Project Management.* Belmont, CA: Lifetime Learning Publications, 1981.
> Chapter 9, pages 99–114, contains many examples of reports from a computer-based project planning system.

L. A. Smith and J. Mills. "Project Management Network Programs." *Project Management Quarterly* (June 1982), pp. 18–29.
> A comparison of forty computer programs that can be used to assist with network diagram use.

Part 3

LEADING THE PEOPLE

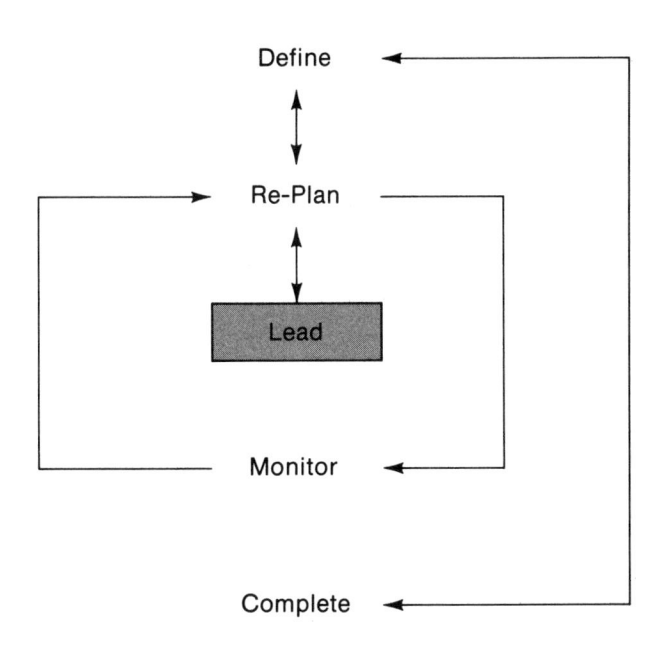

```
            Define ←─────────┐
              ↕              │
    ┌──────→ Re-Plan ──┐      │
    │         ↕        │      │
    │      ┌─────┐     │      │
    │      │ Lead│     │      │
    │      └─────┘     │      │
    │                  │      │
    └─── Monitor ←─────┘      │
                              │
         Complete ←───────────┘
```

10

Computer Software Project Organization Options

In this chapter, we describe the three main organizational forms—functional, project, and matrix—and three other forms by which projects may be managed. Finally, we discuss the informal organization.

THREE PRINCIPAL ORGANIZATIONAL FORMS

Projects have a finite life, from initiation to completion. Conversely, a company, government department, or other organization expects to exist indefinitely. This temporal difference makes it difficult to organize and manage a project within a larger organizational entity.

In addition, projects frequently require the part-time use of resources; whereas permanent organizations try to use resources full-time. Typical project requirements include the following: one hour of computer time each week, use of a terminal next Tuesday for the afternoon, one-quarter of Jane Programmer's time this month and three-quarters of her time next month, use of Joe Technician full-time as soon as the project's hardware designer completes the design. No economically viable organization can afford to stockpile these resources to serve the project's needs instantly. Thus, it is important to organize for project work in adequately responsive ways, and it is important for project managers to recognize this is a compromise that is not fully responsive to project needs.

Although no organizational form is perfect, it is important to recognize the existence of projects when they are present. This means the organization must plan to accommodate this temporary disturbance and accept some disharmony.

Organizational forms differ in response to projects.

There is a variety of ways companies, their divisions, or government organizations can be organized and effectively manage projects. The three most common of these organizational forms are functional, project, and matrix.

Functional

Functional organizations (Figure 10-1) are common in companies dominated by marketing or manufacturing departments (whenever there is a large amount of repetitive work) and exist in other kinds of companies as well. The person asked to manage a project in a company with a functional organization has generally been oriented and loyal to the functional group to which he or she belongs. Specialists are grouped by function, encouraging the sharing of experience and knowledge within the discipline. This favors a continuity and professional expertise in each functional area.

From a project management point of view, the functional organization is least desirable.

Because such an organization is dedicated to perpetuating the existing functional groups, however, it can be difficult for a project to cross functional lines and obtain required resources. It is not uncommon for hostility to exist between different functions; that is, there are barriers to horizontal information flow, and open channels tend to be vertical, within each function. Absence of a project focal point may trouble a customer interested in understanding the project's status, and functional emphasis and loyalties may impede completion. In software projects, a functional organization can result in duplication of effort and resources and often results in failure.

Project

A project organization (Figure 10-2) emerges from a functional organization when the latter impedes project needs. The solution is to move many of the people working on the project from their functional group to the project manager. Line authority for the project is clearly designated, providing

Three Principal Organizational Forms 149

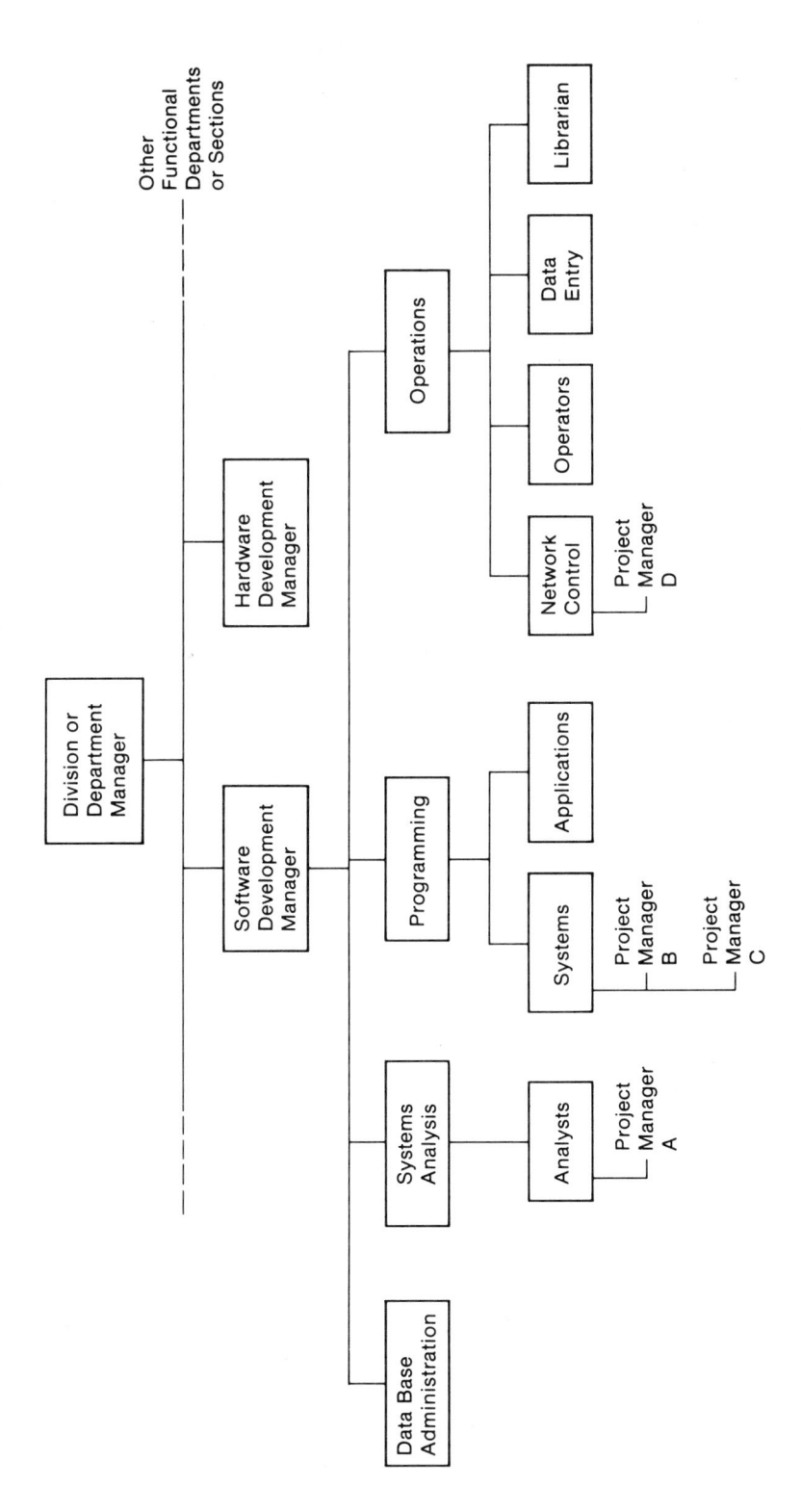

Figure 10-1. Typical organization chart of a functional organization.

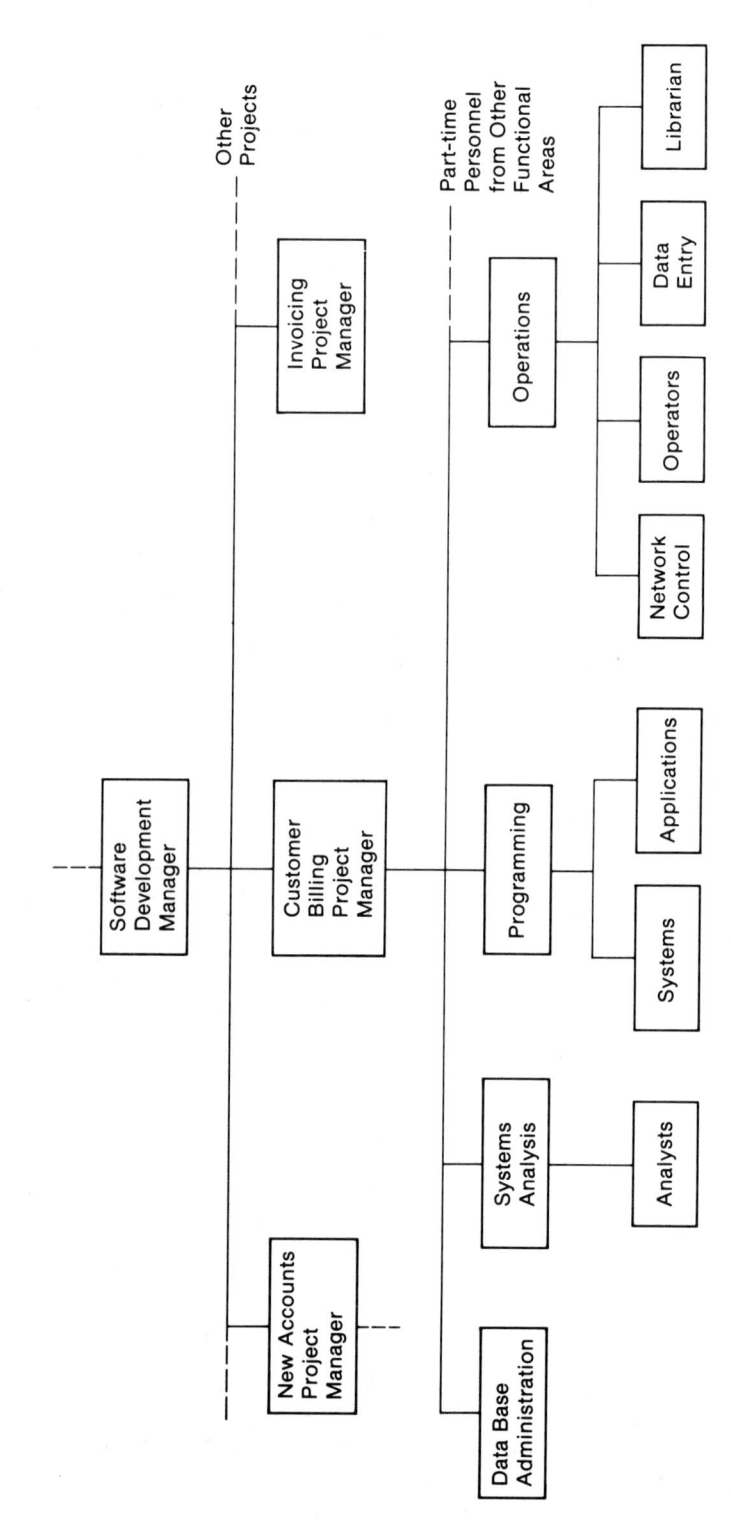

150 Computer Software Project Organization Options

Figure 10-2. Typical organization chart of a project organization.

a single focal point for project management. All full-time personnel are formally assigned to the project, thus assuring continuity and expertise.

A major difficulty with this kind of organization is the uncertainty these people feel about where they will go when the project is completed. There is also a tendency to retain assigned personnel too long. In addition, it is a rare project that actually has all the required resources assigned to it. Thus, such an organization still requires the project manager to negotiate with the remaining functional organization for much of the required support.

If the organization develops additional projects, managing them in this way leads to a splintering, with many separate project centers existing apart from the functional organization. Duplication of facilities and personnel can result. Managers within the functional organization may feel threatened as people are removed from their functional group. This produces another series of stressors. Project organization often inhibits the development of professional expertise in functional specialties and may not effectively utilize part-time assistance from them.

The project organization form is most useful on large projects of long duration.

Matrix

The matrix organization (Figure 10-3) is a hybrid that may emerge in response to the pressures resulting from inadequacies with a functional or a project organization. It attempts to achieve the best of both worlds, recognizing the virtues of having functional groups but also recognizing the need to have a specific focal point and management function for each project. Line authority for the project is clearly designated, providing a single focal point. Specialists, including project managers, are grouped by function, encouraging the sharing of experience and knowledge within the discipline. This favors a continuity and professional expertise in each functional area. The matrix organization recognizes that both full-time and part-time assignment of personnel are required and simplify allocation and shifting of project priorities in response to management needs.

The main drawback is that matrix organization requires an extra management function; so it is usually too expensive for a small organization. It is even possible to have a matrix organization within a matrix organization (for example, the matrixed management information systems department). In addition, the extra functional unit (that is, project manage-

The matrix is probably the best organizational option if you have many projects.

152 Computer Software Project Organization Options

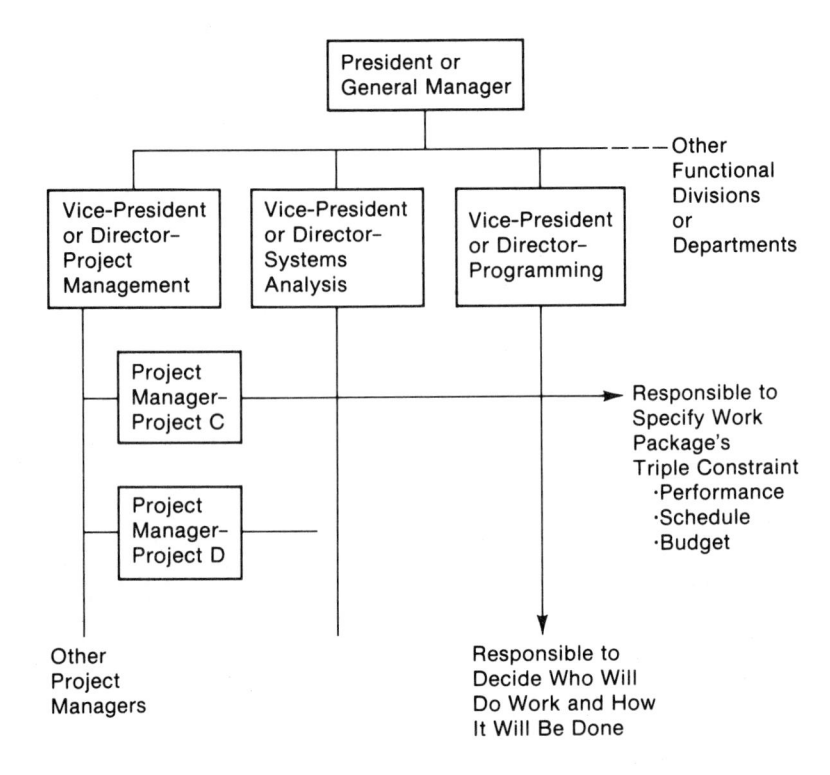

Figure 10-3. Typical organization chart of a matrix organization.

ment) can proliferate bureaucratic tendencies, and the balance of power between project management and functional units can exacerbate conflicts.

OTHER ORGANIZATIONAL FORMS

Quasi Matrix

The quasi matrix (Figure 10-4) is a compromise way to obtain the benefits of the matrix form in a functional organization otherwise too small to afford it. In this compromise organization, when someone is designated project manager, he or she remains part of the functional group for project work done in that group (which is the same as in the functional organization). However, for project management work, he or she reports directly to top management.

Thus, the project focus has top management's support to cut across functional group boundaries. In some cases, the

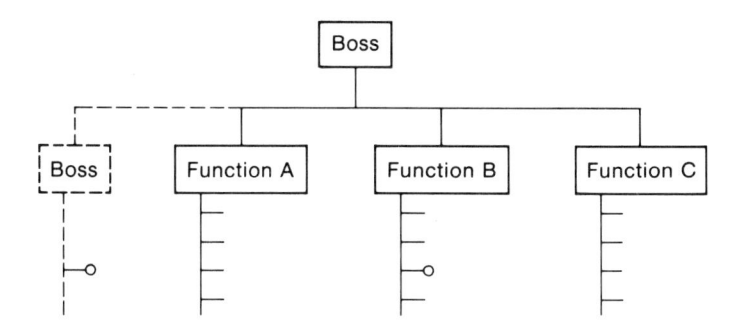

Figure 10-4. Typical organization of a quasi-matrix organization.
Source: "Basic Management Skills for Engineers and Scientists." Lecture notes by Milton D. Rosenau, Jr. Copyright © 1982 by the University of Southern California. Reprinted by permission.

quasi matrix will have a manager of projects (just as in the matrix organization), rather than the boss, to whom the project managers report for project (as distinct from functional) matters.

Venture

The venture organization, common in several very large, commercially oriented companies, is especially appropriate for projects aimed at new product development. Basically, the goal is to set up a tiny functional organization within a giant corporation, thus achieving the advantages of compact size, flexibility, and the entrepreneurial spirit of the small company within and supported by the financial, physical, and human resources of the larger company. Where such a management organization exists, it is common to team up an engineer or researcher with a marketing person and a manufacturing person in the earliest phases of new product development. As the effort moves forward, the venture organization grows, ultimately becoming a functionally organized division within the parent company. Two practitioners of this managerial form are 3M and DuPont. Control Data Corporation also practiced this when developing its supercomputers.

Venture organizations provide small company advantages to large companies.

Task Force

Organizations frequently use a task force to cope with an unexpected project. Hence, this response is most commonly utilized by a functional organization because the other organizational forms are already able to deal with projects. A task force may be thought of as a rarely used, one-project organization within the functional organization. It can be formed quickly, usually by a very senior officer.

Although the people selected to serve on the task force may be highly motivated by their selection, they frequently are not relieved of their usual duties and thus may not have sufficient time for the task force. If they are relieved of their normal duties, they may be anxious about their assignment when the task force has completed its job. In general, a task force is not an appropriate form for dealing with software development because of the problem requirements and the composition of the task force.

THE INFORMAL ORGANIZATION

Regardless of the formal organizational structure, there is always an informal organization (Figure 10-5). Where friendships and common interests are present, these create channels through which information flows easily and cooperation is encouraged. Conversely, rivalries and animosities can inhibit cooperation.

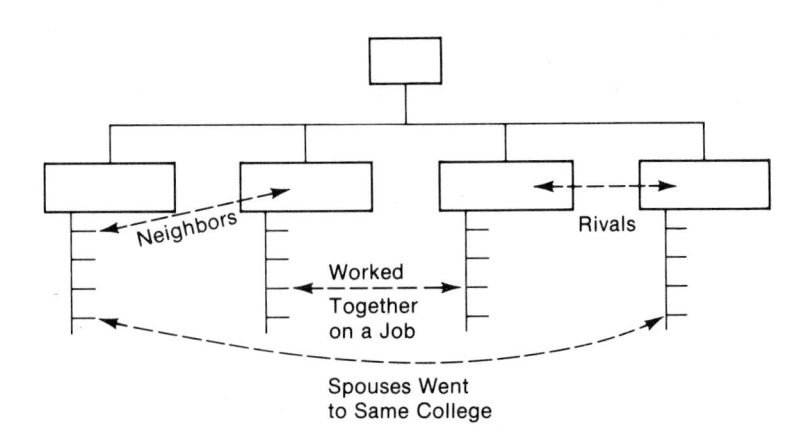

Figure 10-5. The informal organization.
Source: "Basic Management Skills for Engineers and Scientists." Lecture notes by Milton D. Rosenau, Jr. Copyright © 1982 by the University of Southern California. Reprinted by permission.

TYPICAL PROBLEMS

> Each organizational form has its advantages and disadvantages. The only real problem occurs when a project manager believes that a different organizational form will solve all the organizational problems he or she is experiencing.

HIGHLIGHTS

Three common organizational forms for project management are functional, project, and matrix.

Three other forms that may be used are quasi matrix, venture, and task force.

The informal organization is always present and affects how well the formal organization works.

FURTHER READING

T. M. Adams. "Matrix Management—Panacea or Pandemonium?" *IEEE Engineering Management Review*, vol. 8, no. 1 (March 1980), pp. 55–64. (Reprinted from *Personnel Psychology*, vol. 30, no. 1 [Spring 1977], pp. 55–64.)
 This is a breezy article that compares functional, project, and matrix organization forms in terms of very practical issues.

R. D. Archibald. *Managing High-Technology Programs and Projects*. New York: Wiley-Interscience, 1976.
 Chapter 5, section 4, is a thorough discussion of organizational options with many examples.

E. B. Daly, "Organizing for Successful Software Development." *Datamation* (December 1979), pp. 107–116.
 This article nicely points out that software managers increase their chances of success enormously by setting up effective organizations.

S. M. Davis and P. R. Lawrence. "Problems of Matrix Organizations." *Harvard Business Review*, vol. 56, no. 3 (May-June 1978), pp. 131–142.

> The article summarizes the main points in their book, providing a thorough treatment of the matrix form.

W. Jerkovsky. "Functional Management in Matrix Organizations." *IEEE Transactions on Engineering Management*, vol. EM-30, no. 2 (May 1983), pp. 89–97.

> Although academic in tone, this article touches upon some of the problems functional managers have in a matrix organization.

J. Keen. *Managing Systems Development*. New York: Wiley, 1981.

> Chapter 11, pages 214–235, discusses project organization in the data processing environment and has some illustrative organization charts for different time phases during a project.

R. L. Nolan. "Managing Information Systems by Committee." *Harvard Business Review* (July-August 1982), pp. 72–79.

> This is a discussion of the need for an organization to have an executive steering committee to guide information systems projects.

H. E. Pywell. "Engineering Management in a Multiple- (Second or Third Level) Matrix Organization." *IEEE Transactions on Engineering Management*, vol. EM-26, no. 3 (August 1979), pp. 51–55.

> This is a good discussion of matrix's value in larger projects.

W. E. Souder. "Project Management: Past, Present, and Future—An Editorial Summary." *IEEE Transactions on Engineering Management*, vol. EM-26, no. 3 (August 1979), pp. 49–50.

> This is an overview of matrix pros and cons.

M. A. Verespej. "Mission Extraordinary? Call for a Task Force." *Industry Week* (October 19, 1981), p. 67.

> This brief article discusses issues in ad hoc project management.

R. Youker. "Organization Alternatives for Project Managers." *Management Review* (November 1977), pp. 46–53.

> This is a succinct and graphic summary of organizational options.

11

Organizing the Project Team

The project team consists of those who work on the project and report administratively to the project manager. This is in distinction to the support team (people who work on the project but do not report administratively to the project manager), which we discuss in Chapter 12. First, we review sources of project personnel and consider the frequent necessity to compromise by using whoever is available. Then we deal with how much control a project manager can exercise over project personnel and provide some practical tools to help him or her gain effective control. The last section discusses the use of task assignments both as a means to assign the work packages and to obtain commitments from personnel to carry out the work.

DEGREE OF ASSOCIATION WITH THE PROJECT

Figure 11-1 shows eight categories of personnel assignment to projects. They result from all possible combinations of three factors: (1) whether personnel report directly to the project manager or are administratively assigned to someone else, (2) whether they work full-time or only part-time each day (or week or year) on the project, and (3) whether they work on the project from its inception to completion or for only some portion of the project.

Project Team

The project team is composed of the people who report administratively to the project manager (the four cells so designated on the left side of Figure 11-1). We consider this the

Nature of Reporting Relationship / Duration of Project Assignment	Reports to Project Manager		Works on Projects but Reports to Another Manager	
	Works Only on Project	Also Has Other Assignment(s)	Works Only on Project	Also Has Other Assignment(s)
From Start to Finish	P	P	S	S
Only a Portion of Project's Duration	P	P	S	S

P = Project Team
S = Support Team

Figure 11-1. The project team and the support team.

Project team members report to the project manager.

project team because the project manager can assign work packages to these people rather than having to negotiate with other managers to obtain commitments for their work.

This is an organization structure that varies among firms. In some cases, documentation may be part of the project team, and in other organizations, it may be part of the support team. Generally, it is better to keep the test and evaluation (or quality assurance) function on the support team to maintain perspective; however, it is sometimes part of the project team.

Team Mix

The amount of project labor obtained from each category depends on the project contractor's organizational form (that is, functional, project, or matrix) and project size. In a matrix organization, no one may be assigned to work for the project manager; the entire labor pool may be drawn from the support team. In a pure project organization, the vast majority of project labor, perhaps all of it, may be assigned to the project manager. This is especially likely for a large project of long duration. As a practical matter, small projects are not likely to have their own personnel, regardless of organizational form. The majority of those assigned to a project from start to finish is either managerial or administrative because most other skills are required for only some portion of the project.

A key point that emerges from consideration of Figure 11-1 is that the project manager must provide eight different kinds of management attention to people working on the project. People who work on the project for only a portion of its duration must be managed to be ready when needed; then orientation to the project must be provided; finally, the project manager must recognize that they may be frustrated at leaving the project prior to completion. People who have other assignments must be persuaded that the work on the project deserves their attention each day (or week). Because they may have a lower stake in the project, they often require better or more forceful leadership. People on the support team must be managed through other managers, and there are often issues of priorities, performance standards, and loyalty, which require the project manager's attention.

The nature of personnel assignments varies.

There are no absolute organizational forms to mandate. However, there are rules of thumb that can be applied. The project team should be organized so that there is a common purpose to each group within your team. This grouping in fact often maps out onto the phases of the project life cycle. For example, the user requirements analysis might be done by a systems analysis group, and the following product specifications might be done by a product design group. The organizational form should follow along with the size of the data processing work force and the way it will be used. For example, organizing into systems software and applications software would be appropriate for a project where the deliverables include both a set of application specific programs and a new operating system, which will have to be designed and maintained by individuals with different types of knowledge and experience. A sample organization is shown in Figure 11-2.

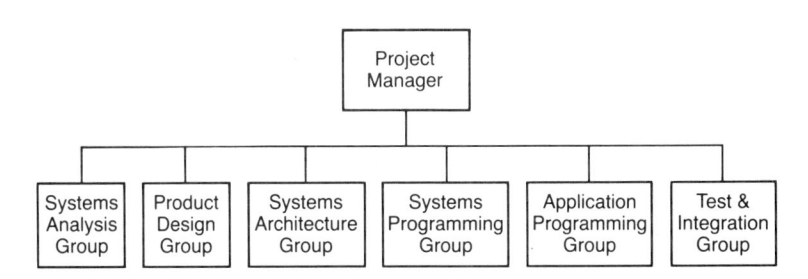

```
                    ┌─────────┐
                    │ Project │
                    │ Manager │
                    └────┬────┘
   ┌──────┬──────┬──────┼──────┬──────┬──────┐
┌──┴──┐┌──┴──┐┌──┴──┐┌──┴──┐┌──┴──┐┌──┴──┐
│Systems││Product││Systems││Systems││Application││Test &│
│Analysis││Design││Architecture││Programming││Programming││Integration│
│Group││Group││Group││Group││Group││Group│
```

Figure 11-2. Organization of a project team.

SOURCES OF PERSONNEL

There are many sources of people, including the proposal team, other people already employed by the organization, and people from outside the organization (hired personnel, contract personnel, consultants, and subcontractors).

The Proposal Team

The proposal team is the best source of project personnel.

By far the best source of project personnel is those who worked on the proposal. They are familiar with the subject matter of the proposal and perhaps to some extent with the customer's specific problems. Being already "up to speed," they require minimal indoctrination. They will, for example, presumably understand the company's business needs and its special requirements.

Other Organization Employees

Other employees of the organization are the second best source of personnel. Those people are at least familiar with company policies and procedures; they know where the library, the back-up file storage, and such are located. Although they may not be familiar with the specific subject matter of the project, they are at least familiar with how the company does business and know its strengths and weaknesses. They know whom to call for help and where to go to get something done. In fact, they have probably worked on similar projects in the past.

The project manager may know their strengths and weaknesses and thus be able to assign them to appropriate work packages. The project manager will not ask them to do more than their capabilities permit or give them a work package so trivial as to be demeaning or demotivating.

People From Outside the Company

There is a variety of outside sources for personnel (see Figure 11-3). Consultants, contract ("body shop") personnel, and subcontractors can be obtained quickly, whereas it often takes months to hire a new full-time employee. The newly hired person, who can work for and be fully under the admin-

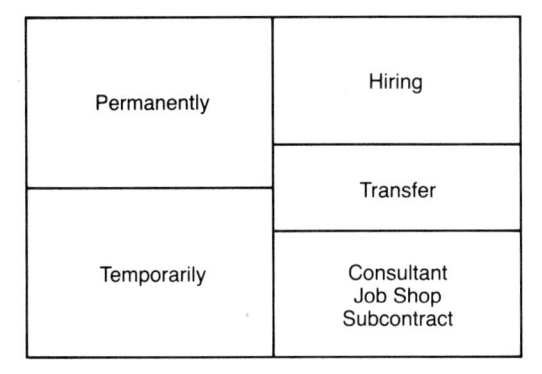

Permanently	Hiring
	Transfer
Temporarily	Consultant Job Shop Subcontract

Figure 11-3. Outside sources of personnel.
Source: "Basic Management Skills for Engineers and Scientists." Lecture notes by Milton D. Rosenau, Jr. Copyright © 1982 by the University of Southern California. Reprinted by permission.

istrative control of the project manager, may be thought of as part of the project team in the sense we are using that term. To hire a person, a project manager has to have a personnel requisition approved, typically must advertise the position, interview several people, make one or more offers to get an acceptance, and wait for the person to relocate (if required) before coming to work. Then there is an indoctrination period while the new employee becomes familiar with company practices. A project of short duration rarely can afford the time to hire personnel and thus depends on the support team. And when a critical employee departs in the midst of a project, the replacement process is even more deleterious to the project schedule and resources.

COMPROMISE

It is indeed rare that a project manager can staff the project entirely with personnel who (1) already work for him or her, (2) worked on the proposal, and (3) represent exactly the right distribution of skills to carry out the project. Usually, the project manager must staff the project from whoever is currently available either full- or part-time. Many of these people will not completely meet the requirements. It is often a case of fitting square pegs into round holes.

Staffing compromises are usually necessary.

Growing Your Own

One way to solve the problem of insufficient personnel to staff your project is to train people from other parts of the company. These people may not even be in computers or data processing. However, for projects where knowledge of the business or industry is very important and where the project itself is of long enough duration to train these people and then be able to use them effectively, this method often is helpful. Computer manufacturers usually have adequate training programs in major cities. You can take advantage of these if your company is not large enough to have its own technical training department.

Training existing employees will not work when you need a particular expertise and do not have the talent in-house available within the time frame upon which your project depends. In that case, competent external help should be acquired.

Qualifications

Avoid accepting other managers' cats and dogs for your project team.

The newly appointed project manager confronted with the urgent need to staff a project team is often victimized by other managers in the company who offer their "cats and dogs." These people may be marginally employed; so company management may pressure the project manager to accept them into his or her group.

This is a very tricky situation. There is pressure from above to accept the people and there is another manager offering them as freely available. But if these people are known to be marginal workers, it is probably better to terminate their employment than to shift them from one project to another, burdening these projects and retaining marginal workers for long periods of time. Nevertheless, it is common for a newly appointed project manager to be offered all kinds of personnel for transfer. On a short duration project, it may be better to accept these workers, unless they are clearly unqualified, than to recruit better qualified assistance.

Motivation

Some projects that offer high pay (such as overseas deployments at computer installations in Saudi Arabia and Iran) frequently attract workers whose primary motivation is money. The project manager may be besieged by candidates who wish to go to work on his or her project. Their motivation, however, may not be best for the project. So confronted, the manager should seek to staff the project team with a few high quality people and confine the money seekers to support team roles, where they are someone else's problem, or to hire this expertise on a consultant basis, so that when the immediate need for their services is over, they are no longer an organizational liability.

Conversely, a project with high scientific content or one of national importance (such as the Apollo project) often attracts highly dedicated, altruistic people. A common correlate of this altruism is a lack of practicality, which the project manager must watch for and temper.

Some projects have an unsavory reputation (fairly and unfairly earned) that makes it very difficult to recruit personnel. They often require portions of the work be performed at an unattractive or remote location. To overcome this drawback, various inducements may be required. Where possible, however, it's the role of the project manager to create doable, practicable jobs for his or her employees.

Some project personnel may be poorly motivated and some may be unrealistic.

Recruiting Qualified Help

Some compromising is clearly required in staffing the project team, but there may be some skill requirements that cannot be compromised. If you need a particular person, and he or she does not work for you, you have only two options: (1) have the other manager agree to transfer this unique person to you, at least for the duration of the project or (2) have the person become a member of the support team.

Most project managers prefer to have people on the project team because it seems to improve project control. People on the project team cannot be given other distracting work assignments unless the project manager approves it, but people on the support team may be given other work that detracts from their ability to honor support commitments.

Nevertheless, such a transfer could well be undesirable for the project if you do not need participation by the person 100 percent of each day. What would he or she do the rest of the time? It can also be undesirable if he or she is a difficult person to supervise. Conversely, if your organization has a matrix form, you can obtain a firm commitment to assign a needed person only as long as the project requires him or her.

CONTROL

Supervision

In talking about the project team, we are talking about people who work for the project manager. They may not work full-time on the project, either for its entire duration or full-time within any given workday or workweek. Nevertheless, they are under the project manager's direct supervision, unless there are intermediate levels of supervision. Some of these people may have been transferred from other managers.

Projects go through different phases, which implies that personnel must be changed. For instance, the system architect, the creative design person, so valuable in the early phases of system design, is not needed when the project is moving toward completion and the team is trying to finish the design rather than figure out additional clever ways to redesign it.

People must join and leave the project as needed.

An administrator or junior project manager assigned to work under the project manager may be needed the entire time, but other personnel may need new assignments. They will either go to work on another project full-time after completing their work or work on two or three projects part-time. It is therefore important that the project manager exercises control over the timing of these assignments so as to have people with the right skills available when required and have other assignments for them when they are not required. This is one reason a resource allocation analysis is desirable.

Proximity

One of the project manager's most powerful tools for improving control of project personnel is to locate everyone in a common area. This aids communication, and where there is increased communication, there is increased understanding. This also assures the project manager that everyone on the team understands the Triple Constraint.

Programmers need both solitude and proximity to other project team members.

However, the art of software design requires quiet and often solitude to proceed efficiently. Thus, proximity does not mean "bullpen" arrangements; instead, programmers should be able to walk only a few steps to discuss common issues with co-workers. This informal conceptual communication usually saves endless hours at formal review sessions.

Distance

A relatively new phenomenon, and growing in usage, is remote programmers, working out of their homes using terminals and direct dial-up capabilities that place them logically as close to the computing capabilities as if they were in the same building. This eliminates time-consuming commutes and enables the programmers to work at the times most productive according to their individual time clocks (which may be all night rather than daily from 9 A.M. to 5 P.M.). This is an effective use of programmers, but it requires that the manager carefully monitor the work produced to ensure that it is proceeding as scheduled and of the quality needed. Weekly on-site meetings with the rest of the staff are appropriate to maintain the conceptual communications needed during the project.

Off-site technical workers require more managing.

Problems

Most project managers would rather staff the project with many project team members and fewer support team members. However, this staffing forces the project manager to contend with many personnel problems, such as people quitting (either the company or organizational unit) to work elsewhere, sickness, higher management reassignments, lack of interest in the project, or other conflicting assignments.

TASK ASSIGNMENTS

We have previously emphasized use of the work breakdown structure and network diagram to divide projects into small pieces of work. Each of these pieces, or tasks, has a corresponding cost estimate. In the ideal world, the persons responsible for each task have prepared both the schedule and the budget estimate. They should also have played a significant role in defining the exact Triple Constraint of their small work package. In any case, the project manager must assign tasks to many different people. As these tasks are assigned, some give and take in the exact scope may be accepted, but whatever is finally agreed upon must be committed to paper. That is, there should be a minicontract between the project

All work assignments should be written.

manager and the people responsible for tasks. This minicontract defines the Triple Constraint of the task.

The project team member who now has his or her task assignment should provide the project manager with a detailed plan of how that task will be performed and periodically review progress against the plan. To the extent that the task performer has played a major role in creating and initiating the task assignment, he or she is likely to be highly motivated to carry it out. Conversely, if the task was assigned without negotiation, the person may have a low sense of involvement and be largely demotivated by the assignment.

TYPICAL PROBLEMS

> The usual problem is what to do with marginal personnel. This is one reason you should have inserted schedule and budget contingency—because sometimes you have personnel who must be used in an area outside their competency, which renders them temporarily marginal. In the case of truly marginal personnel, you can simply refuse to accept them on the project team.

HIGHLIGHTS

The project team is people who work on the project and report administratively to the project manager.

Sources of project personnel include the proposal team, others employed by the organization, and people from outside the organization.

Compromise is required in forming project teams.

People must join and leave the team as required during the project.

Having team members in close proximity improves the project manager's control.

FURTHER READING

F. B. Brooks, Jr. "The Mythical Man-Month." *Datamation* (December 1974), pp. 44–52.
> This is an amusing but accurate analysis of the allocation of personnel on a software project.

C. L. Buck. "Managing the Most Valuable Resource: People." *Project Management Quarterly*, vol. 8, no. 2 (June 1977), pp. 41–44.
> This is a useful, brief discussion of building project teamwork.

C. Cammann and D. A. Nadler. "Fit Control Systems to Your Managerial Style." *Harvard Business Review*, vol. 54, no. 1 (January-February 1976), pp. 65–72.
> This article contains excellent suggestions for improving control of personnel.

"Computer people": Yes, They Really Are Different. *Business Week* (February 20, 1984), p. 66.
> This report of a study conducted by Columbia University for Business Week shows that hardware and software designers and data-processing workers rate job factors differently than managers. The "computer people" feel that learning new skills, security, location, and better hours are substantially more important than managers feel. Conversely, managers rate responsibility, autonomy, and job title substantially higher than computer people.

E. Raudsepp. "Delegate Your Way to Success." *Computer Decisions* (March 1981), pp. 157–164.
> This is a wonderful summary for managers who need to delegate, with a good checklist of questions.

H. J. Thamhain and D. L. Wilemon. "Leadership, Conflict, and Program Management Effectiveness." *Sloan Management Review*, vol. 19, no. 1 (Fall 1977), pp. 69–89.
> This has research data on effective management techniques for project managers.

12

Organizing the Support Team

The support team is the people who work on the project either full-time or part-time for a part or all of the project but do not report administratively to the project manager. This chapter discusses how to obtain their involvement and commitment and how their efforts can and must be coordinated with the project team. Then we consider interaction between the project team and support groups and subcontractors.

INVOLVEMENT AND COMMITMENT

Participation in proposal writing builds team spirit.

As with the project team, the best way to develop a sense of involvement and obtain a commitment from the support team is to have had its members participate in the proposal. Participation also builds a team spirit that continues beyond the project. Failing this, their involvement in planning their own work and committing those plans to writing should also elicit involvement and commitment.

The User

User involvement increases chances for a successful project.

On any project, it is helpful to try to treat users as members of the support team. This is easier on projects being done within your own organization. Clearly, users are also customers, a role for which some formal distance is also appropriate. However, the more they feel that their stake in project success is the same (or greater) than yours, the better off everyone will be. There should be a user representative at least at project reviews, except for detailed design reviews, both to elicit emotional involvement and to monitor project direction.

Early Support Group Involvement

Project managers and the project team often ignore support requirements, which other groups must provide, until it is too late. Unless support personnel understand that their services may be required, they cannot anticipate the extent to which they will be needed. Consequently, the support a project demands may not be available when needed. When support is sought tardily, support groups feel left out, and it may be difficult to obtain their commitment.

This kind of situation may arise because the project team has some degree of parochialism or is not aware what support is readily available. The project team may not understand the potential roles others can play or may assume it knows better than the support groups what kind of effort will be required. This latter situation frequently arises because the project team feels that a support group will "gold plate" the amount of work they propose to do, exceeding project budgets.

As stated earlier, these problems can best be mitigated by involving support groups in the proposal phase. If this cannot be done, involve them as early as possible in the project work. Give them an opportunity to participate in planning their task and employing their best thinking and expertise.

The most common software support groups are quality assurance, technical documentation, data center (operations), training, and library. By bringing in representatives of these groups early, you can avoid countless errors and glean efficiencies. For example, the testing and integrating experience of the quality assurance department can serve as an effective guide for developing your project's test and evaluation plan. The documentation produced by your project can be structured for ease in maintainability, timeliness, and accuracy if you incorporate the experience of the technical documentation group.

The same applies to the time and cost estimates. The support group should make time and cost estimates for their task, and the project group should approve them. These estimates may require a negotiated revision to adjust other project tasks to accommodate support group plans if they differ from the project team's first estimate. This is a common

Have support groups make time and cost estimates.

occurrence. Support groups sometimes must perform their role at a pace dictated by other, higher priority commitments, thus scheduling your project support differently than you had planned. Sometimes the support group sees a completely different way to undertake its role, often to the project's advantage. Or the support group's experts may convince the project team that their role must be broader than originally conceived. For all these reasons, involve support groups as early as possible.

Written Commitments

Obtain meaningful commitments from support groups within your organization just as you do from the outside subcontractors, namely, a written agreement. (This is also what you should do with project team member commitments; the only difference is what actions you can take to settle disputes if they arise.) There must be a Triple Constraint and signatures by both parties. Such agreements (inside the organization) lack legal standing and enforcement provisions, but if the support group manager must sign a written agreement, he or she will be motivated to make a group live up to its commitment. Although there does not have to be a formal contract written up, at the very minimum, an unambiguous, clear, and complete statement of work, Triple Constraint, and mutual commitments should be put in memo format and signed by both parties.

Put all agreements in writing.

There are just so many machine and programmer hours for the data center to offer, for example. However good the initial intentions may be, conflicts normally arise. Having a written agreement delineating your requirements and schedules often precludes your resources from being temporarily reallocated to another project. Also, as managers change, the written agreement provides the continuity you need to do your job.

Support Team Advantages

As we said in the previous chapter, most project managers seem to prefer to staff their project entirely (or mostly) with project team members. However, a project manager (especially in a matrix organization) might prefer to have a large support team rather than a large project team for the following reasons:

1. The project manager does not have to worry about the support team after the project ends.
2. In the case of subcontractors, the support agreement is embodied in a legally binding instrument, namely, the subcontract or purchase agreement.
3. The project manager has the whole world in which to find specialists or experts with the required skill.

COORDINATION

Once the support groups have been identified and their work has been planned properly and phased in with that of the project team, there is a continuing need to coordinate project team work. This is best done with network diagrams (Figures 12-1 and 12-2). In both figures, support group work has been segregated from the main part of the network. There are many other ways to do this, for instance, using distinctive line patterns for each support category. Where color copying machines are available, a color code may be used advantageously.

Network diagrams aid coordination.

Change

Communication and coordination should be primarily in writing. Change should be accomplished by oral communication, over the telephone and/or at meetings involving as many people as required. But the change must then be embodied in the plan revisions and documented.

Consider the case where you are going to be late with your own work on task D, as illustrated in Figure 12-1. Should you inform your subcontractor? It depends. In general, it is probably best to advise subcontractors of your true need date. If you do this, you make it easier for them, and their costs to you will be lower (at least in the long run). But if subcontractors have a history of lateness, it is probably best (1) to have originally allowed time contingency for their work and (2) not to let them know of any delay you have experienced.

Revision

Once committed to paper, plans must be disseminated to and understood by all involved personnel. Plans must also be maintained in a current status. If any out-of-date project

Plan revisions must be written and distributed.

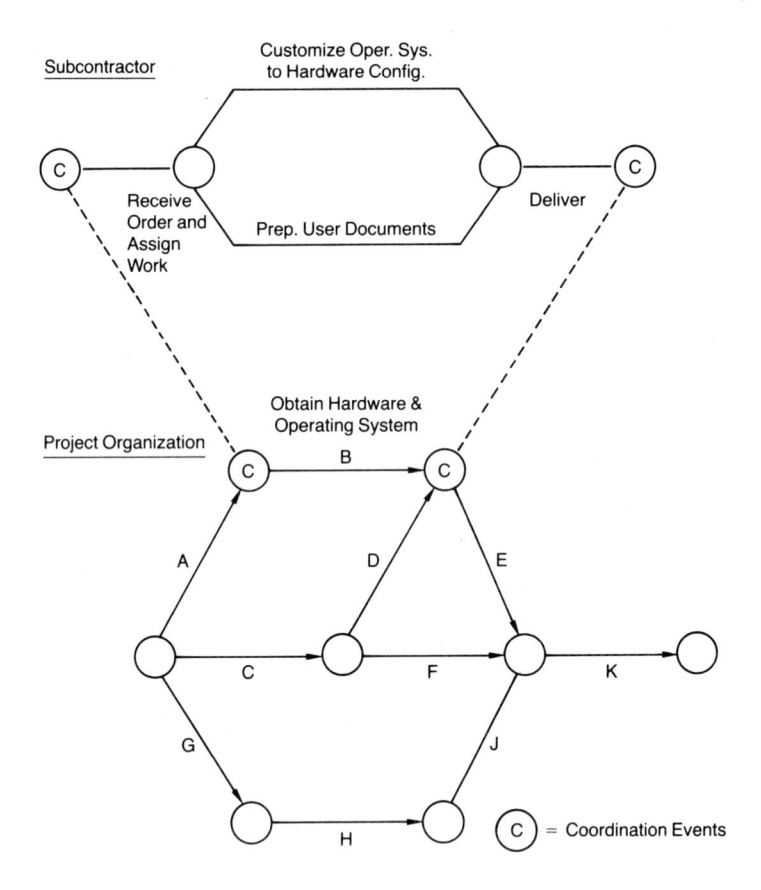

Figure 12-1. Network diagram illustrating use of coordination events.

plans are allowed to remain in circulation, the credibility of all project plans will become suspect. Therefore, everyone who had the original plan must receive revisions. This can be facilitated by keeping an accurate distribution list.

INTERACTION WITH SUPPORT GROUPS

Project team and support group interaction can be difficult. All too often the support group is brought in too late, a situation that reminds us of a story. A commuter comes dashing onto the train platform just as the morning train into the city pulls out. A bystander, observing that the commuter has just missed the train, comments, "Gee, that's too bad. If

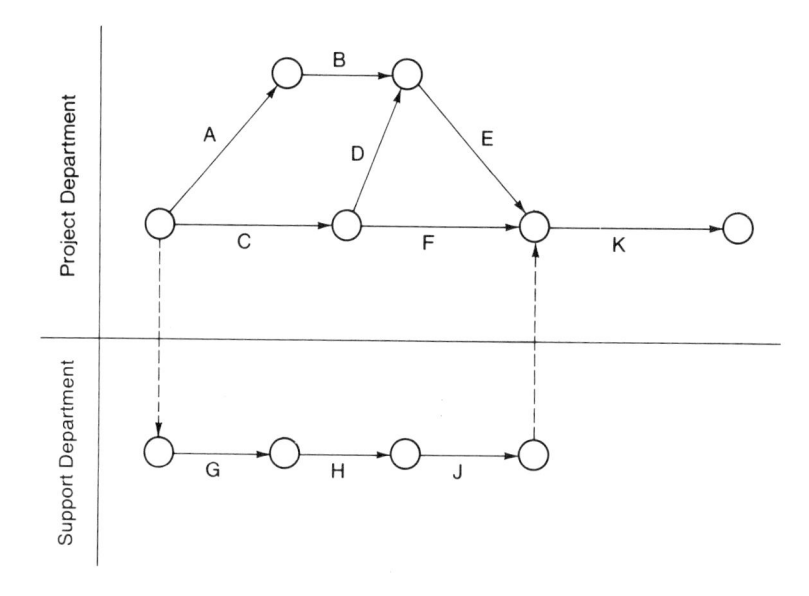

Figure 12-2. Network diagram illustrating use of spatial segregation of a support group's activities.

you'd simply run a little bit faster, you'd have caught the train." The commuter knows, of course, it is not a matter of having run a little bit faster but rather of having started a little bit sooner.

Project Actions

The tardy commuter's situation classically applies where the purchasing department is involved. Purchased software packages arrive later than required, the project is delayed, and project people blame either the subcontractor for delivering late or the purchasing department for failing to place the order early enough. In fact, the blame lies with the people who did not requisition the purchase sufficiently early so the software would be delivered on time. They need not run faster; they should have started earlier.

The experienced project manager copes with this problem in two ways. First, he or she makes certain that the network diagram schedule allows enough time for the support groups to perform optimally. Second, the project manager makes certain that all personnel know when task activities must be completed and holds the task managers accountable for meeting the schedule.

Support Team Viewpoint

These issues can be looked at in a different way, namely, from the point of view of the support groups. They are composed of professionals, in the previous example, purchasing professionals who wish to obtain the best quality of required software at the lowest possible price within the other constraints project personnel impose. They need time to perform their function in a professionally competent way. In the case of government contracts, there are even laws and regulations that require three competitive bids.

Support groups labor under many constraints.

The same is true, of course, of any support group—technical writers, computer programmers, systems designers, or machine operators. Everyone wants to do a good job and wants sufficient time in which to do it. But departments have a work load imposed on them by others. They are trying to respond to many projects bringing work to them at random times and in variable amounts. Thus, support groups typically have some backlog they must work through before they can get to new requests. If they did not have this backlog, if they were sitting there idly waiting for the work to arrive, they would not be utilizing a vital organization resource, their own time, in the most effective way.

SUBCONTRACTORS

Subcontractors are basically no different than you. They have a contract from a customer, in this case, you or your project. They want to be responsive to you, but they have the same kind of problems you do: Personnel and resources frequently are not instantly available; they need time to plan their work; they have to interpret the Triple Constraint in the correct way, and so on.

Just as a contract controls your relations with your customer, so subcontractors define their relationship to your project by the contract your company's purchasing department issues to them. Should a change be required, it is certainly all right to tell them about it. But the change becomes effective and meaningful only when it is converted into a contract change.

Another point to consider when working with subcontractors is that your request for a proposal can require that periodic reviews be included in your contract. This is desirable, as it would be if your customer required periodic reviews of your work. You are trying to see how their work is progressing, to understand if changes will be called for as a result of what they are doing or problems they are encountering, in short, to stay abreast of their work. In software development particularly, subcontractor programming and documentation must be satisfactory and bug-free, and often that cannot be established until the subcontracted work is integrated with other work. Where subcontractors are used in one phase, for example, to establish user requirements during definition, the work should not be considered completed until it has been reviewed and accepted by the development management, who must use that requirements statement.

But you must draw a fine line between giving new directions and simply keeping abreast of what they are doing. Remember that the contract dictates the work and the progress reviews or monitoring activities are solely to find out if it is being done, not to provide daily, weekly, or monthly changes in direction.

Your support agreement is a written contract.

TYPICAL PROBLEMS

> Working with the support team probably causes the greatest difficulty, especially for new, inexperienced project managers. The root of this problem is being dependent on nonsubordinates. Two other problems are closely related. First, to negotiate support agreements takes a lot of time, usually at the very busy project inception period. So it is done reluctantly or poorly or even omitted. In the latter situation, the project manager uses his or her own judgment of what the support group will do. Second, even when the support agreements have been intelligently negotiated, later events frequently require that changes be made. Again, this is time-consuming and must be anticipated.
>
> Another issue of great importance, and often beyond the manager's control, is the location of the QA (quality assurance) function—external to the project organization (as a support service) or inside it, as shown in Figure 12-3. Wherever possible, no matter how annoying the conscience-like character of the quality assurance team may become, it should be located
> *continued*

outside the development organization. The natural advocacy situation between the developers—who must get the product out within the Triple Constraint—and QA—who must not allow errors in the product to go out the door—is diluted in effect when the QA manager reports to the project manager.

This is not as true of the location of other support services such as training, user and technical publications, and the data center. For training and publications, company-wide standardized formats are often not as important as having personnel who are project knowledgeable presenting the information. Managers often have more control over their schedule and support personnel utilization when they are within their organization. They can then use them on successive project tasks throughout the life cycle and maintain continuity. For example, having written user requirements and product specifications during the early part of the project, the documentation specialist would be more familiar with the user's terminology than a newly assigned technical writer for the user's manuals. Lastly, having control over the data center eliminates the project's queuing up behind other users with potential schedule slippages and cost overruns. Of course, this would apply only to those projects large enough to warrant such a hardware investment.

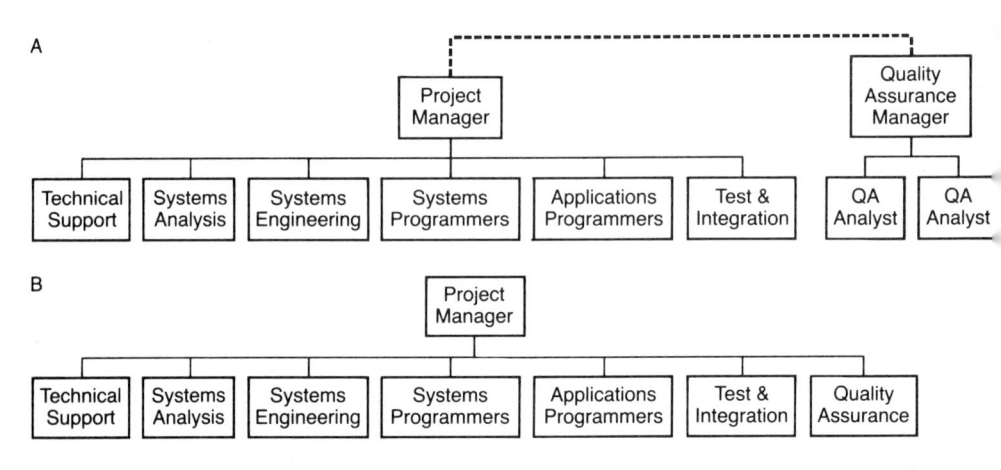

Figure 12-3. Locating the QA group outside the project (A) or inside the project (B).

HIGHLIGHTS

Support teams do not work for the project manager in an administrative sense, but their participation and contributions are vital.

Support groups should be involved in projects as early as possible and allowed to plan their task.

Although they lack legal status, written agreements are an excellent way to obtain commitments from support teams.

Coordination, a continuing need, is best provided by network diagrams.

Every plan revision must be written and distributed to all concerned personnel.

FURTHER READING

R. D. Archibald. *Managing High-Technology Programs and Projects.* New York: Wiley-Interscience, 1976.
   Chapter 8 reviews many of the written devices the project manager can use to control the support team.

A. J. Melcher and T. A. Kayser. "Leadership Without Formal Authority—The Project Department." *California Management Review,* vol. 13, no. 2 (Winter 1970), pp. 57–64.
   This is a case history with some useful ideas on how to obtain cooperation from support groups.

S. L. Stamm. "Assuring Quality QA." *Datamation* (March 1981), pp. 195–200.
   This is a good presentation of the critical role of software QA in a software development project and how to successfully incorporate it into a project organization.

13

The Role of the Computer Software Project Manager

Although the project manager is clearly involved in all phases of the project and is ultimately responsible for satisfying the Triple Constraint, his or her interaction with the project and support teams is a key to the leading (or "people management") phase. This chapter first examines the overriding importance of the project manager's ability to influence other team members. His or her leadership ability depends on motivational skills rather than on authority, regardless of how much hierarchical supervisory authority he or she has over project team members. We also briefly discuss how a manager can gain time to work more effectively with people. Because projects are one-time undertakings, team members must often develop creative solutions. We suggest ways to stimulate creativity.

INFLUENCE RATHER THAN AUTHORITY

Limits of Authority

The project manager lacks control.

As the three previous chapters note, many people working on a project do not report directly to the project manager, and he or she does not even have complete control over those who do. In the first place, people are free to change jobs in our society. If given a command they do not like, some workers will simply quit. Or they may transfer to another division of the organization. Second, modern motivational theory indicates that issuing commands is a poor means to encourage people to perform well on a job. McGregor's Theory X/Theory Y is but one manifestation of the thinking that underlies current managerial practice, which usually substitutes persuasion and participation for command.

Nevertheless, commands are still a way of life, to a greater or lesser extent, depending upon the specific organization and situation. If stated brutally or insensitively, they demotivate and create resentment. If stated politely and reasonably (which is difficult to accomplish), commands may be effective.

Need For Influence

Given these limits to hierarchical authority, project managers must operate by winning the respect of project and support team members. This accomplished, they will find their wishes are accepted voluntarily and frequently with enthusiasm.

There are nine ways to have influence.

A study by Thamhain and Wilemon identifies nine influence bases available to project managers.

1. Authority—the legitimate hierarchical right to issue orders

2. Assignment—the project manager's perceived ability to influence a worker's later work assignments

3. Budget—the project manager's perceived ability to authorize others' use of discretionary funds

4. Promotion—the project manager's perceived ability to improve a worker's position

5. Money—the project manager's perceived ability to increase a worker's monetary remuneration

6. Penalty—the project manager's perceived ability to dispense or cause punishment

7. Work challenge—an intrinsic motivational factor capitalizing on a worker's enjoyment of doing a particular task

8. Expertise—special knowledge the project manager possesses and others deem important

9. Friendship—friendly personal relationships between the project manager and others

The first clearly depends on higher management's decision to invest the project manager with power, regardless of power's intrinsic utility. The next five may or may not be truly inherent in the project manager's position; others' perceptions are most important in establishing their utility to the project manager. The seventh is an available tool anyone may use to influence others. The project manager must earn the last two. Projects are more likely to fail when the project manager relies on authority, money, or penalty to influence people; success is correlated with the use of work challenge and expertise to influence people.

There will be occasions when the project manager must negotiate with team members. A typical approach is to explain the rationale of the effort and to involve the people in planning the detailed work packages. Given this need to influence, an effective project manager must be a superb communicator. He or she must have verbal and written fluency and be persuasive to be effective.

EFFECTIVE MANAGERIAL BEHAVIOR

A manager must plan and manage.

As we said in Chapter 1, the project manager must work with people not of his or her own choosing, many of whom have different skills and interests. Furthermore, the project manager is a manager, not a doer. If the project manager is writing lines of computer code for a programming project, designing a circuit for a new computer circuit board, or assembling boards into a terminal, who is planning the work of others? Who is deciding what approach to take to the support group manager so as to obtain the services of the most senior and best qualified person? And who is trying to devise a contingency plan in case the system test does not produce desirable results? The project manager must spend his or her time working with people and planning their work so nothing is overlooked and contingency plans are ready if needed.

On a very small project, the project manager's participation is also required as a worker, not merely as a manager. If not physically, then at least mentally, a project manager in this situation should have two hats, one labeled "project manager" and the other labeled "worker." The project manager must realize which function he or she is performing at any given moment and wear the appropriate hat.

Qualifications

Generally speaking, one becomes a project manager because one has been an excellent programmer, circuit designer, or analyst rather than because one has been trained or demonstrated competency as a project manager. But a virtuoso technical performance is not a sufficient qualification for managing the efforts of the project and support teams. In fact, one's demonstrated technical or professional skills are frequently problem-solving or performance skills that do not involve an ability to interact with others. But project managers, in common with other managers, need people skills rather than technical skills (see Figure 13-1). Developing people skills can be extremely difficult for many technically trained people who become project managers. Physical systems tend to behave in repeatable and predictable ways; people do not.

The project manager should be chosen because of an interest and skill in human relations.

For instance, some people have an altruistic-nurturing orientation; other people have an assertive-directing orientation; and others have an analytic-autonomizing orientation. Although altruistic-nurturing oriented people are usually trusting (a strength), people of another orientation may see them as gullible (a weakness). Similarly, the assertive-

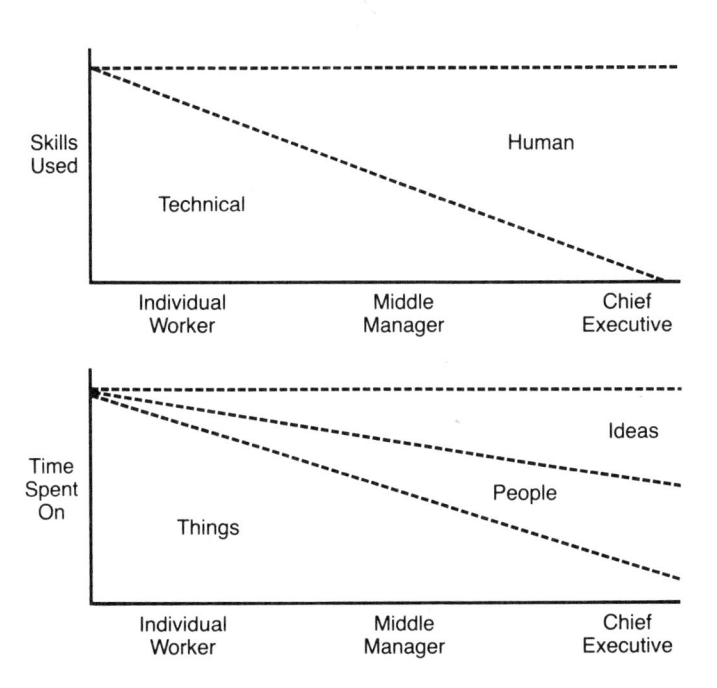

Figure 13-1. Management.
Source: "Basic Management Skills for Engineers and Scientists." Lecture notes by Milton D. Rosenau, Jr. Copyright © 1982 by the University of Southern California. Reprinted by permission.

directing person's self-confidence (a strength) can be seen as arrogance (a weakness), and the analytic-autonomizing person's caution (a strength) may appear to be suspicion (a weakness). A person with a balance of these orientations, who is flexible, may be seen as inconsistent.

To compound this problem, the same thing said to the same person at two different times can produce different reactions. This lack of predictability can be a major pitfall for many prospective project managers. Project managers must deal with both technical and emotional issues. If not already fluent with these human relations skills, they should take a course in behavioral psychology.

Managers manage and workers perform the tasks.

The project manager sets objectives and establishes plans, organizes, staffs, sets up controls, issues directives, spends time working with people, and generally sees that the project is completed in a satisfactory way, on time, and within budget. The project manager does not do the work of others on the project. A project manager who is an excellent programmer may find it frustrating to watch a more junior person carry out the programming on the project. The junior person will take longer, make mistakes, and not do as good a job as could a project manager with that skill. But if the project manager starts to do the programming, it demotivates the junior person, reducing his or her opportunity to gain experience and learn, and lessens the manager's time to function in the most vital role of all, namely, that of project manager.

A computer software project manager is not required to have been a programmer, although some background helps enormously and, in this age of home computers, there is no excuse for a software project manager to be computer illiterate. What is more important by far than the technical expertise is the skill in managing people, by whose work the project will succeed or not. In fact, some of the worst managers we've seen have been such excellent technicians that they couldn't keep their minds off managing the design effort rather than the people who were supposed to be designing! Technical background in systems design and programming is helpful to the extent that the manager uses it as a tool to understand the effort involved rather than to perform the effort.

Communication

Effective communication is one of the most difficult human endeavors. There are so many obstacles it is amazing that any effective communication at all occurs. Words have different meanings, and people often have different perceptions or orientations. The project manager's reputation (be it as a jokester or as a very serious person) will alter the way any message is received. Everyone the project manager communicates with will tend to hear the message he or she wants or expects to hear, which is not necessarily the message the project manager is attempting to deliver. Sometimes people are not listening, are distracted, or have a closed mind. Others, especially upper managers, may filter new technology and its related issues through their outdated filters of experience, reaching erroneous and sometimes disastrous conclusions. For example, how could an IBM 370 orientation allow for the diversity and potential in today's multimicrocomputer networks?

There is an aphorism about how to communicate: First you tell someone you intend to tell them; then you tell them; and then you tell them you told them. There is much truth in this use of multiple message delivery.

Communication must be worked at.

There are several steps you can take to improve your communication with other people:

1. Plan what is to be communicated beforehand rather than trying to decide while communicating. As it is sometimes stated, "Put brain in gear before opening mouth."
2. Use face-to-face meetings in which you can observe the other person's "body language." Allow enough time at an appropriate time of the day.
3. Decide which sequence and combination of telephone discussion, face-to-face meeting, and memo will be most effective.
4. Be consistent and follow through with actions appropriate to your message.
5. Use simple lanaguage.

In addition, you should consider using feedback, notices, and proximity.

Feedback

Communication is very much like a servomechanism in that it is not effective unless there is feedback. Communication can be improved by asking the person to whom the message has been delivered to restate it in his or her own words, which can help overcome a listener's closed mind.

Communication requires feedback.

Another effective technique is to back up any verbal communication with a memo. This may also be done the other way around, first sending the memo and then meeting to discuss it. It is the duality of mode and the recipient's restatement that is most effective, rather than simple redundancy. For example, the process of merely putting down on paper an informal design decision between user and analyst may open side effects not originally thought about. Vital user feedback can prevent countless hours of wasteful programming.

Notices

It is impractical to meet constantly with all participants on a very large project. Even on a smaller project, it may be disruptive to have numerous meetings. It is thus desirable to issue project notices and reminders of priority actions for any given period. Putting such notices on distinctively colored paper or preprinting the project name on the top will set them apart from the other mail. This is especially useful in projects where systems programmers are managed separately from application programmers, but the latter should be apprised of changes in systems programs.

Proximity

Locating the people on the project near each other also aids communication. Because the people are close together, they can see each other more often, which makes communication easier and more frequent. And when people are in frequent contact, their point of view tends to become more uniform.

Follow-Up

It is necessary to have some system of follow-up of the communications, be they face to face or written. Some people simply keep an action log, a chronological listing of all agreements reached with other people for which follow-up action is expected.

Somewhat more effective is a follow-up system keyed to the individual from whom action is expected. A filing card with each key person's name printed on the top may be used to record notations of actions expected of that person. A variant of this is keeping a folder for each key person in which you store records of all discussions or copies of memos for which follow-up action is required or requested. In either event, hold periodic meetings with each key person and use the filing card or folder to plan the topics to be discussed.

A project history is an effective tool for the manager, key personnel, and any replacements throughout and following the project. It may be a chronological or topical file. It should contain a history of the design and other decisions considered during the life of the project. Many of these will be discarded, of course, but for the manager who may have to come on board after the inception of a project, it proves to be an invaluable tool to prevent revisiting issues that were already considered but rejected.

When it is known that project managers (or any manager, for that matter) have such a consistent follow-up system, people who work for or with them will realize that any statements made to them will be taken seriously. Therefore, commitments made to them will tend to receive serious and consistent attention.

Follow up communications.

Conflict Resolution

Projects are fraught with conflicts. They inevitably arise because projects are temporary entities within more permanent organizations. One root cause is thus competition for resources. Regardless of organizational form, project managers and functional managers tend to have momentary interests that are at odds; so project managers must be able to "stomach" conflict. Pride of ownership of design ideas often creates internecine rivalries that have destroyed many a computer systems architecture team. The project manager's critical role in conflict management is to ensure that issues are resolved and that arguments do not become personal.

The project manager must cope with conflict.

The Thamhain and Wilemon study reviews the causes of and ways to resolve conflict. Their findings indicate that many things can be done to reduce conflicts, the simplest of which is having good plans, current and realistic schedules, and thorough communications.

Efficient Time Management

Given the wide range of project managers' duties (in a sense, they must be all things to all people), they can easily end up working nights and weekends unless they are very efficient in the use of time. Of course, they should not make the mistake of being efficient to the point of being ineffective.

Effectiveness is achieving the desired results. Effectiveness is what counts, but project managers are more likely to be effective if they use their time efficiently.

The overriding issue in time management is "first things first." The project manager must know the most important things to do this year, this month, this week, today, and right now. Only when he or she has a clear perception of priorities can a project manager effectively manage his or her time.

Well-planned meetings are essential.

The second key issue in time management is to devote large chunks of time to important single issues. This can be accomplished by maintaining a time log (see Figure 13-2) on how you actually spend your time next week. At the end of next week, examine the record of what actually occurred as you recorded it at the end of each time interval during the week. Then plan how you will alter your behavior in the following week to get fewer, larger chunks of time concentrated on single topics. Do this several times, over a period of several months, and you will master the art of better time management.

Manage time efficiently.

Because project management involved integrating the work of many people, numerous meetings will be held. Conducting them efficiently and effectively is essential. The following are keys to improving meetings:

- Know beforehand why the meeting is to be held and what outcome is expected.
- Determine the minimum number of people required.
- Choose a meeting location with room arrangement consonant with the meeting's purpose (for example, a round table arrangement for discussion among equals, a lecture hall arrangement for a presentation, and so forth).
- Circulate an agenda with topic durations to all attendees, and perhaps discuss this individually with the key participants ahead of time. If this meeting constitutes a document or design review, be sure that numbered copies have been distributed to each attendee with enough lead time for the documents to be read through.
- Be prepared, and open the meeting on time with a restatement of the purpose and agenda.
- If possible, ask each attendee (one at a time) for his or her views on each topic prior to topic completion. Just because some attendees are loud or dominant does not mean they are best qualified to speak on a topic; a quiet, shy, or retiring person will often make a valuable contribution if invited to comment.

Day / Time	M	T	W	T	F
8:00-8:10					
8:10-8:20					
8:20-8:30					
5:20-5:30					

Figure 13-2. Sample time log.

Source: "Basic Management Skills for Engineers and Scientists." Lecture notes by Milton D. Rosenau, Jr. Copyright © 1982 by the University of Southern California. Reprinted by permission.

- Verbally summarize what transpires at the meeting and later distribute published minutes to all attendees.

Although they won't work everywhere, you might try the meeting rules used on the Gossamer Albatross project as reported in *Technology Review* (April 1981, p. 56):

All meetings are held standing in a circle.

All participants are heard in turn.

All meetings must result in a definite decision.

All decisions must be acted on immediately.

THEORIES OF MOTIVATION

Regardless of hierarchical authority, anyone can encourage or stimulate others to contribute to a project and improve their productivity. For project managers, many of whom lack direct authority over all the resources required for project success, an understanding of motivation is essential. A major element of the project manager role is to avoid demotivating others. There are many theories of motivation, the two most important of which we briefly review.

Hierarchy of Needs

People have five levels of needs.

Abraham Maslow's theory of the hierarchy of needs (Figure 13-3) holds that motivation is not external but rather arises within the worker if managerial actions are not in-

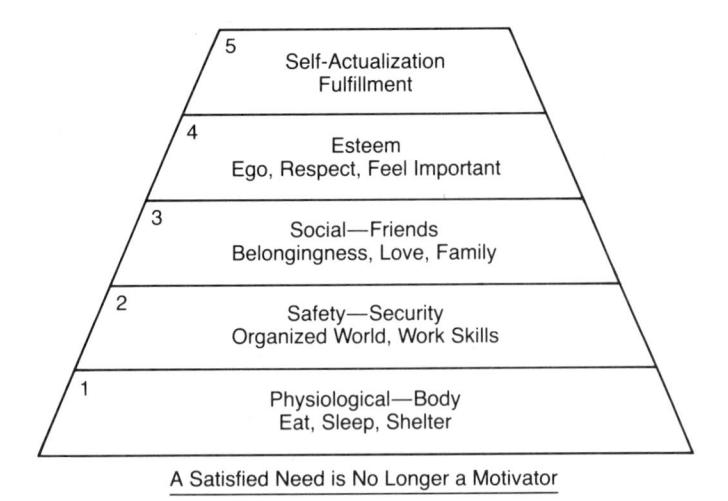

```
            /5\
           / Self-Actualization \
          /    Fulfillment       \
         /4_____ \
        / Esteem                   \
       / Ego, Respect, Feel Important\
      /3_____\
     / Social—Friends                  \
    / Belongingness, Love, Family       \
   /2_____\
  / Safety—Security                       \
 / Organized World, Work Skills            \
/1_____\
/ Physiological—Body                         \
/ Eat, Sleep, Shelter                         \
/_____\
        A Satisfied Need is No Longer a Motivator
```

Figure 13-3. Motivation—Abraham Maslow's hierarchy of needs.

Source: "Basic Management Skills for Engineers and Scientists." Lecture notes by Milton D. Rosenau, Jr. Copyright © 1982 by the University of Southern California. Reprinted by permission.

appropriate. The worker is motivated to achieve a specific goal because of an inherent internal need. Each person has five levels of needs. The lowest of these is physiological or body needs (eat, sleep, have shelter, and so forth). A hungry person will have a goal to eat and will engage in the goal-directed activity of buying and preparing food to satisfy the hunger need. (In fact, if we try to prevent this person from satisfying the need, by denying him or her money to pay for the food, for instance, the person may engage in such antisocial behavior as robbery to satisfy the need.) Once this need is filled, continuing to offer more food, sleep, or shelter has no motivational value. Higher level needs now come into play. Second-level needs are safety and security; third-level needs are social; and fourth-level needs are esteem or ego. The fifth-level needs are for self-actualization or fulfillment.

To take advantage of Maslow's findings, a project manager would have to understand the levels of need an individual has already satisfied. Then he or she could offer satisfiers for unmet needs as an encouragement. Americans generally have unfilled needs on levels three, four, or five; therefore, the project manager would offer satisfiers aimed at these levels.

If the project manager does not offer satisfiers, workers will find satisfiers outside the work environment (Table 13-1).

TABLE 13-1. Satisfiers.

Level	Job Related	Other
5	Setting own goals	Hobbies or volunteer work
4	Winning company award	Election to civic board
3	Staff meetings or committee work	Club membership
2	Insurance packages	Live in safe area
1	Enough salary to purchase necessities and reasonable work hours	Availability of adequate stores

Source: "Basic Management Skills for Engineers and Scientists." Lecture notes by Milton D. Rosenau, Jr. Copyright © 1982 by the University of Southern California. Reprinted by permission.

Note that money is not a motivator, although it may play a role. A person feels good when he or she gets a salary increase because it provides recognition (filling an ego need). However, a person who can fill his or her social needs only by joining a country club will need more money than the person who can satisfy these social needs by being active in community groups.

Motivational Factors

Frederick Herzberg has done an excellent study on work and motivation, examining specific factors that motivate workers. He found many things done (company policies, supervision, work conditions, and salary, for instance) are not motivational at all. He called these "hygiene factors." The absence of hygiene factors is demotivating, but their presence is not motivating.

Instead, there have to be motivational factors present to foster high productivity. The key motivational factors are achievement, recognition, the work itself, responsibility, advancement, and growth. Achievement and recognition are short term, and the others are long term in their impact. Thus, it is important to give workers recognition frequently (but not routinely) for significant accomplishments.

Achievement and recognition are the most powerful motivators.

IMPLICATIONS OF MOTIVATIONAL THEORY

How can you take advantage of these widely accepted theories of how people become motivated? There are many techniques, three of which we briefly review.

Theory X/Theory Y

We have already mentioned Douglas McGregor's work in identifying two managerial styles. Theory X and Theory Y. Theory X is the authoritarian style, in which top management makes decisions and coerces workers to comply. Theory Y is the participative style, built upon the findings that people both enjoy working and want to work. Theory X assumes external control of the workers; Theory Y assumes useful controls are within individuals and managers can draw upon workers' self-direction.

Participative decision making is best.

In working with the support team, over which he or she lacks control, the project manager should try to adopt the Theory Y style (and would probably be well advised to use it with the project team as well). Authoritarian behavior is not usually appropriate, especially to encourage the creative talents of programmers and analysts. Managerial behavior can be based on the assumption that others want to do a good job.

To put it another way, consider how you would like to be managed and how you would respond. Workers are rarely self-motivated in a Theory X environment, but are more likely to be so in a Theory Y environment. Also, each manager has his or her own style of management. Use the style with which you are comfortable.

Behavior Modification

Negative reinforcement can stop negative behavior, but it requires positive reinforcement to promote positive behavior.

B. F. Skinner devised a theory of behavior modification that advocates positive reinforcement, namely, rewards for "good" behavior. Using Skinner's theory, one would induce people to behave differently (that is, consonant with project goals) by rewarding them when they act appropriately. "Rewards" typically are consistent with Herzberg's findings, namely, a sense of achievement and recognition.

Thus, if a technical writer does a fine job on your project, it is appropriate to send her a memo and send a copy to her boss (or vice versa) and perhaps to her personnel folder as well. Conversely, if you have been practicing behavior modification and positive reinforcement consistently, you do not have to do anything if on another occasion she does a poor job. The absence of positive reinforcement will be message enough. Further, that absence may very well motivate the designer to ask you how her performance fell short.

Very early in Rosenau's industrial career, the president of his company sent the following letter (on engraved, personal stationery) to him at his home just after the project team of which he was a member shipped the first unit of an advanced system:

People's behavior can be modified.

> Dear Milt:
>
> I would like to extend to you my hearty congratulations for your contribution to the outstanding technical success of the Satrack Program. I know that you must feel proud of being a member of the team who accomplished a marked advance in the state of the art of aspheric manufacture.
>
> Our Company is now considered to be in the forefront of this development activity, and it has been through your contributions that we have achieved this position.
>
> I know that your efforts were great and there were many long evenings and weekends which you personally sacrificed. It is indeed gratifying that we have the people with the spirit to undertake such a challenging problem and carry forth to a successful conclusion.
>
> Sincerely yours,

The recipient of such a letter will become motivated to put in similar extraordinary efforts in the future and probably will continue to have family support for that effort. Other examples of positive reinforcement include awards (wall plaques, luncheons or dinners, trips, and so forth) or a story or picture in the company newspaper. These promote worker motivation because they provide recognition and validate an achievement.

Management By Objectives

Another practical technique that the project manager can use is management by objectives (MBO). Variations of this technique are management by results (MBR) and management by commitment (MBC). As the names suggest, the techniques focus management and worker attention on the outcome (objectives or results) rather than on the process by which a worker chooses to achieve the outcome. This frees the manager to concentrate on what is desired, and it leaves the worker free to concentrate on how to accomplish it in his or her own style. This is particularly suitable for software development efforts where modules of code can be parceled out to programmers as discrete entities. As long as project standards are observed regarding language, maintainability, accuracy, and interfaces, the programmer can be creative in his or her design and coding.

To use this simple, powerful technique, the project manager negotiates with a worker on the results the worker will agree to achieve. Because the technique is a general one, the worker may be a member of the project team or the support team. The results must be like project objectives, that is, verifiable, measurable, specific, and achievable. These are recorded on paper (perhaps a standard form), and are signed by both the worker and the manager. In the event that changes are required, these must be jointly negotiated, and the paper must then be revised and signed again. Note that this technique is identical to how you would contract with another organization to do subcontract work; the only difference is that the agreements are not legally binding.

MBO involves project team members, thus motivating them.

The technique draws upon the motivational factors of responsibility and achievement. The worker may be motivated because he or she is consulted in defining the task to be carried out. And, as the worker is doing the work, there may be clear progress during the work that provides a sense of achievement.

The only problem with the technique is that it is sometimes difficult to set the objectives or results that are to be achieved. When this is the case, the same technique used for starting a project with unclear objectives can be used. That is, agree on something specific that will be accomplished in a given period, and then try to set longer term goals when more is known about the task.

STIMULATING CREATIVITY

The project manager must also stimulate creativity. This is not applicable only to computer software projects; it is, however especially important in computer software projects.

In general, the less precedent for the project, the more creativity will be required. Both design and programming can be highly creative, but creativity also has a valuable place in documentation and testing.

Motivation

Creativity may be stimulated simply by managing in a way consistent with behavioral and motivational theory. Encouragement by providing recognition and appreciation is the most straightforward technique to stimulate creativity. In addition, one must provide a favorable atmosphere. In a sense, we are looking at positive reinforcement again. People are permitted to fail when asked to produce creative results and are not castigated for doing so. Rather, they are praised when they succeed.

Brainstorming

Brainstorming techniques are often used to deal with some intractable problem. The conventional method for brainstorming is to advise perhaps a half-dozen people of the problem and after one or two days convene a brainstorming meeting. At this meeting, restate the problem and reiterate the ground rules:

Positive reinforcement and brainstorming will stimulate creativity.

1. Absolutely no criticism (including smirking) is permitted.
2. The more ideas produced, the better is the session.
3. Novel, unusual (even impractical) ideas are desired.
4. Improvement or combination of prior ideas is also desirable.
5. No idea, no matter how outlandish, is rejected.

Use a tape recorder to permit more leisurely subsequent consideration of the ideas thus generated. Writing down the ideas, as they are expressed, on a flipchart or blackboard, helps to stimulate more ideas. The basic rule, however, is that each idea is recorded, no matter how strange it may sound.

An alternative method that may work better in some situations is to have a facilitator talk to a few people individually and ask for their ideas on solving the problem. After three or four people have been interviewed, you have a list of ideas to use to start the brainstorming session (like pump priming), which is then carried out in the normal way.

DETECTING BURNOUT

Avoid burnout by making sure project team members don't overwork.

Burnout among software professionals becomes a more severe issue the longer someone has been working on a project and the more trouble the project gets into. Working too long on a problem or working too many hours consistently often dulls discrimination skills, causing less efficiency and usually introducing more mistakes. Another variety of burnout occurs at the end of a project, when everyone seems to want to move onto something new and more exciting. This leads to poor testing, poor documentation, and an incomplete product.

The manager can help reduce burnout by monitoring the hours employees are putting in and ensuring that productivity is not being hampered by overcommitment and overdedication to task. Under no circumstances should the manager ignore the potential harm, both physical and psychological, that such fatigue can do to the employee (not to mention to the project!). Sometimes the best medicine is a twenty-four-hour stint away from the office and the programs to regain perspective on the problem and energy to solve it.

PRACTICAL TIPS

There are a few "tricks of the trade" that project managers should employ to help put the techniques discussed in this chapter to practical use. One is to keep your door open, which encourages people to talk with you and may identify key project issues that you were not yet aware of.

But when you do your planning, close your door and do not answer the telephone to gain high leverage on time use. When you are also a worker on your project, which is a common situation on smaller projects, this is when you do your own technical work.

Another trick is to walk the halls. There are always some people who will not enter your office, even if the door is open. Also, what you inevitably see when you go to the sites where work is supposed to be done is that things are not as you expected them to be.

Finally, plan all meetings. *Never* call a meeting for which you have not circulated an agenda in advance.

TYPICAL PROBLEMS

> Project managers are not normally selected from a pool of trained, qualified people. Rather, projects arise within (or descend upon) the organization, and a person who has demonstrated technical proficiency is asked to become project leader.
>
> Such people are often good "doers," have technical skills, and may think they want to be a project manager; but they usually take the job not knowing what is involved. They may get along with others (as opposed to being hermitlike) but be unable to cope with the inevitable conflicts that bedevil the project manager. What then happens is the organization has a poor project manager and has lost the services of a good technical resource. Also, such project managers tend to have orientations skewed too much to technical requirements rather than the users' true requirements.
>
> One cure for this problem is to be sure candidates for project management read books such as this prior to being offered jobs as project managers. After that, assuming a continuing interest in the job, the selected candidates should be sent to any one of the plethora of seminars on project management. These seminars, typically of two to five days duration, are given throughout the world.

There are many limits to authority; so project managers should learn how to wield influence.

HIGHLIGHTS

Managers must confine themselves to planning and let others perform the tasks.

Human relations skills are vital to a project manager.

Effective communication can be aided by feedback, issuing notices, and locating workers near each other.

Familiarity with theories of motivation will help managers do their job.

Creativity can be stimulated by positive reinforcement and brainstorming.

FURTHER READING

R. D. Archibald. *Managing High-Technology Programs and Projects.* New York: Wiley-Interscience, 1976.
   Chapter 3 is an excellent overview of the many role issues confronting project managers.

B. F. Baird. *The Technical Manager: How to Manage People and Make Decisions.* Belmont, CA: Lifetime Learning Publications, 1983.
   An absolutely superb book, filled with practical advice.

T. H. Bruggere. "Software Engineering Management, Personnel and Methodology." *Proceedings Fourth International Conference on Software Engineering* (1979), pp. 361–368.
   This good discussion of the role of the software manager includes practical problems and the attributes required to solve them.

L. Fried. *Practical Data Processing Management.* Reston, VA: Reston Publishing, 1979.
   Chapter 6, pages 274–338, although a bit abstract, discusses personnel issues in the data processing environment.

A. S. Grove. "How (and Why) to Run a Meeting." *Fortune* (July 11, 1983), p. 132.
   Here are some practical tips on how to run effective and useful meetings.

V. G. Hajek. *Management of Engineering Projects.* New York: McGraw-Hill, 1977.
   Chapter 1 is only five pages long, but it has an overview of the project manager's role, stressing contractual involvement.

P. Hersey and K. H. Blanchard. *Management of Organization Behavior: Utilizing Human Resources,* 3rd ed. Englewood Cliffs, NJ: Prentice-Hall, 1977.
   This is a very good and reasonably nontechnical review of motivation and organizational behavior.

F. Herzberg. "One More Time: How Do You Motivate Employees?" *Harvard Business Review*, vol. 46, no. 1 (January-February 1968), pp. 53–62.
   This is a classic, brief article that summarizes job factors that are "satisfiers" and "dissatisfiers."

J. Keen. *Managing Systems Development.* New York: Wiley, 1981.
   Chapter 12, pages 236–260, is devoted to people management in the data processing environment.

P. S. Licker. "The Japanese Approach: A Better Way to Manage Programmers?" *Communications of the ACM* (September 1983), pp. 631–636.
   This article proposes reducing high turnover among computer professionals by creating a Japanese style Theory Z atmosphere, stressing lifetime employment, nonspecialized career paths, and collective decision making.

P. W. Metzger. *Managing a Programming Project,* 2nd ed. Englewood Cliffs, NJ: Prentice-Hall, 1981.
   Pages 129–145 provide a good but brief discussion of the manager's job on a programming project.

H. J. Thamhain and D. L. Wilemon. "Conflict Management in Project Life Cycles." *Sloan Management Review,* vol. 16, no. 3 (Spring 1975), pp. 31–50; and H. J. Thamhain and D. L. Wilemon. "Leadership, Conflict, and Program Management Effectiveness." *Sloan Management Review,* vol. 19, no. 1 (Fall 1977), pp. 69–89.
   The first article reviews the kinds of conflict project managers encounter and some ways to cope with them. The second article measures which influencing techniques are most effective in given situations.

Part 4

MONITORING PROJECT PROGRESS

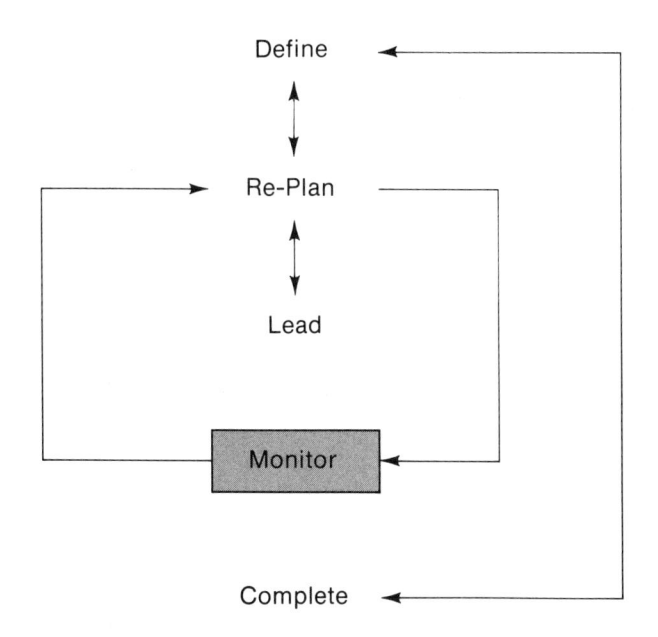

```
        Define ←─────────────┐
          ↕                  │
    ┌──→ Re-Plan ────┐       │
    │     ↕          │       │
    │    Lead        │       │
    │                │       │
    └──[ Monitor ]←──┘       │
           │                 │
        Complete ←───────────┘
```

14

Monitoring Tools for Software Projects

The next phase of project management is monitoring progress. First this chapter discusses various control techniques. Then there is a detailed consideration of the use of reports. Last, the special case of monitoring several projects simultaneously is discussed.

CONTROLLING TO ACHIEVE OBJECTIVES

The word "control" has a pejorative connotation, implying power, domination, or authority. Thus, many project managers (especially new ones) tend to avoid the necessity of installing and using controls on projects. The purpose of such project controls is to measure or monitor progress toward your objectives, evaluate what needs to be done to reach these objectives, and then take corrective actions to achieve the objectives. Thus, you must employ controls (in the measurement sense of the word) as a standard or your project will go off course and you might never know it. Control is the magic word, and measurement for the Triple Constraint is the name of the game.

Controls are needed to monitor progress against the project plan.

CONTROL TECHNIQUES

The first, and in many ways the most important, control is a well-publicized plan for all three dimensions of the Triple Constraint. A work breakdown structure, a network diagram

201

that indicates every element of it, and a cost estimate for each activity indicates how the project should be carried out. All the milestone events, of course, are based on the life cycle (Figure 1-4). Any deviation—and there usually is at least one—from this three-dimensional plan indicates the need for corrective action. Without such a plan, control is impossible.

What you measure is that to which attention will be given.

There are several restrictive control tools available, such as withholding resources or discretionary authority. When the project manager uses these controls, he or she is assured that people working on the project request the use of these resources or authorities, thus providing visibility. As an example, the project manager could require that any expenditure in excess of $1,000 receives his or her specific approval. Or the project manager could require any subsystem test report to need his or her signature. These kinds of controls go beyond the project plan in that they make project workers seek out the project manager for approval during the performance of each project activity or task. Anyone's failure to request approval of a planned major purchase tells the project manager that the project has deviated from the plan.

Controls tell you if the project plan is being followed.

This kind of restrictive control may well be appropriate with an inexperienced team or on a difficult project. But it is normally appropriate only for very small projects. If essentially all decisions on a large project must flow through the manager, the project will get bogged down by his or her lack of time to review a myriad of documents for approval. An effective variation on this restrictive approval control approach is to insist on independent inspection and quality control approvals on test data as a means to verify progress. For instance, you could insist that each module test be approved by people working on other related modules. Usually, in fact, for a large project, only abnormal (imperfect) test reports would get signed, to prevent a paperwork deluge.

Another project control method is to place trust entirely in the person carrying out a particular task. This method is fine if that person is able to recognize deviations from plan and realizes they must be reported promptly to the project manager. The person must also be capable of reporting the problem clearly. Because these three preconditions are rarely satisfied, this control tool should not normally be used.

Control is best exercised by examining the status of tasks.

A far better approach is for the project manager to examine the work being done under the direct control of the project team and support teams. This kind of control is based on the Theory Y assumption that people working on project tasks will be trying to do a good job (which can often become a self-fulfilling prophecy) rather than on the Theory X assumption that people will not do a good job. These examinations of activity work are accomplished by reading reports and conducting project reviews.

The optimum report type for monitoring project progress, in our experience, has been the exception report. The larger the project, the greater the number of reports management must plow through, making it terribly difficult to note easily just where the problem areas are. For example, if programming and testing of eight modules are going as scheduled but one module is well behind schedule, the manager would need to know just what type of module was delayed. If it was a major transaction processing module upon which the other eight depended, then the report that "eight out of nine modules are ready on schedule" would be exceptionally misleading. Exception reports should also be supplemented by occasional spot checks, in addition to scheduled reviews. One manager among one of our clients used to walk the halls during critical phases to chat with the programmers and find out the perceptions of the folks actually doing the work; he felt that gave him more of a sense of the true progress than the written word.

REPORTS

Reports fall into three broad categories: those concerned with the accomplishments along the performance axis, those concerned with schedule progress, and those concerned with cost. Reports may be written as summaries to provide an overview or be detailed about a particular task activity or some other element of project work. Reports may be strictly for the use of the organization performing the project or be intended for people outside, such as the customer or other contractors. If the project organization is in an industrial company, there is a wide spectrum of people to whom reports might be addressed, as shown in Figure 14-1.

Report Recipients

Within the software development organization, reports would be addressed to vice-presidents or directors of development, managers of test and evaluation, support services, su-

204 Monitoring Tools for Software Projects

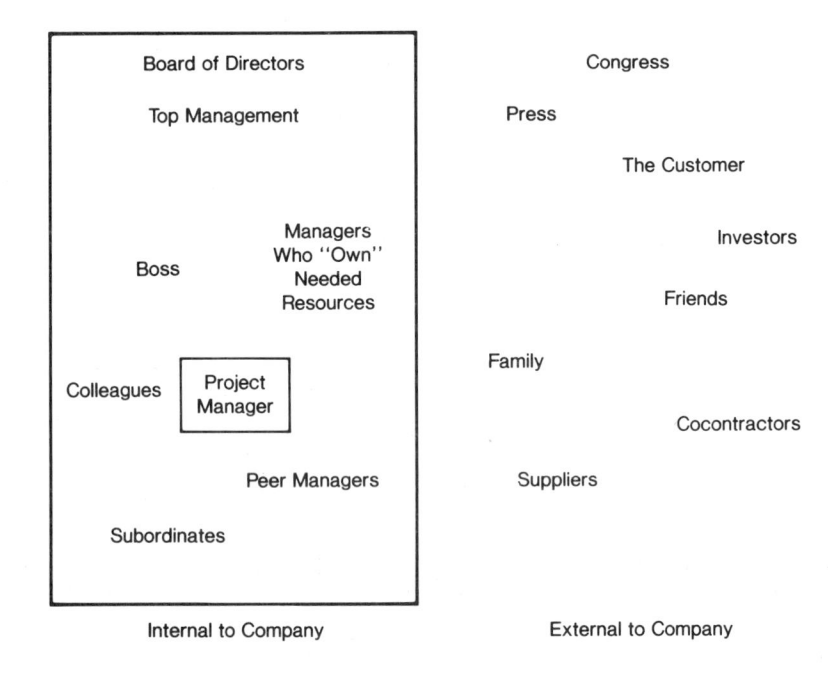

```
┌─────────────────────────────────────────┐
│        Board of Directors                │      Congress
│                                          │
│        Top Management                    │      Press
│                                          │
│                                          │      The Customer
│                     Managers             │
│            Boss    Who "Own"             │      Investors
│                     Needed               │
│                    Resources             │      Friends
│                                          │
│                                          │  Family
│         Colleagues  ┌─────────┐          │
│                     │ Project │          │      Cocontractors
│                     │ Manager │          │
│                     └─────────┘          │
│                                          │
│                  Peer Managers           │  Suppliers
│                                          │
│         Subordinates                     │
│                                          │
└─────────────────────────────────────────┘

         Internal to Company               External to Company
```

Figure 14-1. Report recipients.

pervisors, and project managers—depending upon the form of the project organization and the company. Smaller projects would use fewer different formats and probably have fewer associated support groups with which to interface. Government projects would require more frequent and more structured reports than most private sector company projects.

Regardless of which axis you are reporting against, the reports should be geared toward the recipient. A common failing is that the senior management report is too detailed. The degree of granularity needed increases the closer the manager is to the people actually performing the work in question. A vice-president of development, for example, has much less interest in the nature of a programming bug than the responsible supervisor. Wherever possible, condense and summarize, emphasizing key trends; supporting detail can always be provided when the problem is researched.

Problems

Do not confuse activity with progress.

The project manager cannot depend entirely on reports. In the first place, they may be inaccurate, a common failing of cost reports, which are prone to arithmetical errors and data entry errors if a computer-based system is being employed. On the other two axes, the people who write reports are prone to unwarranted optimism. Software project workers generally assume a well-advanced task is nearly complete; in fact, no task is complete until it is truly finished. Thus, most task reports will indicate a task is 80 or 90 percent complete, implying it will require additionally only a small fraction of the time already spent. Unless the task is as simple as drilling a hundred holes in a plate, it is normally impossible to measure what percentage of the task is truly complete. (And, as we said before, even in this case, there is no assurance the last hole won't destroy the plate, forcing the task to be completely redone.) In general, completing any given task requires more time than the person working on it forecasts. For instance, a report that X lines of code have been written for a computer program originally planned to be Y lines long tells you nothing about the percentage of completion. You know you are truly complete only when Z lines of code (which may be either more or less than the Y lines planned) actually run properly and adequately. Failure to predict when software is indeed fully debugged, as opposed to initially written, is the most common project reporting chimera.

Even though the task manager's report expresses a high degree of confidence that the task will be completed when scheduled, such a promise is not deliverable. Reports are one-way communication and lack the give and take possible in a meeting; so it is hard to judge the status of a task in progress solely from written data.

Consider the schedule situation illustrated in Figure 14-2. There is a long period of time in the middle of the project when there are no scheduled task completions. Thus, there are no certain checkpoints available, leaving considerable uncertainty as to the actual status. This illustrates another reason to break a project into many small tasks. There will be less uncertainty as to schedule status.

Dividing a project into many small tasks aids precise determination of its status.

If the work breakdown structure divides the project into many small tasks, the manager can look at each of them individually and decide whether they are complete. Only those tasks for which all work has been done are considered complete. No other task, regardless of the amount of effort applied so far, is complete. A task that is 80, 90, 99 percent complete is not complete. This two-state (bivalued) approach to examining tasks simplifies the project manager's job tremendously. He or she can accept as complete only those tasks for which reports (oral or written) guarantee the activity is complete. With many small tasks rather than only a few

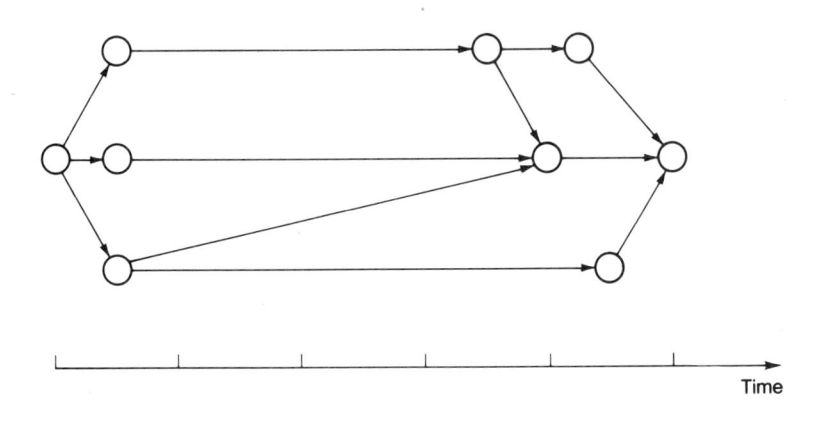

Figure 14-2. Time-based network diagram.

larger ones, there is much less uncertainty about overall project status.

Unfortunately, even this approach can lead to unwarranted optimism because there may be a ripple effect on programs concatenated with a delayed program. A previously 100 percent completed program may be found to have serious bugs when it finally gets data inputted from its precedent program.

Detail Level

Write reports for their specific audience.

Reports should always be as brief as possible and written for the audience for which they are intended. Because many people concerned with the project will wish to receive reports, there is a tendency to try to circulate one report to many recipients. This is a mistake. Many who wish to be kept abreast of progress are not interested in small details. This is especially true of busy management, both project organization and customer, for whom the project manager should prepare brief summary level reports. Such reports might also be circulated to people concerned with some specific aspects of the project but who do not require all the details in any particular report. Whenever possible, try to include a solution for problems encountered so that your management knows you are on top of an unexpected situation and that you are not stymied.

Pictures, demonstrations, and models should also be encouraged, especially for high-technology or geographically remote computer software projects. It is often hard for people not intimately concerned with the project to visualize the expected outcome or even the concept. For them, tangible descriptions, pictures, and such are by far the most appropriate means for providing reports. If your organization has closed-circuit television, this may be an excellent use of it. Whenever possible, try to define screen formats and sequences early in the project so that users can get a sense of the system under development.

It is always important to avoid the pitfalls of excessive reporting. Clearly, this is a gray area requiring judgment. The "convenience" of copying machines can easily lead to too many copies of overly detailed reports being circulated to too many people.

Cost Reports

Cost planning and reporting are important because they provide a guide for management action. They permit comparison of actual accomplishments in terms of cost incurred and planned accomplishments. Thus, they aid in determining whether there will be a cost overrun or underrun at completion. In some instances, they may aid in determining whether a specific task is on schedule.

Unfortunately, in many organizations, there is a tendency to look at actual cost versus planned cost as virtually the only measure of project progress. This is useless because there may be offsetting overruns and underruns, which we discuss in the next chapter.

MULTIPLE PROJECTS

As a project manager, you may eventually be responsible for more than one project. You may have many project managers reporting to you or there may be so many task managers reporting to you on a single project that you cannot personally attend all the task reviews and critically examine all the necessary detail. In this case, you must receive some kind of summary information that indicates the status of the several projects (or the many tasks) for which you have responsibility. When you cannot personally get into details, you are

The value of summary status indicators is questionable.

completely at the mercy of those who summarize information for you. Robert A. Howell indicates one way you might receive summary briefing information. In essence, his proposal is that, for every project (or task) for which you have responsibility, there should be a red, yellow, or green status indicator for each of the technical, schedule, and cost dimensions of the job. He also suggests these for funding status and would display in this summary form whether project review meetings have been held and at what point the program plan obtained approval. Such a system is certainly graphic, but it is no better than the judgment of the person who prepares the information.

Probably a better approach is to visit the various project reviews personally. Imagine you have three projects reporting to you, each of which is being managed by another project manager who reviews it monthly. You might sit in on each of these in a rotating fashion; so you attend the review of each project once every three months.

A useful concept to help in project monitoring is critical success factors. These are the six or seven key indicators (of many possible measures) that, when monitored, allow a manager to determine how well he or she is performing and what progress is being made. For the software project manager, some critical success factors would be schedule, cost, performance by project life cycle phase, personnel changes, customer involvement and satisfaction, facilities readiness, and usage. In a large project, there might be more data and figures to support each area, but probably not more critical success factors.

The importance of each factor might vary over the project life. For example, great increases in hiring should occur during design to accommodate the implementation requirements of a large project. However, they would be unusual during the conceptual phase or before the design phase, when commitment to proceed with implementation has been achieved.

Properly identified critical success factors can help monitor project progress.

Critical success factors also differ from company to company and often between managers. In a company doing a software research and development project, budget may not be as critical because of a prior commitment to support product development at any cost.

Critical success factors also depend upon the industry. Additional factors for computer software personnel would be the price of hardware, firmware, and off-the-shelf software packages.

TYPICAL PROBLEMS

> Problems arise because of too much or too little control. The former may demotivate personnel, consume too much time, or cost too much. In addition, there is a cost (and other) report time lag that delays news of problems. Further, there are inaccurate reports, even from conscientious people. In other cases, unclear reports will mask the deviation that has actually occurred.
>
> Even if the reports are prompt, accurate, and clear, the deviation may be noticed when you are busy with other urgent activities. Whenever a deviation is noticed, it takes time to react. Finally, you may be distracted by a human tendency to search for a guilty party on which to blame everything.

HIGHLIGHTS

Comparison with the project plan provides the basis for control.

Project managers may exercise control by requiring their approval or trusting task managers, but the best approach is to examine the status of tasks.

Reports, which may concern any axis of the Triple Constraint and be detailed or general, provide a means to examine the status of tasks.

Managers in charge of several projects can best exercise control by periodic personal reviews.

FURTHER READING

R. D. Archibald. *Managing High-Technology Programs and Projects.* New York: Wiley-Interscience, 1976.
   Chapters 8 and 9 provide several illustrations of control techniques.

C. W. Burrill and L. W. Ellsworth. *Modern Project Management.* Tenafly, NJ: Burrill-Ellsworth Associates, 1981.
> Chapter 3, pages 27–59, provides a detailed review of work control in the data processing project environment.

R. H. Clough and G. A. Sears. *Construction Project Management,* 2nd ed. New York: Wiley-Interscience, 1979.
> Chapters 9 and 10 stress time and cost control, also illustrating several reporting techniques.

M. S. Deutsch. *Software Verification and Validation.* Englewood Cliffs, NJ: Prentice-Hall, 1982.
> This entire book is devoted to the control of technical quality in a software engineering project, but the emphasis is primarily on aerospace projects and, in particular, the author's work at Hughes.

J. Gido. *An Introduction to Project Planning.* Schenectady, NY: General Electric, 1974.
> Chapter 5 briefly treats control, with concentration on the schedule aspect.

R. A. Howell. "Multiproject Control." Managing Projects and Programs Series. Cambridge, MA: Reprint from *Harvard Business Review,* no. 21300 (1971).
> This article clearly illustrates a method for controlling several projects simultaneously. As noted in this chapter, there are some problems with Howell's approach, but it is still the best concept if there are several projects.

J. Keen. *Managing Systems Development.* New York: Wiley, 1981.
> Chapter 13, pages 261–285, is devoted to project control.

R. Pilcher. *Appraisal and Control of Project Costs.* London: McGraw-Hill, 1973.
> Chapters 11 and 12 provide a detailed discussion of cost controls.

J. F. Rockart. "Chief Executives Define Their Own Data Needs." *Harvard Business Review* (March-April 1979), pp. 81–93.
> This classic article defines the critical success factor approach and its usefulness for senior managers. The approach is likewise useful for project managers.

J. D. Wiest and F. K. Levy. *A Management Guide to PERT/CPM,* 2nd ed. Englewood Cliffs, NJ: Prentice-Hall, 1977.
> Chapter 6 is a brief discussion of PERT/Cost as a control tool.

15

Software Project Reviews

There are two kinds of project reviews: periodic (typically monthly) and topical (usually milestones). Reviews can cover status or design issues or solicit problem resolution or an approval. Reviews are the most important control tool available to the project manager; they assure that he or she and the project team will actually be meeting to discuss progress. This chapter deals with both types of reviews and the general necessity to conduct reviews.

THE NECESSITY FOR REVIEWS

Having reviews is very much like having a navigator on an airplane. Reviews and a navigator are unnecessary if everything is proceeding according to plan. The purpose of both is to uncover deviations and correct them. Experienced project managers know the project will not proceed as planned, but they do not know how it will deviate. Only the naive project manager believes the plan is sufficient and no further navigation is necessary to arrive at the project's Triple Constraint point destination.

Another purpose of reviews is communication. Especially in topical reviews related to the software development life cycle, there will be representatives of different constituencies—users, systems architects, managers, quality assurance—all of whom may have different ideas of just what they have read. The words "interactive transaction processing" in

Reviews enhance communication and motivation.

a banking system, for example, may mean to the user that he or she can switch money between accounts and to the systems architect that there will be a series of screen formats that the user will have to reply to before money can be withdrawn from the account. The attendees at the reviews will try to ensure that their understanding of the document, and functions it represents, are indeed correct, and to take steps necessary to align those areas where miscommunications have occurred. A rule of thumb that we have found to be effective is that whenever you have an interface between two or more groups—for example, between users and analysts, between application programmers and systems programmers—it is valuable to have a formal review. This enables all parties to clarify their expectations and requirements.

Before each phase of the project life cycle can, in fact, be said to be completed and the ground work done for the succeeding phase, a review, as described later in this chapter, must be held to achieve necessary consensus that the work done thus far is accurate, complete, and unambiguous. It is precisely those inaccuracies and ambiguities that cause costly overruns later in the development process.

Reviews are your off-course alarm.

The project manager's boss and other senior management will want to know about the project status. This is more common in large projects, projects being performed on contract for others, and time-critical projects undertaken to comply with regulatory changes. The customer (in external projects), too, may wish to have periodic or topical reviews. These requirements for reviews and their nature and thoroughness should have been included in the negotiated contract for the work. The people working on the project will also wish to have reviews of the overall project from time to time. This is their means of learning whether their effort has to be adjusted from plan to conform with some new reality or everything is still proceeding according to the original plan (which never occurs). Reviews with the project and other personnel in attendance are a means for communication and can enhance motivation.

THE CONDUCT OF REVIEWS

Whether reviews are periodic or topical, they should be planned. Certain questions are almost always appropriate to raise.

Planning

Reviews may be thought of as a very small project. The goal is acquisition of all relevant information. There is a schedule and cost. The schedule may be a simple statement that the review will consume two hours on a particular afternoon. The cost depends on the number of people who participate and the preparation time.

There should be a plan for reviews. Everyone involved should understand the Triple Constraint for the review and be prepared to carry out his or her assignment. This means the project manager must make specific assignments to various individuals, who must know how much time and what level of detail are appropriate for their participation. Reviews may also be thought of as a particular kind of meeting. As such, all the care of preparation and follow-up discussed in Chapter 13 is relevant.

Think of a review as a small project.

Conducting the Review

To ensure the best review possible, a clear statement of purpose should always be made to avoid initial misconceptions that can waste everyone's time. If problem identification is the key purpose, rather than the actual decision making, state that right away. If tasks are to be assigned, be sure to give them due dates. Information dissemination and decision making should usually be separated at reviews, with decisions made separately, based on the results of the review.

Another helpful technique is to ensure that attendees truly understand and are concerned about the position they represent. For example, if the user's requirements document is being reviewed, users should not be represented by a systems analyst; a user must be present.

Third, a secretary or scribe should be appointed to be responsible for noting all the problem areas, points raised and by whom, committee appointments, due dates, and so forth. Subsequent memos should document very carefully exactly what occurred so that changes can be made as necessary and monitored. Some of the more critical issues should be saved as part of the project history.

In general, running a good review follows the rules for chairing a good meeting: stay on the subject; avoid becoming personal; identify the salient issues; assign knowledgeable people to work on the problem outside the review meeting and report back by a given date. But good reviews depend on prior distribution of documents so that attendees are talking to a common set of data. For example, a review of the user requirements would be of little help without a document that contains report contents, definitions and frequencies, information flows, and screen contents and occurrences, where applicable. Otherwise, the user would not know which requirements had been included and which had been overlooked.

Questions

Ask "why" questions.

The smart project manager learns to ask questions at project reviews. You are not asking questions to embarrass or pillory anyone but rather to find out how the project is deviating from the plan so you can take corrective action. If you (or others, such as configuration management or quality assurance) don't ask questions, some people won't volunteer critical information. Thus, ask questions nonthreateningly. Such nondirective questions often start with "why." A very good question is, "Why are you doing that?" You can follow this with successive "why" questions. Some other helpful questions to ask are the following:

What persistent problems do you have, and what is being done to correct them?

Which problems do you anticipate arising in the future?

Do you need any resources (people or things) you do not yet have?

Do you need any information you do not have now?

Are there any personnel problems now or that you anticipate?

Are there any environmental problems now or that you anticipate?

Do you know of anything that will give you schedule difficulties in completing your task? If so, what?

Is there any possibility your task will be completed early?

Will your task be completed within the allowed budget, or do you anticipate some overrun?

Is there any possibility your task will be completed with an underrun?

Is this documentation complete, accurate, and unambiguous?

Is there any possibility that completion of your task will lead to any technological breakthroughs for which patents might be appropriate?

Has any work done on your task led to any competitive edge we might use to gain other business elsewhere?

The thing to remember about project reviews and these questions is that you are almost assuredly going to hear some bad news. Most of us do not cope with bad news in a very positive way; so the project review can easily become a recrimination and blaming session. This will not be productive. It will destroy the review and much additional effort on the project. Be businesslike and factual in conducting the reviews, and keep asking questions to gather information. If it is appropriate to assess blame, do that in a different meeting, preferably privately with the person who must be blamed.

Plan to conduct project review meetings and expect problems to surface.

PERIODIC REVIEWS

In general, every project should be reviewed once a month. It may be appropriate to review some projects once a year or once every three months; others may require weekly or even daily reviews. Periodic reviews catch deviations from plan before they become major disasters, and the nature of your project will determine the appropriate review frequency. Unless there are compelling reasons to do otherwise, schedule periodic reviews for a few days after the monthly project cost reports are available.

Task Review

A task is in one of two conditions: complete or not complete. For tasks whose performance axis dimension has been completed, examine the actual versus planned cost and schedule, as illustrated in Figure 15-1. Unless there is something unique about the cost deviations on any completed activity, the accumulated actual cost versus plan can be used to forecast the cost at the end of the project. In Figure 15-1, actual cost for the five complete tasks ($42,000) is less than planned cost ($44,100), and the ratio of these indicates that the final actual costs will be approximately 97.5 percent of the plan.

Software Project Reviews

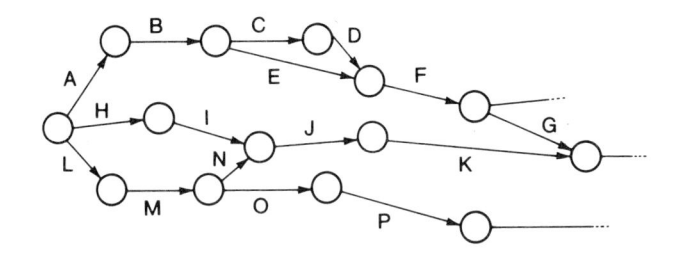

1 - Identify technically complete activities.
2 - Examine actual versus planned cost and schedule:

Completed Activity	Cost Act	Cost Plan	Cost Var	Schedule Act	Schedule Plan	Schedule Var
A	3,000	3,200	200	7	6	⟨1⟩
B	4,100	2,900	⟨1,200⟩	9	5	⟨4⟩
C	6,000	8,400	2,400	6	11	5
D	9,700	12,600	2,900	12	17	5
E	19,200	17,000	⟨2,200⟩	24	23	⟨1⟩

Figure 15-1. Measuring progress.

Watch the critical path.

Actual versus plan ratio may not be meaningful in the case of schedule variations because many of the completed tasks will not be on the critical path. An activity not on the critical path will often be completed later than plan simply because it was not necessary to complete it within the planned time. Thus, the project manager can make predictions about the schedule only by looking at those completed tasks on the critical path.

It is appropriate to ask which incomplete tasks are in progress and which have not yet been started. For those under way, find out whether there have already been any difficulties that would preclude their being completed on time within the cost plan.

In the case of the project illustrated in Figure 15-1, the next concern would be the status of tasks H, L, and F. Do these tasks not yet completed indicate that the project is hopelessly behind schedule? After exploring that, we want to know about the critical path for this particular project. In this case, the concern is whether the completed activities have already caused the project to slip hopelessly or whether the schedule variations have no significance with regard to the overall project.

In the case of cost review, it is necessary to examine the details of each task individually, as shown in Figure 15-2. The project manager who looks only at the overall project may be deceived. Project cost can appear to be in harmony with the plan, but that may conceal compensating task overruns and underruns or other difficulties that must be explored.

Examine individually the cost of each task.

Commitments

Project cost reports are always plagued by certain problems. First, they are not issued instantly at the end of the month. It takes time to gather the data, process it, print it out, and distribute it, whether the system is manual or electronic. Second, these reports are never the highest priority in any corporation's accounting department, coming after payroll and usually after customer billing. Thus, project cost reports typically follow completion of the monthly period by two or three weeks (at least a week and a half, and, in some cases, five or six weeks).

In addition, cost reports are nothing but a record of the apparent charges to a project, which may be in error. Even if the cost charges to the project are correct, they do not necessarily reflect the corresponding amount of performance accomplishment. Even if the actual costs for each task agree completely with the plan for each task, there is no assurance

Commitments are future costs.

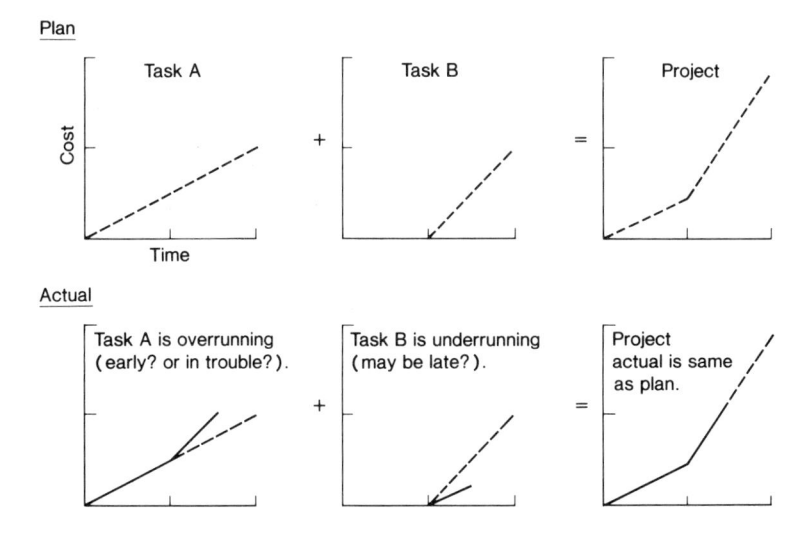

Figure 15-2. Details matter.

that the work accomplishment has a corresponding degree of completion. Within an individual task, where there is no detailed further subtask breakdown, the project manager has only judgment to guide whether progress and cost are consistent. But if a project is divided into many tasks, the ambiguity is reduced because the project manager can look at completed tasks and compare their actual cost with plan. In looking at these costs for tasks, the manager must also look at commitments. Commitments are obligations for which the project will be billed but that are not reflected on the actual cost reports. Figure 15-3 illustrates two common problems.

A task apparently completed with an underrun may in fact have outstanding bills charged against it. To preclude surprises, look at the commitments charged against the task. You may do so with either a manual or computer-based commitment report. If these reports do not exist, the project manager must maintain these manually to avoid unpleasant surprises.

To summarize, review the Triple Constraint:

- Technical dimension—Task is either complete or not.
- Schedule dimension—Compare actual and planned time for completed tasks. Slippage is significant only if the schedule is delayed.
- Cost dimension—Compare actual and planned cost for completed tasks. Include commitments.

Month	Event	Commitment Report	Cost Report
1	$10K purchase order issued	$10,000	-0-
2	$1K trip authorized	11,000	-0-
3	Traveler paid $900	10,000	$900
4	Vendor delivers	10,000	900
5	Vendor sends bill	10,000	900
6		10,000	900
7	Vendor's bill paid	-0-	10,900

Figure 15-3. Commitments are future costs.

Cost to Complete

Periodically, the project manager should request estimates of the cost (and time) to complete all incomplete tasks. You might do so quarterly or semiannually and also whenever the plan is revised substantially.

Do not make these estimates by simple subtraction of cost to date from the planned cost, as in method 1 in Figure 15-4. Have each task manager totally reestimate the task in light of everything now known, as shown by method 2 in the figure. Unfortunately, this often indicates that the project will overrun its budget, but it is important to learn of that possibility early enough to do something about it. As the project progresses, the participants learn about what is involved. Also, replanning may occur, and the necessity for new tasks may become apparent.

Periodically request estimates of the cost of completing all unfinished tasks.

Follow-Up Actions

During any review, a variety of actions will be identified to cope with the various problems uncovered. The project manager should always record these actions, the person responsible, and the expected completion date. This might be done on a register (Figure 15-5). All concerned people should receive copies, and the status of these action assignments should be reviewed no later than the next project review.

Follow up reviews.

TOPICAL REVIEWS

There are many kinds of topical reviews. The one used depends on the undertaking and customer requirements. You

Method 1			Method 2		
Plan (or Allowed) Cost	=	$10,000	Task Q	=	$1,632
Cost to Date	=	6,000	Task R	=	2,149
Cost to Complete	=	$4,000	Task S	=	1,910
			Cost to Complete	=	$5,691

Figure 15-4. Estimated Cost to Completion.

Assigned Actions for Completion		
Project: _____		
Action	Responsibility	Due

Figure 15-5. Typical action follow-up form.

will always have milestone reviews and may be required to do high level management reviews. You should also ensure walkthrough reviews of design.

Milestone Reviews

The most critical are those milestone reviews that are identified within the work breakdown structure and reflect the completion of the formally documented part of a phase of the project life cycle, as shown in Figure 1-4. Again, the particular documents will vary according to corporate standards and the particular life cycle cleavage used. However, our life cycle phasing of concepts, definition, feasibility, systems design, detailed design, and implementation produces the set of documents that must be reviewed as shown in Figure 15-6.

Because each document is aimed at a separate audience, the content of the review board for each document likewise should change. Our review board composition suggestions are shown in Figure 15-7. In many companies, to provide continuity when the reviewers shift, there is a permanent chairperson assigned for reviews. The format of the reviews, however, should be consistent regardless of the composition of the review board, as described earlier. The review process is iterative and should be repeated until the parties reviewing the documents (and ostensibly the work they reflect) concur on the contents. Failure to do so will perturb the development process later on and can be counted on to affect budget and schedule and possibly performance.

Keep review format consistent.

All these milestone reviews should be mandated in the contract and made a precondition to carry out further work on the project. Thus, the reviews themselves would clearly be designated as task activities on the network diagram and itemized in the work breakdown structure as well as being identified as major milestones.

Management Reviews

Such reviews are often onerous, but they may stimulate participation and involvement on the part of all people working on the project. They are usually attended by upper management, and their chief purpose is to impart general information regarding project performance, schedule, and cost.

To gain the stimulation benefit, the project manager must solicit ideas from all project personnel as to what should be discussed during the review. Rough ideas for the review should be delineated in a smaller group of key staff. At this point, the manager should delegate portions of the review to other people. (Be sure there are not so many people making presentations at the formal review that it becomes a circus.) Next conduct a trial run with a fairly large group of project participants invited to criticize. Following this, materials can be prepared for the formal presentation, before which it is desirable to conduct a second dry run with a peer management group that represents the same range of skill backgrounds as the audience that will attend the formal review. The people attending this dry run review will provide addi-

Management review presentations can be an opportunity to stimulate project personnel.

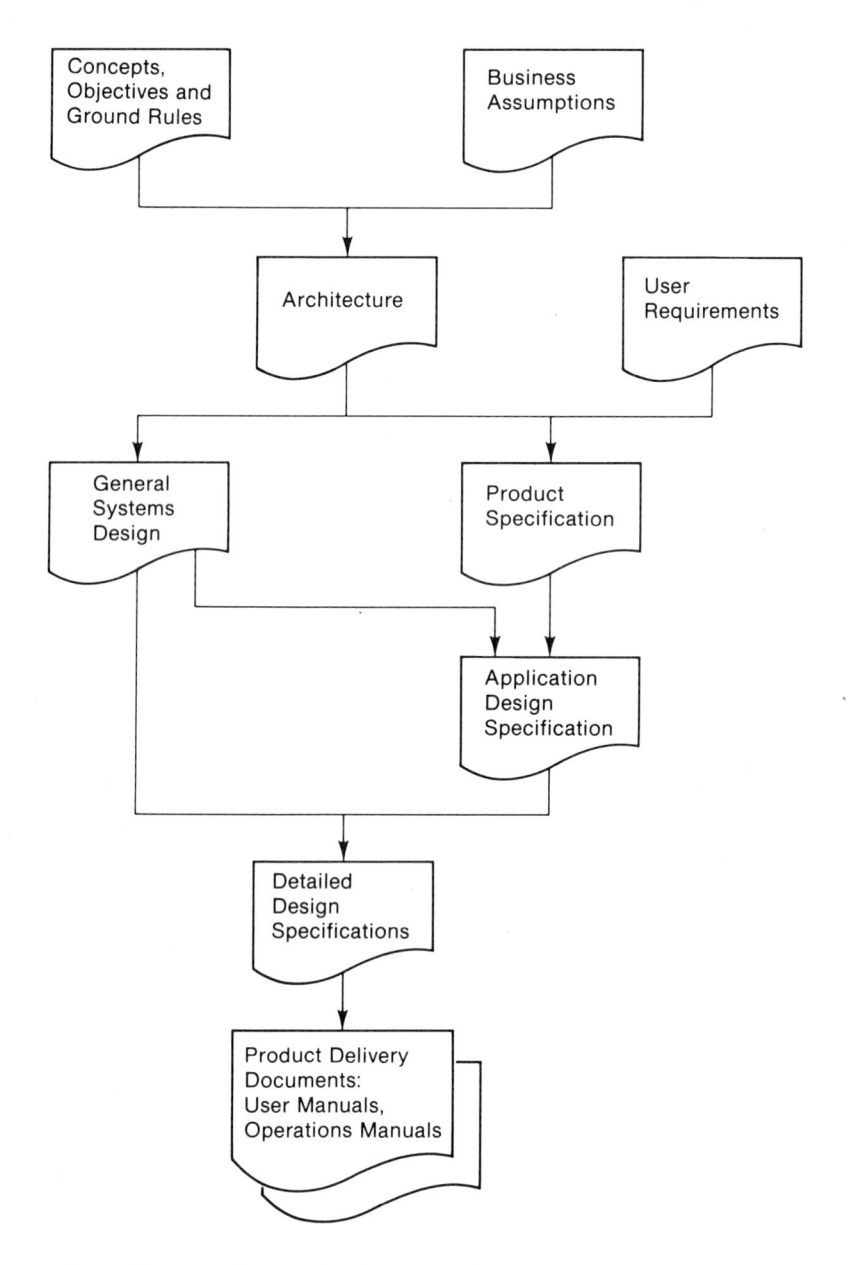

Figure 15-6. Software development documentation.

tional insights as to how materials can be better presented or changed. If possible, videotape the presentation for later review.

Now you are ready to conduct the formal review, after which it is desirable to conduct the entire review again for the

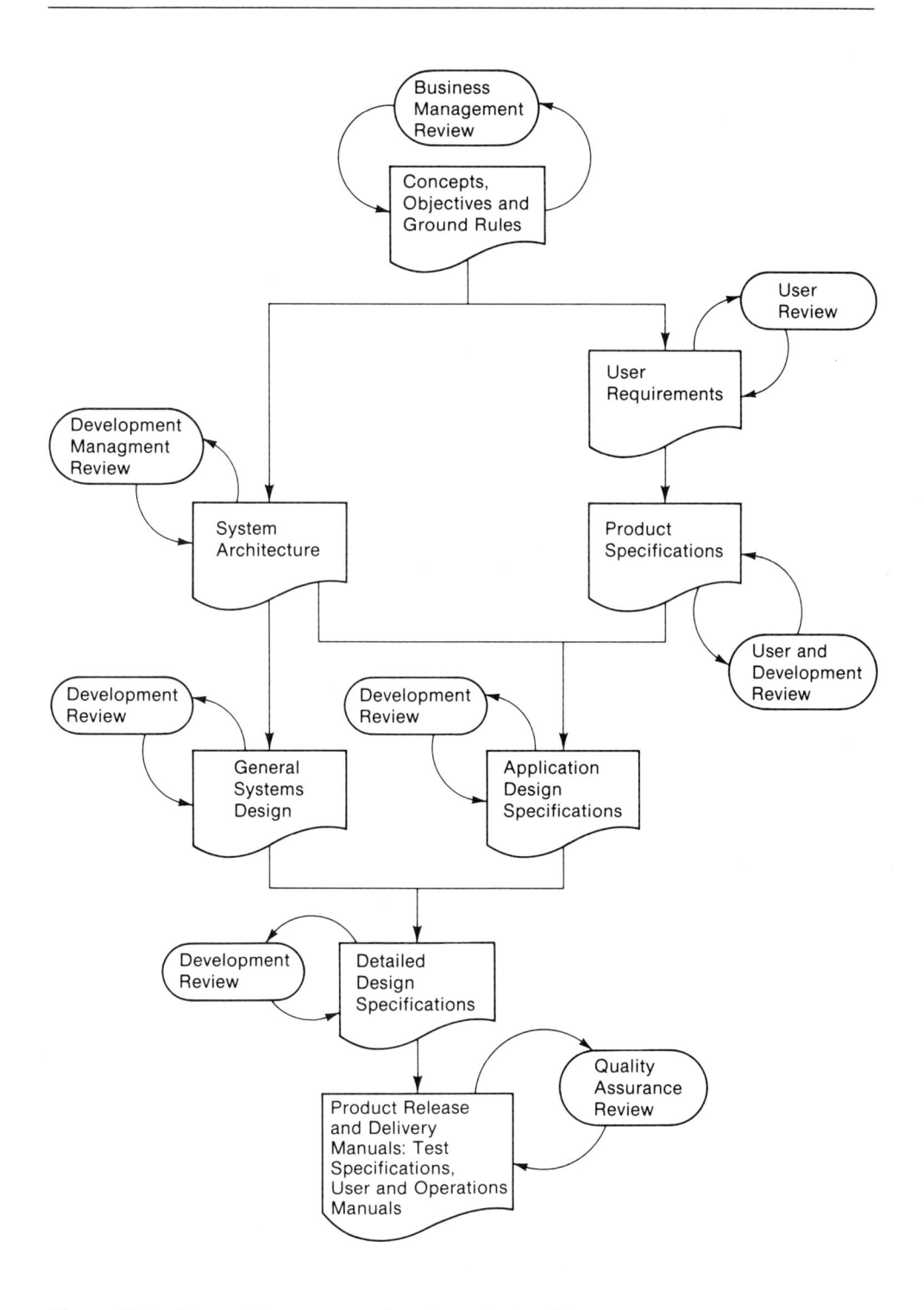

Figure 15-7. Formal document and review relationships.

benefit of everyone working on the project. They are just as interested as you in the kinds of questions the important people asked and will find it just as interesting and motivating to spend some time hearing what happened and getting an overview of the issues covered in the review.

Structured Walkthroughs

Do not confuse technical reviews with management reviews.

Structured walkthroughs are reviews where programmers read and critique each other's code. They are one of the most popular technical reviews today. Although this topic is covered in many technical books on software engineering and structured design, we mention it here to remind project managers to schedule such reviews and identify them as milestones to ensure that the development effort is proceeding appropriately. Managers certainly don't have the time to attend each of these, but they should ensure that their programming staffs do such a peer review to reduce errors.

TYPICAL PROBLEMS

> Reviews are plagued by four common problems. First, there is always a concern as to whether the information being presented or discussed is accurate. Cost reports, as previously noted, are especially prone to error. Beyond this, there is often speculation about the exact status of some task, test, module, or report. Clearly, good planning for reviews can reduce if not eliminate this problem.
>
> The second problem is the poorly conducted review. Aimless discussion, attacks on people rather than on the validity of their ideas, and recriminations are common. Running a review like any other well-planned meeting greatly reduces the possibility of getting off the track.
>
> Another problem is customer requirements that change at every meeting. Reviews are based upon previously established requirements and schedules. If the requirements change, their impact on the Triple Constraint (performance, schedule, and budget) must be
>
> *continued*

> determined. This reevaluation should take place outside the review process itself, however.
>   A fourth problem is involving all review attendees—making them participate rather than observe. No one should be part of a review if his or her participation is not crucial to the project being reviewed. However, tacit acceptance of specifications or budget does not indicate understanding. Often it helps to have those individuals responsible for an area (for example, the user representative for a new personnel system, data base administrator, or quality assurance representative) present at the review of those portions that are relevant to their needs and to allow for discussion by the others as to impact. Participation encourages revelation!

HIGHLIGHTS

Reviews uncover the inevitable deviation from plan and allow a consensus as to the needed corrective action.

Reviews, like projects, must be planned.

Ask nondirective questions and expect problems to surface at project review meetings.

Periodic reviews should be conducted as appropriate for the project, but once a month is a good rule of thumb.

The kind of topical review used depends on the project and the customer's requirements.

Questionable accuracy and poor procedures are common problems with reviews.

FURTHER READING

M. E. Fagan. "Design and Code Inspections to Reduce Errors in Program Development." *IBM Systems Journal* (1976), pp. 219–248.
>   This is a good discussion of the role a code review has in reducing software coding errors.

R. W. Jensen and C. C. Tonies. *Software Engineering.* Englewood Cliffs, NJ: Prentice-Hall, 1979.
This is a concise description of how to conduct a design review.

R. C. Tausworthe. *Standardized Development of Computer Software,* Part 1: *Methods* and Part 2: *Standards.* Englewood Cliffs, NJ: Prentice-Hall, 1977 and 1979.
This excellent reference book should be part of every software development manager's library.

E. Yourdon. *Structured Walkthroughs,* 2nd ed. Englewood Cliffs, NJ: Prentice-Hall, 1980.
This is the definitive work on this important topic.

16

Cost Reports

Actual project costs must be measured to control the cost dimension and may reveal schedule or performance dimension problems. We discuss these topics in this chapter and include typical examples of cost reports, which are normally generated as computer printout.

COMPUTER COST REPORTS

Large organizations commonly have computer-generated reports that summarize project cost. They may also cover schedule deviations. There is a variety of report systems available for purchase or lease. Figure 16-1 shows how such reports can be useful for project control. Actual cost (and schedule) data are collected from labor time cards, purchase orders, and other direct charges to the project. These are compared with plans; noted variances are analyzed; and required corrective actions may then lead to replanning. Comparing reality to the plan may suggest that certain trends will lead to future variances, which again is a cause for replanning. To be useful, this comparison must be done for each cost center (for example, department) and work breakdown task.

The project manager must steer a careful line between having too many forms and too much information and having too little information to control the project, although it is probably better to have more information than less. Neither the project manager nor top managers should be trapped into

Variance from plan is a danger signal.

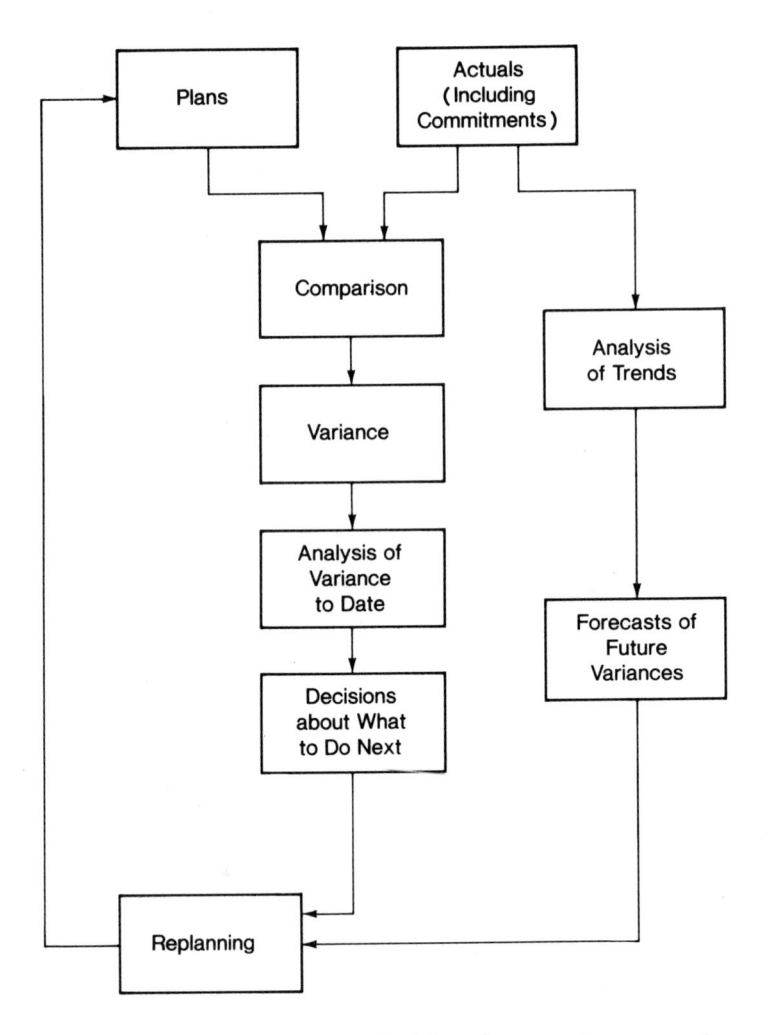

Figure 16-1. Replanning is called for whenever future trends or past actuals indicate significant deviation from plan.

believing actual cost data (which can be reported with great precision) are the only measure of project health (which requires difficult three-dimensional measurements).

Most organizations with computer support for project management issue a weekly labor distribution report. This report lists the names of people charging time to each project during the previous week. This is a key report for a project manager, providing an early warning signal. Examination of the report may reveal people charging your project who should not be charging to it or people not charging your project whom you expected to be working on it.

CONTROL

This section reviews a few of the cost reports for a hypothetical project, illustrating some issues in project control. These reports are typically prepared with a computer, working with the planning data base such as that discussed in Chapter 8. But it is not absolutely necessary to use a computer, although the amount of data to be handled can otherwise be a substantial burden, even to a well-qualified project cost accountant.

Variances Due to Timing

Figure 16-2 is the project cost report for task B being performed by the information services group, at the end of the first month. Typically, this report would be available about the middle of the second month (February, in this case). In this case, labor and the overhead thereon are in accordance with plan. But there is a favorable variance in the nonlabor expense. That is, there was a plan to spend $4,400, but nothing has been spent.

Figure 16-3 shows the corresponding task and period commitment report for the group. Commitments in the amount of

A variance between actual cost and plan may be due to payments being made later than plan rather than work variances.

PROJECT COST REPORT

PROJECT _____ PAYROLL TAXES _____ TASK __B-DETAILED DESIGN__ DEPARTMENT __INFORMATION SERVICES__

	CATEGORY	MONTH 1 - JAN			TOTALS TO DATE		
		PLAN	ACTUAL	VARIANCE	PLAN	ACTUAL	VARIANCE
HOURS	SR. PROGR. -ANAL.	40	40	0	40	40	0
	JR. PROGR.						
	QA ANAL.						
	CLERK						
DOLLARS	LABOR	1,000	1,000	0	1,000	1,000	0
	OVERHEAD	1,000	1,000	0	1,000	1,000	0
	NONLABOR	4,400	0	4,400	4,400	0	4,400
	PRIME COSTS	6,400	2,000	4,400	6,400	2,000	6,400
	G & A	960	300	660	960	300	660
	TOTAL COSTS	7,360	2,300	5,060	7,360	2,300	5,060

Figure 16-2. Cost report for first month for task B work by the information services group.

Cost Reports

PROJECT COMMITMENT REPORT

MONTH ___1___

PROJECT _Payroll Taxes_   TASK _Detailed Design_   DEPARTMENT _Information Services_

Commitment Date	Item	Amount	Estimated Payment Date
21 Jan 84	P.O.—Microcomputer Co.	$4,000.	30 Apr 84
21 Jan 84	Travel Auth.—C. Williams	400.	15 Feb 84
		$4,400.	

Figure 16-3. Commitment report for first month for task B work by the information services group.

$4,400 have been incurred. Thus, the cost variance merely indicates that bills have not yet been paid rather than being a variance due to activities not yet undertaken. To put it another way, it is anticipated that the $4,400 expense will occur later. This demonstrates the impossibility of making intelligent use of project cost reports without also examining commitment reports.

Figures 16-4 and 16-5 are the same reports for the end of

PROJECT COST REPORT

PROJECT ___PAYROLL TAXES___   TASK ___B-DETAILED DESIGN___   DEPARTMENT ___INFORMATION SERVICES___

	CATEGORY	MONTH 2 - FEB			TOTALS TO DATE		
		PLAN	ACTUAL	VARIANCE	PLAN	ACTUAL	VARIANCE
HOURS	SR. PROGR. -ANAL.	4	4	0	44	44	0
	JR. PROGR.						
	QA ANAL.						
	CLERK						
DOLLARS	LABOR	100	100	0	1,100	1,100	0
	OVERHEAD	100	100	0	1,100	1,100	0
	NONLABOR	0	350	⟨350⟩	4,400	350	4,050
	PRIME COSTS	200	550	⟨350⟩	6,600	2,550	4,050
	G & A	30	83	⟨53⟩	990	383	607
	TOTAL COSTS	230	633	⟨403⟩	7,590	2,933	4,657

Figure 16-4. Cost report for second month for task B work by the information services group.

```
                    PROJECT COMMITMENT REPORT
                         MONTH    2
PROJECT  Payroll Taxes   TASK  Detailed Design   DEPARTMENT  Information Services
```

Commitment Date	Item	Amount	Estimated Payment Date
21 Jan 84	P.O.—Microcomputer Co.	$4,000.	30 Apr 84
21 Jan 84	Travel Auth.—C. Williams	All	Paid
		$4,000.	

Figure 16-5. Commitment report for second month for task B work by the information services group.

the second month. Once again, the labor hours and costs as well as the overhead are in accordance with the plan. In this case, there is an unfavorable variance during the second month with regard to nonlabor costs because the travel voucher is paid now but the plan had the expense in the first month. For the totals to date, that is, through the end of the second month, the nonlabor variance is favorable. This favorable variance is composed of the unpaid $4,000 purchase order, which is variance only because of payment timing, and a $50 favorable variance because the travel voucher payment was $50 less than plan.

Variances Due to Actual Work Not as Per Plan

Figures 16-6 and 16-7 are the project cost reports at the end of the third and fourth months for the same task. In this case, labor hours exceed plan in the third month, with attendant unfavorable cost variances, which happen to offset exactly the previous favorable variance on nonlabor due to the travel variance. In the fourth month, the purchase order is paid, and the net variance for the completed task becomes zero.

Figures 16-2 and 16-7 illustrate that variances occur because of the payment timing and that actual performance differs from plan. They also indicate the necessity of examining the details in project cost reports and commitment reports to understand the reported variances and their significance.

Actual work may differ from plan.

Each computer-based system differs in detail; so the proj-

PROJECT COST REPORT

PROJECT: PAYROLL TAXES   TASK: B-DETAILED DESIGN   DEPARTMENT: INFORMATION SERVICES

	CATEGORY	MONTH 3 - MAR			TOTALS TO DATE		
		PLAN	ACTUAL	VARIANCE	PLAN	ACTUAL	VARIANCE
HOURS	SR. PROGR. ANAL.	2	3	⟨1⟩	46	47	⟨1⟩
	JR. PROGR.						
	QA ANAL.						
	CLERK						
DOLLARS	LABOR	100	125	⟨25⟩	1,150	1,175	⟨25⟩
	OVERHEAD	100	125	⟨25⟩	1,150	1,175	⟨25⟩
	NONLABOR	0	0	0	4,400	350	4,050
	PRIME COSTS	200	250	⟨50⟩	6,700	2,700	4,000
	G & A	30	38	⟨8⟩	1,005	405	600
	TOTAL COSTS	230	288	⟨58⟩	7,705	3,105	4,600

Figure 16-6. Cost report for third month for task B work by the information services group.

PROJECT COST REPORT

PROJECT: PAYROLL TAXES   TASK: B-DETAILED DESIGN   DEPARTMENT: INFORMATION SERVICES

	CATEGORY	MONTH 4 - APR			TOTALS TO DATE		
		PLAN	ACTUAL	VARIANCE	PLAN	ACTUAL	VARIANCE
HOURS	SR. PROGR. ANAL.	0	0	0	46	47	⟨1⟩
	JR. PROGR.						
	QA ANAL.						
	CLERK						
DOLLARS	LABOR	0	0	0	1,150	1,175	⟨25⟩
	OVERHEAD	0	0	0	1,150	1,175	⟨25⟩
	NONLABOR	0	4,000	⟨4,000⟩	4,400	4,350	50
	PRIME COSTS	0	4,000	⟨4,000⟩	6,700	6,700	0
	G & A	0	600	⟨600⟩	1,005	1,005	0
	TOTAL COSTS	0	4,600	⟨4,600⟩	7,705	7,705	0

Figure 16-7. Cost report for fourth month for task B work by the information services group.

ect manager should understand exactly how the reports are prepared (that is, to what errors the reports are prone) as well as the specific meaning of each column of data.

Variances Due to Overhead Rate Changes

Figure 16-8 is the project report for task E in the technical support section, as reported at the end of the fourth month. In this report, there are favorable variances in labor but an unfavorable variance in overhead. How can this be? If labor is favorable, why should overhead be unfavorable?

Figure 16-9 shows the cause of this. A planned overhead (namely, 100 percent) was based on a planned work load for the technical support section (or perhaps the division). But the actual overhead at the end of the fourth month is higher (namely, 130 percent) because the work load base for the entire section has been reduced from plan. The overhead expenses have been somewhat reduced, but not in the same proportion as the direct labor because overhead is partially composed of fixed expenses that cannot be reduced. Thus, the actual overhead rate turns out in this case to be 130 percent

Factors outside the manager's control may cause costs to vary from plan.

PROJECT COST REPORT

PROJECT PAYROLL TAXES   TASK E-REWRITE USER'S MANUAL   DEPARTMENT TECHNICAL SUPPORT

	CATEGORY	MONTH 4 - APR			TOTALS TO DATE		
		PLAN	ACTUAL	VARIANCE	PLAN	ACTUAL	VARIANCE
HOURS	SR. PROGR. -ANAL.						
	JR. PROGR.						
	QA ANAL.	200	120	80	200	120	80
	CLERK	400	400	0	400	400	0
DOLLARS	LABOR	7,000	5,800	1,200	7,000	5,800	1,200
	OVERHEAD	7,000	7,540	⟨540⟩	7,000	7,540	⟨540⟩
	NONLABOR	0	0	0	0	0	0
	PRIME COSTS	14,000	13,340	660	14,000	13,340	660
	G & A	2,100	2,001	99	2,100	2,001	99
	TOTAL COSTS	16,100	15,341	759	16,100	15,341	759

Figure 16-8. Cost report for fourth month for task E work by the technical support section.

Planned

| Project Example $100,000 Labor Cost | Project Otherone $300,000 Labor Cost |
|---|---|ರ

Overhead ($200,000 Fixed + $200,000 Variable) / $400,000 = 100%

Revised

Project Example $100,000 Labor Cost	Project Otherone $150,000 Labor Cost

Overhead ($200,000 Fixed + $125,000 Variable) / $325,000 = 130%

Figure 16-9. Overhead rate changes are the cause of overhead variance.
Source: "Project Management." Lecture notes by Milton D. Rosenau, Jr. Copyright © 1981 by the Association for Media-based Continuing Education for Engineers, Inc. (AMCEE). Reprinted by permission.

rather than the planned 100 percent. (Such a change in overhead is extreme; we use it simply to dramatize the possible effect of overhead rate changes.) Overhead changes can also be caused by the amount of overhead expense differing from plan. The variances could be summarized as follows:

- A quality assurance analyst was planned full-time but was not released from the previous project at the start of month 4. If labor is not added, the project will be late.
- Overhead is now 130 percent, not 100 percent, as planned. This will cause a cost overrun unless compensating savings can be found.

Figure 16-10 is the project cost report for this task in the technical support department at the end of the fifth month. The quality assurance analyst category continues to have a favorable variance, which is partially offset by an unfavorable variance in the clerk category and the continuing unfavorable variance in the overhead. The overhead variance is again attributable solely to the overhead rate now being 130 percent rather than 100 percent, as per plan. Examination of these variables might lead to the following kind of information:

PROJECT COST REPORT

PROJECT _____ PAYROLL TAXES _____ TASK E-REWRITE USER'S MANUAL _____ DEPARTMENT TECHNICAL SUPPORT

	CATEGORY	MONTH 5 - MAY			TOTALS TO DATE		
		PLAN	ACTUAL	VARIANCE	PLAN	ACTUAL	VARIANCE
HOURS	SR. PROGR. -ANAL.						
	JR. PROGR.						
	QA ANAL.	40	20	20	240	140	100
	CLERK	80	120	⟨40⟩	480	520	⟨40⟩
DOLLARS	LABOR	1,400	1,500	⟨100⟩	8,400	7,300	1,100
	OVERHEAD	1,400	1,950	⟨550⟩	8,400	9,490	⟨1,090⟩
	NONLABOR	0	0	0	0	0	0
	PRIME COSTS	2,800	3,450	⟨650⟩	16,800	16,790	10
	G & A	420	518	⟨98⟩	2,520	2,519	1
	TOTAL COSTS	3,220	3,968	⟨748⟩	19,320	19,309	11

Figure 16-10. Cost report for fifth month for task E work by the technical support section.

- The quality assurance analyst is still below plan.
- A clerk, previously unplanned, has been added to complete the work on schedule.
- Overhead is still 130 percent, but final dollars are okay.

The clerk was able to accomplish in fewer hours the work previously planned for a quality assurance analyst. This net effective saving in labor hours was sufficient to compensate for the increased overhead dollars. The end result in this case is a small, favorable variance.

TYPICAL PROBLEMS

In addition to management's tendency to presume that cost status is the only measure of the project's progress, a problem previously mentioned, there are two other
continued

Cost reports are late and sometimes incorrect.

common problems. First, cost reports are never available immediately after the end of the reporting period (typically the fiscal or calendar month). They are usually issued about two or three weeks after the close of the report period. Thus, there is always a time lag with which the project manager must contend. This problem cannot be solved but must be accepted because of other accounting priorities. An alert project manager can recognize the situation and make full use of other available data to stay more current, including weekly labor distribution reports (indicating who did or did not charge time to the project), purchase orders, travel vouchers, and module completions.

The second problem is that cost reports often have errors, such as charges that should have been allocated to other projects or overhead accounts. The project manager or an administrative assistant must study the reports carefully and not merely accept them as gospel.

HIGHLIGHTS

Computer-generated cost reports show variances from plan, which usually require corrective action.

Reports can show variances due to timing, actual work deviating from plan, or overhead rate changes.

Three problems with cost reports are that management tends to assume they are the only measure of progress, they never appear immediately after the reporting period, and they may contain errors.

FURTHER READING

R. H. Clough and G. A. Sears. *Construction Project Management*, 2nd ed. New York: Wiley-Interscience, 1979.
> Chapter 10 has an extensive discussion of the project cost system in the construction industry, with much that is generally applicable in any industry.

J. A. Maciariello. *Program-Management Control Systems.* New York: Wiley-Interscience, 1978.
> *Chapter 11 contains a good overview of PERT/COST and C/SCSC cost control approaches.*

R. Pilcher. *Appraisal and Control of Project Costs.* London: McGraw-Hill, 1973.
> *Chapter 11 provides a clear and thorough discussion of cost control, with an emphasis on the need to tie this into the work breakdown structure and network diagram.*

M. D. Rosenau. *Successful Project Management.* Belmont, CA: Lifetime Learning Publications, 1981.
> *Chapter 15, pages 165–179, contains many examples of reports from two computer-based project planning and control systems.*

17

Handling Changes

Change is a reality of project management. This chapter first reviews why project plans are altered and then discusses techniques for making changes.

REASONS FOR CHANGES

Change is a constant on projects.

Deviations from the project plan occur because Murphy was an optimist. Or there is a Rosenau's law of revolting developments: There will be at least one. Then there is Lewin's law of perversity: There will always be more changes than you want. A large body of data convincingly demonstrates that presumably conscientious program managers have been confronted with changes in many situations. This has led to missing both the schedule and the cost dimensions of the Triple Constraint, with the overruns typically being a factor of approximately two above plan. In software development, changes occur and are, in fact, to be expected, planned for, and controlled.

Although not illustrated in Table 17-1, Mansfield's data also show that the situation is somewhat worse than average for large projects and better than average for small projects.

TABLE 17-1. Time and Cost Overrun Data, Expressed as Multiple (X) of Plan.

Project Type	Time	Cost	Source
50 new products (new chemical entities, compounded products, or alternate dosage forms) in ethical drug firm	1.78X	1.61X	E. Mansfield et al., *Research and Innovation in the Modern Corporation*, W. W. Norton, New York, 1971, p. 89
69 new products in proprietary drug laboratory	2.95X	2.11X	E. Mansfield et al., op. cit., pp. 102 & 104
20 management information systems projects	2.10X	1.95X	R. F. Powers & G. W. Dickson, "MisProject Management? Myth, Opinions, and Reality," *California Management Review*, XV, no. 3, 147–156 (Spring 1973)
34 Department of Defense systems from "planning estimate" from "development estimate"	– –	2.11X 1.41X	G. R. McNichols, D.O.D. Report (November 1974), as quoted in R. A. Brown, "Probabilistic Models of Project Management with Design Implications," *IEEE Trans. Engr. Mgmt.*, vol. EM-25, no. 2, 43–49 (May 1978)
10 major construction projects completed 1956–1977	–	3.93X	W. J. Mead et al. (1977), as quoted in E. W. Merrow et al., "A Review of Cost Estimation in New Technologies," Rand Corporation Report R-2481-DOE (July 1979), p. 38
10 energy process plants	–	2.53X	E. W. Merrow et al., op cit., p. 87

This seems to make sense; intuition tells us that the more ambitious undertaking is less likely to be estimated accurately. This is another reason to break a large project down into many small tasks. It will be easier to estimate a small task accurately.

Special Software Problems Leading to Changes

Software projects are not unique in a project management sense, but there are special problems that are particularly prevalent in software development. The project manager should be alert for these. Software bugs often arise because of logic errors. Memory or CPU overload results in slow response or problems of inadequate storage, which may require a complete system redesign. Real-time systems can have timing and queuing problems. There can also be rapid technological changes that render work obsolete very quickly, errors in translating user requirements into technical solutions, and changes because the user has a better understanding of what he or she wants after finally seeing some output. In common with all projects, but with a different impact for software projects, the project manager must be alert for standards and documentation errors.

Real Changes in the Planned Project

Changes can be imposed indirectly.

One of the causes of both time and cost overruns is that deviations from the plan occur in the job. They may be externally imposed, by the customer or user, for instance. A change might include a request for preparation of multiple reports from a computer program.

In addition, schedule changes can be imposed, and these frequently have attendant cost implications. If delivery of new hardware is delayed (or even worse, it is delivered with the glitches still not ironed out), there is typically a cost consequence. Conversely, the customer may impose a change in project funding. Although a delay in project funding to the project organization may not appear to change the total available funding, it almost always is accompanied by a schedule rearrangement, which normally leads to undesirable cost consequences.

Environmental, health, and safety regulations that change during the course of the project may cause other changes in scope. Inflation may exceed plan, causing a cost problem, particularly on major projects originally planned to take several years. There may be changes in resource availability, either people or facilities. These do not constitute changes in project scope, but they do constitute changes from plan that will have an impact, usually unfavorable, on schedule and cost.

There may be legal changes, such as those that occurred in the banking industry in 1980, when saving and loan (S and L) institutions were granted what amounted to consumer checking account privileges. Commercial banks had to repackage their set of consumer banking products, and S and Ls were required to add all the processing that interest-bearing checking accounts require.

Estimation Inaccuracy

Several factors affect estimation accuracy. Of these, an imperfect definition of project scope is the most common. Either a customer (or user) or a contractor (or developer) may be the cause of the error, but it usually is attributable to both.

There may also be poor estimates of either time or cost. The rush to prepare a proposal and submit it in accordance with the bidding requirements may preclude there being sufficient time to do a good job of estimating. There is so much inherent uncertainty in some tasks of some projects that a poor estimate is almost a foregone conclusion.

Many jobs are proposed with deliberate underestimates of the amount of time or money it will take to perform them. This is the so-called "buy-in" situation in which a bidder attempts to win a job by making a low bid. This does not require an illegal misrepresentation, although that may be the case. It may result from a deliberate attempt to make optimistic assumptions about all the uncertainties in the proposed project as well as to omit all contingency from the estimates. In a sense, the bidder is making an estimate of time and cost that could occur perhaps 1 or 0.1 percent of the time rather than attempting to make an estimate near the mid range of possibilities.

Buy-in bids are much more prevalent where the contemplated contract will be a cost reimbursible form and the bidding contractor will not bear the financial burden of having made a low bid. They can also occur in a fixed price contract situation where the bidding contractor is confident that the customer will request changes in scope. Such changes will provide a "get well" opportunity: increases in both time and cost for the main project can be added onto or concealed in renegotiations necessitated by changes of scope.

In software projects, the underestimates more than likely occur due to a failure to understand the programming complexity, programmer talent, hardware features, or political requisites of the system proposed. Using new hardware, a new system architecture (arrangement of software functions among hardware components), a new or uncommon lan-

Uncertainty, "buy-ins," and inadequate technical resources can cause poor estimates.

guage, or inexperienced programmers will cause time and cost overruns. It is the project manager's skill, however, in assessing the benefits of innovative return that makes the risk taken pay off.

ADOPTING CHANGES

At this point, it should be clear that projects normally require changes of plan, although the specific reason or reasons cannot be forecast. Given that change will occur, despite prior planning to avoid it and our greatest optimism, the issue becomes, simply, how to plan for change by controlling it when it does occur.

Change Control

The method for controlling change is to design a change control system that suits your company and your project. Elements of such a system may vary, but they must include the following:

- Effective date
- Initiation
- Authorization
- Implementation

A change control system is a formal approval cycle for changes to an approved milestone document (including program code). Thus, a change to the format of an accounts payable report would require formal approval because the formats are included in the design documents of the programs that prepare it, as well as in the requirements and product definition documents.

Design Freeze

A decision must be made as to just when to initiate a change control system. Too early—during the conceptualization phase, for example—and you will always be making changes because not enough detail is available about the project as yet. Too late, and the work done earlier may not reflect crucial higher level changes. For example, if there is no change control system in place when the detailed design is altered, the product definition may need to be changed as well, but there is no method of controlling the impact of the change.

In general, implement a change control system when the definition phase has been completed and the requirements have been reviewed and accepted. Subsequent changes to the conceptual documents from the first life cycle phase, such as in a business rule, would be reflected in a change in user requirements rather than in a change to the conceptual documents.

Institute change control when requirements are defined.

Change Initiation

Usually a change authorization form is prepared. It describes the change, who requests it and why, when it is required by, and the documents it will affect (so that documentation can stay current). A sample form is shown in Figure 17-1. Change requests would be initiated by a programmer to correct a bug in a program already being used by the customer, by a customer to be able to print a new report, or by a customer to add a new transaction processing capability. These change authorizations are requests and must be authorized by the appropriate reviewing body before they are implemented. The changes should be initiated by the actual requestor. For example, users should request the change in report formats rather than asking the programmer to make the change request for them. That eliminates possible misinterpretations of the users' requirements.

Those who request changes should initiate them.

Each organization has its own detailed version of a task authorization form, but the essential elements are a description of the Triple Constraint, which defines the task being authorized, and a place for signatures of the person authorizing the work and the person accepting responsibility for the work. This form thus constitutes a "contract," defining in writing the agreement reached to authorize a task to be performed within the same organization in support of a project. In the case of a subcontractor, the subcontract document or purchase order authorizes the task.

Change Authorization

Although anyone can initiate change requests, only an authorized body should be able to approve them. A change review board is the usual mechanism, although in smaller projects, the review board could in fact be a single individual.

Handling Changes

TASK AUTHORIZATION			PAGE 1 OF 1
TITLE CHANGE INTEREST CALCULATION			
PROJECT NO. PBM 12	TASK NO. 1451	REVISION NO. —	DATE ISSUED 2.15.84

STATEMENT OF WORK:

CHANGE RATE OF INTEREST CALCULATED FOR PASSBOOK ACCOUNTS FROM 5¼% TO 5½% COMPOUNDED DAILY EFFECTIVE JULY 1, 1984.

APPLICABLE DOCUMENTS:

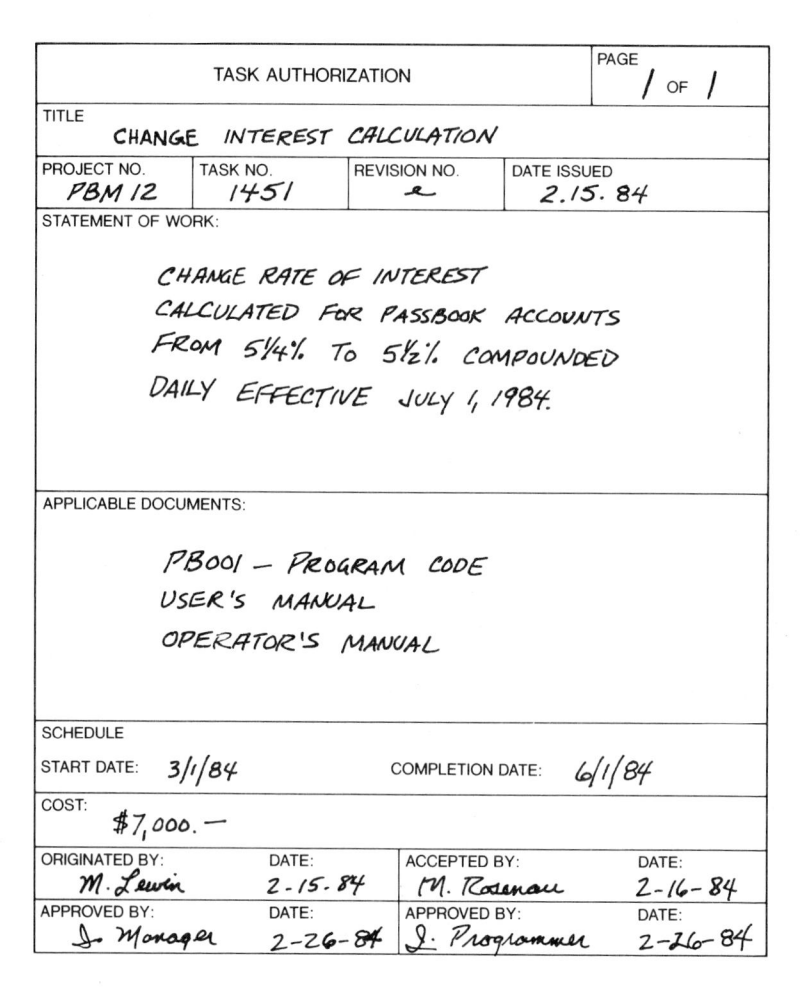

PB001 — PROGRAM CODE
USER'S MANUAL
OPERATOR'S MANUAL

SCHEDULE
START DATE: 3/1/84   COMPLETION DATE: 6/1/84

COST: $7,000.—

ORIGINATED BY: M. Lewin	DATE: 2-15-84	ACCEPTED BY: M. Rosenau	DATE: 2-16-84
APPROVED BY: J. Manager	DATE: 2-26-84	APPROVED BY: J. Programmer	DATE: 2-26-84

Figure 17-1. Typical task authorization form.

The review board's composition should be such that it can evaluate the impact of the requested change on the rest of the project. If insufficient data exist to evaluate that impact, then the board should study the matter before making a determination. Unlike the review boards for milestone documents throughout the project life cycle, which change in composition, the change review board should have stable membership, at least during development. (When the project is completed and the developed system is being maintained, the review board can be composed differently. Maintenance is, in fact, a separate project.)

The mechanics of the change review process differ from company to company. Some have computerized printouts of changes requested, disposition, and assignee; others may use a handwritten list or only copies of the changes themselves. However, the basic process is usually as follows:

1. Determine the importance of the need for the change.
2. Determine the Triple Constraint impact.
3. Assign the change to one or more parties.
4. Change all relevant documentation to reflect the change.
5. Record the change when it is completed.

In essence, the change process, as distinct from the change control process, is a project in itself and can be managed as we've discussed in this book. Obviously, no unauthorized changes should be made or allowed.

Authorized changes become projects themselves.

Sometimes changes cannot be authorized because the resources required are not currently available. In this case, they may be tabled and reviewed again at a later date. In some cases, the benefit accruing from the change may be of little value, and the change is denied. In general, changes usually are allowed because the trouble of going through the formal review process discourages capricious requests.

Systems under development usually have different types of changes than those already in production. The former may have, unfortunately, changes in the design as it is successively refined. That is preferable to design changes after coding and implementation have been started. The review board may decide not to approve changes, even though change control has been initiated, until the design has been stabilized. In completed, installed systems, changes tend to be for increased functionality for the user or system optimization, rather than to correct bugs and design flaws (which should have been eliminated by the testing during its initial development!).

Changes vary in type and impact.

Changes, just like originally intended work, must be defined, planned, managed, and monitored before they can be completed. Thus, some, if not all, of the originally issued task authorizations must be changed when a change has occurred and a decision has been made as to how to alter the plan to carry out the remainder of the project. This may seem to be a lot of work, but it is far less onerous to take the time to make sure each agreement with people working on the project has been changed than to discover later that some people have been working according to their prior understanding of the project plan.

Never hesitate to publicize plan changes if these are required.

There is a natural reluctance to make a formal plan change. Such a change not only requires work to issue plan revisions, but it forces us to admit we were wrong (in the original plan), and often brings this to the attention of higher management. Conversely, such information, if given to higher management, may result in your project receiving more help, better access to resources, or higher priority.

Figure 17-1 shows a one-page form, but an actual task authorization, in common with a subcontract, might be many pages long. The form might be part of a carbon set, providing copies for the initiator, the task manager, and the project cost accounting section.

Hence, the task authorization documents initially used to authorize work are also a major change control document. A large project may generate many of these, and the amount of time it takes to issue them may be so great as to suggest that there first be telephonic or other speedy notice of forthcoming changes.

TYPICAL PROBLEMS

There is always a reluctance to tell the customer and your boss that a revolting development (such as the discovery of unexpected "bugs" in the program) has occured and there are many reasons to justify delay. But you should deliver the bad news carefully, thoughtfully, and promptly, before someone else does it. What you should do is inform your customer as soon as possible after you have completed a reasonable comparison of alternative solutions to the problem. Because there is a natural reluctance to be the bearer of bad tidings and because there may always be more alternatives to consider, there is a tendency to delay. No one likes surprises of that nature. Once the customer has been informed and has a chance to consider the issues, it is usually necessary to amend the contract in some way. Verbal redirection is not binding, although it may be acted upon (if customer relations are satisfactory) while the contract is actually being negotiated.

A second problem is that task authorizations are often verbal rather than written. Because they promote

continued

> misinterpretation, verbal authorizations should be avoided. But they are employed in the real world of project management. When you must use them, be sure you are clear, ask for feedback, and then try for written confirmation.
>
> The third problem with changes is their impact on resource allocation. There is nothing to do but face up to reality that resources must be rescheduled, as inconvenient as this may be. If you do add labor on your project, remember that the schedule is not likely to be shortened in proportion to the amount of labor that is added.

HIGHLIGHTS

Changes will occur on every project, but smaller projects usually face fewer difficulties from them than do larger projects.

Changes must be controlled with a formal change control process.

Changes may result from customer requests; extenuating circumstances, such as a strike; altered environmental, health, or safety regulations; inflation; or resource unavailability.

The composition of the change control board should be stable.

Uncertainty and buy-ins can result in inaccurate estimations.

Authorization documents can be used to communicate planning and change control.

Three problems that changes can cause are managers may be reluctant to inform the customer and higher management of them, verbal authorizations often cause misunderstanding, and resources must be reallocated.

FURTHER READING

R. D. Archibald. *Managing High-Technology Programs and Projects.* New York: Wiley-Interscience, 1976.
  Chapter 8, section 2, very briefly discusses change control.

C. W. Burrill and L. W. Ellsworth. *Modern Project Management.* Tenafly, NJ: Burrill-Ellsworth Associates, 1981.

Chapter 8, pages 175–197, covers how to introduce change in a data processing project.

P. W. Metzger. *Managing a Programming Project,* 2nd ed. Englewood Cliffs, NJ: Prentice-Hall, 1981.

Pages 116–120 and 208–209 discuss change control and implementation.

18

Coping With Unexpected Problems

This chapter is concerned with solving problems as your project encounters changes during execution. First we discuss some general approaches to coping with problems. Then we describe decision trees, a powerful analytic technique for problem analysis. Following that, we review use of a matrix array and then discuss the kind of meetings in which problem-solving approaches are most likely to be effective.

THE GENERAL APPROACH

In general, the options available are either deductive or inductive logic. In the former, the solution is derived by reasoning from known scientific principles, using analytical techniques, and the conclusions reached are necessary and certain if the premises are correct. In practice, the project manager is rarely confronted with problems for which this approach is appropriate and must rely on inductive techniques, for which the scientific method is the typical prototype. Inductive methods reach conclusions that are probable. This straightforward approach entails seven steps, described in the following sections.

Good solutions require a seven-step approach.

249

State the Real Problem

The key to problem solving is understanding the real problem rather than the apparent symptoms. Smoke may be emerging from the hardware you built or the computer may refuse to obey a subroutine command, but the actual problem may be an overheated component or an improper line of code in the computer program. You will have to decide how and perhaps why these particular problems occurred.

Identify the true problem.

Determining the real problem is one of the basic underpinnings of software development. If the user's real requirements are not determined, then the subsequent software product developed won't satisfy his or her real needs. The entire debugging process in writing software pivots around identifying the true problem: is it placing the numbers in the wrong positions on the report or has it just printed wrong numbers?

Gather the Relevant Facts

A fact-gathering phase is usually necessary to clarify the problems. People trained in engineering, mathematics, and science tend to want to engage in this step ad infinitum. Although it may take a good deal of time to locate information sources, there is also a law of diminishing returns. Because you will never have a 100 percent certainty of obtaining all the information, you must learn to exercise judgment as to when to truncate a search for additional information. At that point, you begin to converge on a solution using the information already gathered.

Propose a Solution

Once a plausible or possible solution has been identified, the winners and losers rapidly separate in their approach to problem solving. The losers inevitably adopt the first solution that comes to mind, possibly leaping out of the frying pan and into the fire. Admittedly, the pressures to come up with a solution quickly are great. No one likes to walk into his or her boss' or customer's office and say, "We have a problem." Such a crisis generates psychological pressure on the project manager to come up with a solution quickly so he or she can say, "We have a problem, but don't worry about it because we have a pretty good solution in mind." But it is best to take a different approach.

Develop Several Alternative Solutions

The winning approach to problem solving is to develop several alternative solutions. Thus, when the problem has arisen and must be reported, the successful project manager will say, "We have a problem. We may have a possible solution, but I am going to take three or four days to consider other alternatives. Then I will report to you on the options and our recommended course of corrective action." Although such an approach to reporting the bad news may make you initially uncomfortable, it is invariably associated with reaching better solutions.

Developing alternatives is the key to problem solving.

For example, the decision has been made to automate some accounting functions. The form of the automation can be one of many. Alternative solutions would be in-house hardware and software facilities, service bureau with in-house terminal and printer, and service bureau only. The software could be purchased along with the hardware from a single vendor; the hardware could be obtained separately, and the software could either be custom developed or bought already coded as a package. The "best" solution, of course, is determined by the Triple Constraint of performance, schedule, and cost.

When seriously behind schedule, the possible alternatives a manager might consider would be slipping the schedule, renting time on another computer, or subcontracting out some of the work.

Adopt the Best Alternative

After deciding what is the best alternative, you must adopt a course of action.

Tell Everyone

As an effective project manager, you have earlier made certain that everybody involved in your project had one or original project plan. Now, because you have ch must tell more dimensions of the Triple Constraint, the previous everyone what the new plan is. As discusse some people chapter, if you fail to do this, there v-tion, producing working in accordance with obsolet something useless and out of date.

Audit the Outcome

As you implement the best alternative solution, watch how it is working out. Auditing will improve your ability to solve problems by showing you how your solutions actually work out. And as you learn more about the problem you are solving and the approach you have adopted, a better alternative may become clear, which may necessitate a further change in the plan.

DECISION TREES

Choosing the best alternative often requires estimating the possible outcomes and their probabilities. An organized way to cope with the situation is to use a decision tree. This technique is both simple and powerful. If you use it often enough, it will improve your average performance in adopting alternatives. Consider the decision whether to go to a movie or walk on the beach. This decision and its possible outcomes are shown in Figure 18-1.

Each possibility has chance future events, which have to do with the quality of the movie or the weather. There are also different outcomes, which are illustrated. Outcomes such as those shown, which have more than one dimension to them (happiness and money, in the figure), must be reduced to a

Decision trees require you to quantify the outcome.

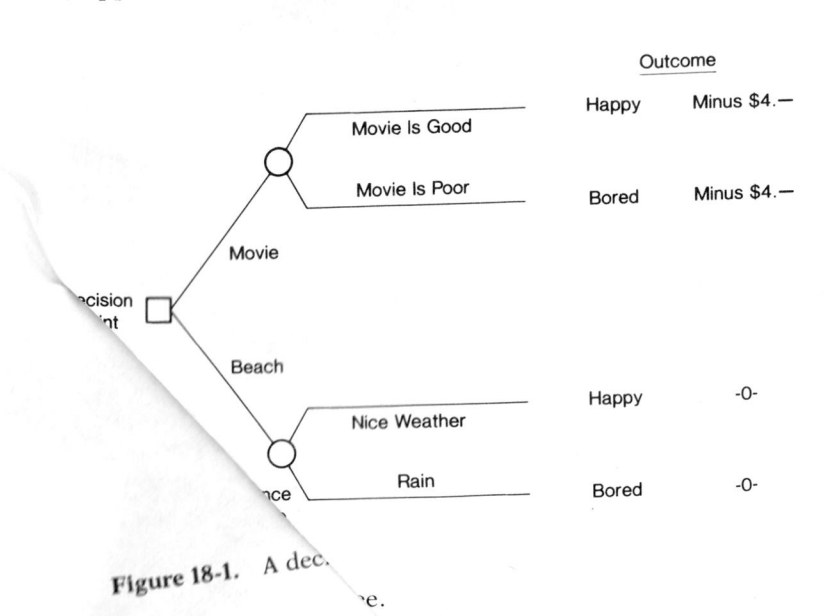

		Outcome	
Movie Is Good		Happy	Minus $4.—
Movie Is Poor		Bored	Minus $4.—
Nice Weather		Happy	-0-
Rain		Bored	-0-

Figure 18-1. A dec...

single numeric value. This can be done by utility or preference techniques, which we shall not discuss (see Moore and Thomas, 1976, Chap. 9).

Figure 18-2 is a general representation of the kind of decision trees with which you must work. A decision tree always starts with a decision for which there are two or more possible choices. Each choice may be followed by chance future events or subordinate choices (decisions) in any order and with two or more branches following each node. There is a single numeric value outcome, which is typically the present value of the cash flows along the various branches to that outcome.

Decision trees are used routinely in many situations, such as the decision whether to drill an oil well at a given location or whether to locate a new warehouse in a new geographic region. In both of these typical situations, the correctness of the decision depends on the probabilities of things happening in the future (oil being found or business growth), and decision trees are designed to maximize the likelihood of choosing the correct course of action. In a software project, you might have to choose which of two yet-to-be-developed computers

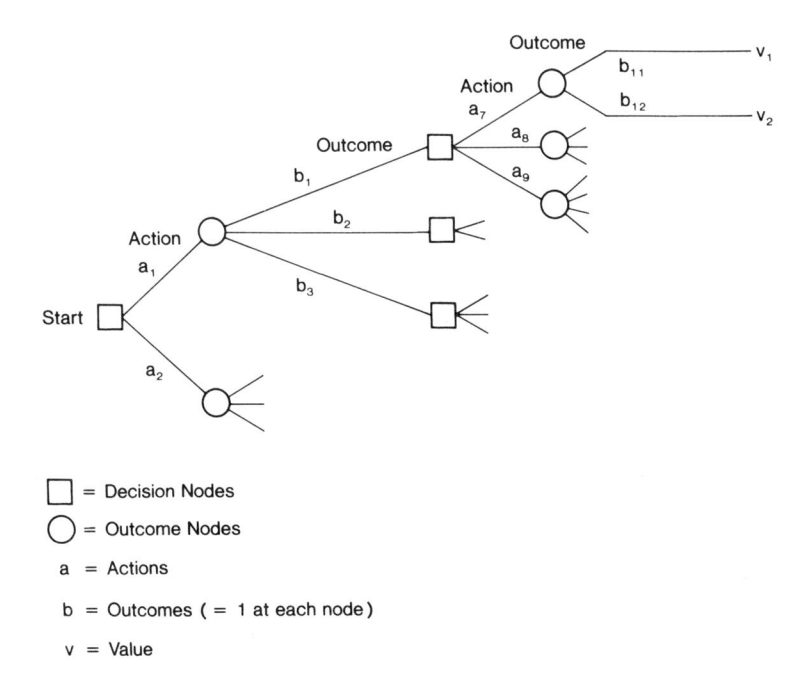

Figure 18-2. A generalized decision tree.

254 Coping With Unexpected Problems

to commit to; and there would be uncertainty about delivery and performance.

Consider the following situation, which often confronts a project manager. You have just received an unsolicited request for a proposal that will yield a $300,000 before-tax profit if you can win the job. Checking with the marketing manager, you learn that your company and two others were both solicited suddenly and you all have an equal opportunity of winning the job. Thus, you appear to have one chance in three of winning $300,000 if you write the proposal.

After discussing this, you and the marketing manager realize you have the opportunity to quickly develop a computer model for $45,000 and doing so increases the odds of your winning to fifty-fity. The decision with which you are confronted is whether to develop the model (at a cost of $45,000) to increase the odds of winning a $300,000 before-tax profit from one in three to one in two. Figure 18-3 shows the decision tree and the problem analysis for this situation. Figure 18-4 is an alternative representation. In both cases, the

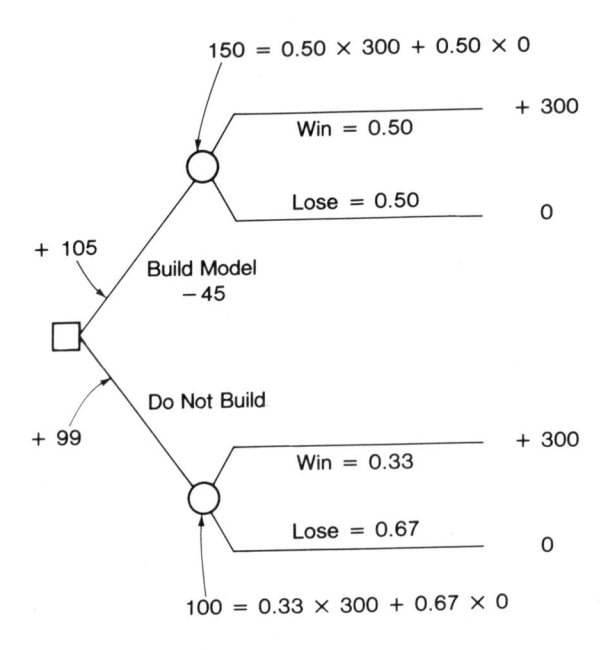

There are two ways to draw decision trees.

```
                150 = 0.50 × 300 + 0.50 × 0
                                            + 300
                    Win = 0.50

                    Lose = 0.50
                                            0
        + 105
              Build Model
               -45
        □
              Do Not Build
        + 99                                + 300
                    Win = 0.33

                    Lose = 0.67
                                            0
                100 = 0.33 × 300 + 0.67 × 0
```

Methodology:
- Construct diagram from left to right.
- Insert $ values from right to left.

Figure 18-3. Decision tree for illustrative example (thousands of dollars omitted).

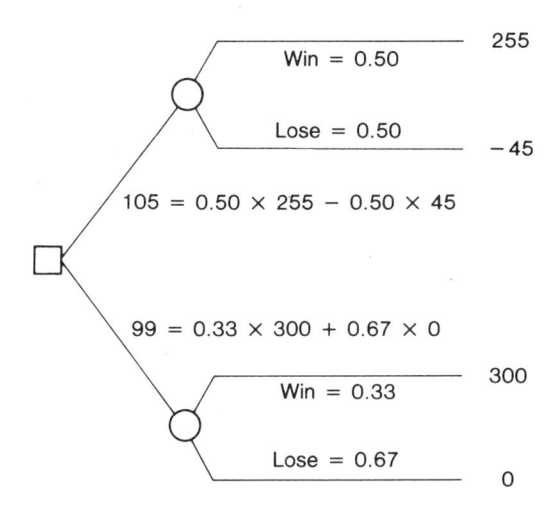

```
                           255
         Win = 0.50
      ○
         Lose = 0.50
                           −45
    105 = 0.50 × 255 − 0.50 × 45
 □
    99 = 0.33 × 300 + 0.67 × 0
                           300
         Win = 0.33
      ○
         Lose = 0.67
                           0
```

Figure 18-4. Alternative representation of Figure 18-3 decision tree.

branch in which the model is developed has a higher value than the branch in which the model is not developed. Therefore, your decision would be to develop the model because it has a higher expected value. This does not guarantee that you will win the job. Rather, it gives you a higher expected dollar value. If you use decision trees in enough cases, you will do better over the long run. But you might very well develop the model and still lose the job, thus ending up losing $45,000. (Note that, for simplicity, we have ignored the cost of writing the proposal in both situations.)

Sometimes you are confronted with decision choices, for example, how to remove a resource constraint on two projects, for which a qualitative decision tree (Figure 18-5) is useful. In this, you may be unable to quantitatively estimate outcome values, odds of occurrence, or costs of actions. However, you may be able to clarify the alternatives to the point where a better choice is possible.

MATRIX ARRAY

Quantitative

In situations where decision trees are not practical or are unwieldy for the analysis and comparison of alternatives, the matrix array may be a satisfactory aid. Figure 18-6 illustrates

A matrix must list all significant criteria.

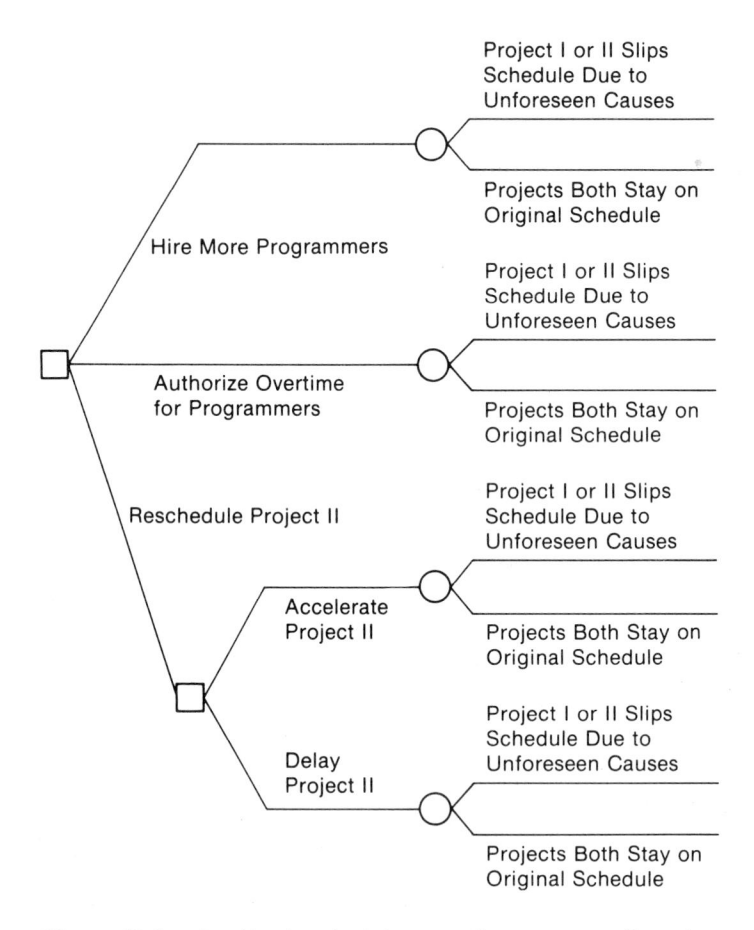

Figure 18-5. Qualitative decision tree for resource allocation.

a quantitative weighting (or scoring) array. The key considerations in the particular problem are listed on the left margin. In a computer programming project, the performance criteria might include processing speed, size of memory required, response time, and reliability. In addition to performance targets criteria, the listing should include the schedule and cost implications of adopting that particular solution.

Next, weighting factors (the sum of which is equal to one) are attached to each criterion (or target). Then a percentage, indicating the degree to which the solution satisfies the particular criterion target, is entered for each solution. Finally, each percentage for each solution in the body of the matrix is multiplied by the corresponding weighting factors, and the result is entered at the bottom of the solution column (for example, for solution approach 2, $[0.20 \times 90\%] + [0.15 \times$

Criteria	Weighting Factor	Solution Approach 1	Solution Approach 2	Solution Approach 3
Performance Target A	0.20	60%	90%	80%
Performance Target B	0.15	90%	70%	70%
Performance Target C	0.15	90%	50%	90%
Schedule Target	0.20	70%	70%	90%
Cost Target	0.30	90%	80%	70%
Weighted Percentage Value		80%	74%	79%

Figure 18-6. Quantitative decision matrix.

70%] + [0.15 × 50%] + [0.20 × 70%] + [0.30 × 80%] = 74%). There are four problems with this approach:

1. Deciding on weighting factors may be difficult.
2. Choosing percentages may be difficult, especially for the schedule and cost targets, where the solution approach may exceed plan.
3. The highest ranking or weighted percentage value may still be inadequate.
4. It does not consider people, in particular, the possibility that one solution approach is championed by an ambitious person who will work nights and weekends to accomplish it.

Qualitative

Because of the manipulation to which the quantitative approach is subject, it is often better to use a slightly more qualitative matrix. Such a matrix can explicitly consider people issues, especially where there are advocates for or opponents to a particular solution approach, and it can use quantitative data where these are available (Figure 18-7). Note three aspects of this approach:

1. Numbers are used whenever possible.
2. People are given explicit consideration.
3. The summary identifies both favorable and unfavorable issues.

Also, this kind of matrix can always be used, even early in the decision analysis, before all relevant numerical data are available.

Be honest about solution shortfalls.

To use this kind of matrix, list each solution across the top. You must do this conscientiously. When you write down the first solution and it clearly falls short with regard to one or more of the key criteria, seek additional solutions designed to overcome the shortfall of the ones presently conceived. Usually, after you have written down two, three, or four solutions, each of which has one or more aspects of shortfall, you will identify some hybrid or new variant that comes close to satisfying all the key considerations identified. Even if the matrix array does not lead to a hybrid that clearly satisfies all significant considerations, using the array will clarify available trade-offs and options.

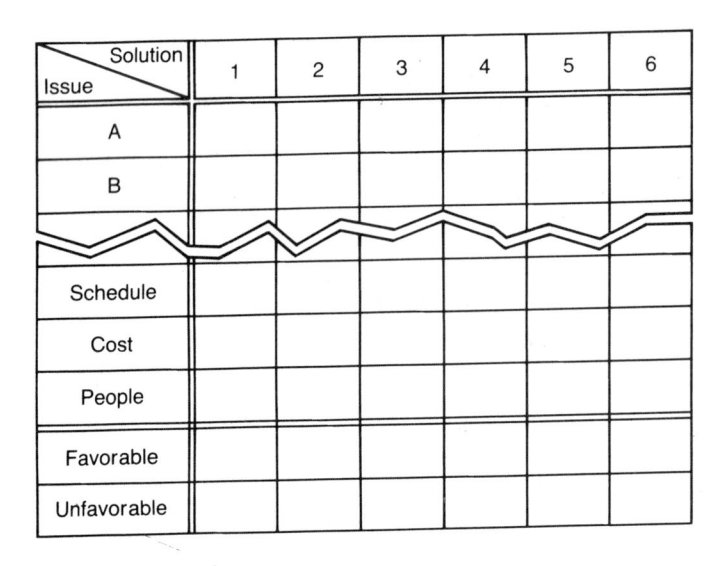

Issue / Solution	1	2	3	4	5	6
A						
B						
...						
Schedule						
Cost						
People						
Favorable						
Unfavorable						

Figure 18-7. Qualitative matrix.
Source: "Basic Management Skills for Engineers and Scientists." Lecture notes by Milton D. Rosenau, Jr. Copyright © 1982 by the University of Southern California. Reprinted by permission.

PROBLEM-SOLVING MEETING STYLES

C. J. Margerison, in *Managerial Problem Solving*, identifies four meeting styles for use when solving problems:

1. Command (issuing orders)
2. Negotiative (different groups horse trading to reach agreement)
3. Collegiate (peers reaching decision by consensus)
4. Advisory (exchanging information and making subsequent decision)

He also identifies five approaches to problem solving. If the information to solve the problem is readily available, a solution-centered approach to problem solving may be adopted. Three of these are indicated. First, the managerial authority is accepted and the manager has the information and the ability to solve the problem, a directive approach is appropriate and a command meeting, one in which the manager issues orders, is the most appropriate meeting style. This does not mean a different meeting style cannot be used, but a command meeting will most likely produce an effective solution under these conditions. Second, the negotiative approach to problem solving is bargaining with different objectives but common interests, and in this case a negotiative meeting is most likely to be effective. Third, the prescriptive approach to problem solving is one in which a solution is solicited, and the presented answer may only be a tentative trial. For this, a negotiative or collegiate meeting style is most useful.

There are two problem-centered approaches to problem solving, those in which information is still needed. The first of these is the consultative approach, in which trust exists and information sharing is useful to diagnose the problem. The second is the reflective approach, which is useful if the problem is unclear and nonjudgmental restatements are acceptable. In both of these approaches, the advisory meeting is most likely to be productive.

Single-purpose meetings are the most effective.

Meetings have different purposes. Reviews of milestone documents throughout the project life cycle are different from the change review meetings, for example. But meetings are most effective when they have a single purpose: decision making or information dissemination, rather than both. Also, the composition of the meetings and the speaker will alter the meeting's format and purpose. Thus, a project review conducted with subordinates will be different from one presented for senior management; the attendees are present to give information in the former and to receive information in the latter.

TYPICAL PROBLEMS

> In most project management problem-solving situations, it is not possible to find *the* answer, only a most acceptable (or least objectionable) answer. This may be caused by the inherent uncertainty or lack of quantitative data. It is thus a matter of judgment about when to choose among the identified solutions and when to keep looking for more, better solutions. Honest people will differ (as they will in their perception of the problem and their evaluation of solution alternatives), and this must be both expected and tolerated. Use of a qualitative matrix or a purely qualitative decision tree can reduce, if not eliminate, this problem.
>
> Quantitative techniques are valuable when there is ample time for analysis. Usually that is in the proposal stage, when the determination is being made to bid or not and effective resource allocation is being weighed against returns on investment. During the actual management of a project, there is little time for such analyses. The best problem-solving tools are the manager's own common sense and the experience of his or her staff, resources, and customer requirements.

HIGHLIGHTS   The seven steps in problem solving are identify the problem, collect the data, develop alternative solutions, select a best solution, implement the solution, audit the outcome, and inform everyone.

Decision trees help you choose the best alternative.

Matrices, another aid to alternative selection, may be qualitative or quantitative.

There are appropriate meeting styles for different problem-solving approaches.

FURTHER READING

V. G. Hajek. *Management of Engineering Projects*. New York: McGraw-Hill, 1977.
> Section 14.11 is a good one-page summary of decision making to solve problems.

C. J. Margerison. *Managerial Problem Solving*. Maidenhead, Berkshire, England: McGraw-Hill, 1974.
> This is an outstanding book on all aspects of problem solving.

P. G. Moore and H. Thomas. *The Anatomy of Decisions*. New York: Penguin, 1976.
> This is a well-written, clear, complete treatment of decision trees. It is brief but thorough.

Part 5

COMPLETING THE SOFTWARE PROJECT

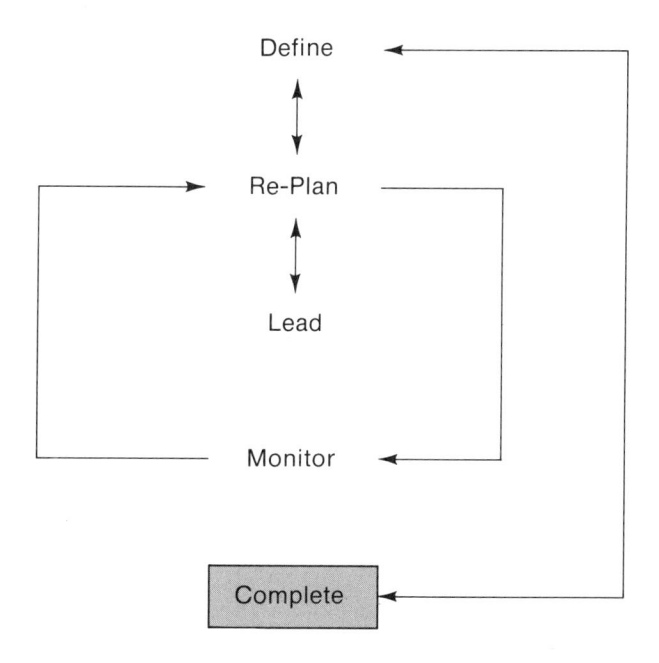

Define
↕
Re-Plan
↕
Lead

Monitor

Complete

19

Computer Software Project Completion

The fifth and last step in project management is project completion. To introduce this topic, this chapter reviews the project life cycle, first introduced in Chapter 1. This discussion then reviews activities required to complete the project. Then the consequences of project completion are discussed, and we show that all personnel do not necessarily have the same stake in ending the project.

PROJECT STAFFING CYCLE

Phases

Figure 19-1 shows a project staffing cycle in a generalized way. The three phases are arbitrary, but they are sufficient to illustrate the point that activities change during the duration of any project, including computer software projects. This has implications for the illustrated personnel head count and means that the kind of personnel used in different phases will have to change. For instance, creative designers, very useful in the early phases, can easily become an obstacle to completion if they are retained during the later phases.

That projects have different phases emphasizes that personnel needs will change throughout the project staffing cycle.

Termination

There is a variety of ways to stop projects. Resources can be withdrawn, for instance, by reassigning personnel or re-

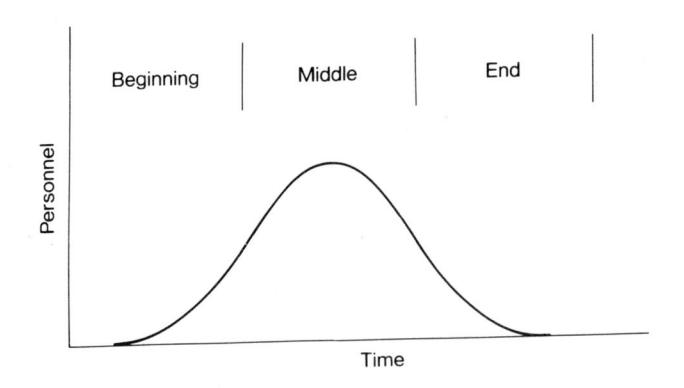

	Beginning	Middle	End
Construction	Site	Erection	Landscaping
Product Development	R&D, Market Research	Engineering and Manufacturing	Product Introduction
Aerospace System	Engineering	Assembly	Customer Test and Sign-off
Computer Software	Definition and Design	Programming	System Test and Acceptance

Figure 19-1. Project staffing cycle.

quired facilities. Higher priority projects may gain at the expense of a low priority project, which may be allowed to wither on the vine. These approaches are not as desirable as an orderly and carefully planned termination. Project success, that is, satisfying the Triple Constraint, can be obtained only by such an orderly ending. During the last few months of a project, weekly reviews may be required; and during the last few weeks, daily reviews may be required.

Acceptance

The goal of project management is to obtain customer or user acceptance of the project result. This means the customer or user agrees that the performance dimension specification of the Triple Constraint has been met. Unless the acceptance criteria have been clearly defined in documentation agreed to by the customer and the contractor, there will be discord at the end of the project. Thus, an accurate, complete, and unambiguous statement of requirements early in the project is so necessary; it reflects what the customer (or user) asked for. The milestone reviews are likewise important because the customer signed off on the product(s) specified. Lastly, the worth of concurrent documentation is felt because without an up-to-date specification, neither customer nor contractor can argue effectively about acceptance criteria. When agreement is lacking, the customer will typically want more (unless it costs unacceptable amounts of time or money) and the contractor will argue for less. This is why an unstated or undefined amount of maintenance should not be included in a project.

Therefore, the acceptance phase must start with the initial contractual definition of the work to be undertaken. This is not to say there cannot be changes of scope during the contract to alter or clarify the acceptance criteria.

The acceptance phase begins with the definition of the job.

In some projects, it may be impossible at the beginning to agree upon final acceptance criteria. This is typical of high-technology development projects and not uncommon for computer software projects. When this is the case, the contract should call for an initial effort of an adequate duration to clarify the entire system design and acceptance criteria. At the end of this first phase covering requirements and feasibility, a customer review is conducted and a contract is negotiated for the final implementation phase of work, including acceptance criteria for the end of the project. This approach requires the customer to bear a large risk during the initial phase because the contractor may decide during the initial phase that the final phase will be lengthy and costly. Nevertheless, there is no reasonable alternative to this two-phase approach.

Because there are many possible completion points and delivery conditions for a project, it is necessary to think these through. Completion of an automated teller machine (ATM) network for a bank would differ depending on whether it was defined as the development of the distributed software for the network, the fabrication of the ATM machines, or the completion of the application software that updates customer account records.

Objectively measurable criteria for completion (such as move these two hundred books to the next room before 9:30 a.m.) are best. Subjective criteria (such as paint an attractive portrait of me) are risky. The former allow little or no room for ambiguity; in the latter, the customer and contractor could easily have different standards.

Completion requires objective and measurable criteria be attained, which ideally solves the customer's problems.

It is also important to be clear about what the project output is supposed to accomplish. For instance, three very different results occur when the product performs the specified functions, the product was built according to the specified designs, and the product really solved the customer's problem.

Test Criteria

The most difficult aspect of software development, in our experience, is the test process. Random perversity strikes by contributing faults not one's own, such as faulty hardware and bugs in another vendor's software. The project manager must be aware of the eventuality of these occurrences and establish the test criteria early on in the project.

The test issues concern testing by whom, against what, for how long, and how much. Where applicable, the contractor should do as much testing as possible in-house before going to test at the customer site. But the ultimate user should be made responsible for determining just what test data he or she wants to see run through the system (live data is usually preferable because the results can be compared to those from an existing manual or automated system).

Bugs often do not show up in a system until certain critical times have passed and the system must use data it has created, such as occurs when doing month end accounting processing. Without attention to the length of time testing is required, the customer could end up accepting software that performed well but, alas, not for long.

A manager of testing is sometimes appointed, and, where applicable, a single point of contact with the customer is appointed to monitor the preparation of the test data and the validation of results. The template for all the testing, however, is the test plan, which is either an important part of the requirements documentation, produced early in the project, or is issued separately during the design phase. Whenever it is issued, though, the customer must approve it and assume responsibility for some part of the test preparation process. The contracting organization knows how to create test data, but the customer knows which are meaningful test data and is in the best position to create data with the type of errors most likely to happen. Often, in fact, the errors introduced are not thought of by programmers, who understand the innards of the programs and use them as they intended when writing them.

The user and operator manuals written by the contractor must also be accepted by the customer. This involves actually using them on-site, ensuring that they are comprehensible to users and operators alike. This must be included as part of the test process and the acceptance criteria.

The customer must be involved in the test process.

Project completion clearly depends upon the precise wording of the acceptance criteria. There should be no room for doubt or ambiguity, although in practice this is extremely difficult to accomplish at project inception. Both parties may enter into a contract with goodwill, but the contractor may have assumed and perhaps even included in the contract the jointly agreed priority to use customer facilities to validate product output. Such a priority can easily become an ambiguous issue toward the end of the project. Other difficulties in wording arise when the word "appropriate" is used. Appropriate tests or demonstrations that seem clear and simple at the beginning of a project have a way of becoming the opposite toward the end.

Delivery

Delivery may or may not be completion. Project completion often requires the product function after delivery at a location the customer designates. Even if not explicitly the case, there may be an implied warranty that requires it. Thus, responsibility for delivered goods after they leave the contractor's facility is always an issue to be considered at project inception. It is to the benefit of both user and developer to define acceptance as the product operative on the *user's* hardware at the user's site.

Delivery is not necessarily the last step.

Consider the situation where the customer has witnessed final system tests at your company and accepts the computer software program. After delivery to and installation on the customer's computer, the program does not perform adequately. What can the project manager do? As a minimum, you are going to have to participate in fact finding. At one extreme, the acceptance criteria will have been absolutely clear; the tests at your company will have been unambiguous; participation in and witnessing of these tests will have been done by qualified and responsible senior personnel; and the performance shortfall at the customer's facility will be attributable entirely to the customer's actions. The developer runs the risk of wasting huge resources debugging the customer's hardware, which may not even be part of the contractual agreement.

Stipulate clear conditions for acceptance.

More likely, questions will arise about the acceptance test, the specific equipment used to perform it (for example, CPU loading, timing, calibration procedures, or even the possibility of stray magnetic fields), or what might have occurred to change the program during delivery. Regardless of contract form or your desire to obtain more business from that customer, the customer's final happiness with how well the program solves his or her problem will affect your reputation; so you may have to engage in a lot of extra, perhaps unpaid, effort to help get the program working. In some cases, you may be able to show that the fault was theirs and get them to pay you for your extra effort.

Once the contractor has turned over possession of the goods, the contractor's control is greatly diminished. Therefore, it is important to have clearly stipulated conditions for acceptance, including payment terms.

Documentation

A software project requires documentation to enable users to understand it, operators to run the software, and programmers and analysts to subsequently change it. When contracted for, the product delivered includes the user and operations manuals, installation manuals, the actual code listings, and a copy of the software on a magnetic medium such as tape or disc. Software without documentation, especially at the functional (what it does) and user (how to use it) levels, is not a completed product.

Project documentation must be accepted by the customer before the project is completed.

Although concurrent documentation is a contemporary principle of software project life cycle management, in practice, it is not quite as concurrent as one wants. This occurs because changes have to be retrofitted to many documents, there are inadequate technical documentation resources, and many other reasons. Some documents, like the user's manual, may not be completed until the acceptance test, where user training is part of the acceptance criteria. However, the project is not complete until the documentation that reflects it has been delivered and approved by the customer.

COMPLETION CONSEQUENCES

Project completion may be viewed as a boon or doom. The customer, the contracting organization, the project manager, and the project personnel may not all see it the same way.

Four Affected Parties

For the project manager, completion may be an opportunity for promotion, but many project personnel may find themselves laid off if there is not other work. If the project was badly managed, its manager may receive a less favorable assignment in the future, and personnel who did an outstanding job may have a choice future assignment. The contracting organization's view of project completion depends on customer approval and project profitability. The customer may be unhappy because he or she specified the wrong acceptance criteria but admit the contractor has met the specifications.

Thus, there is no reason to assume that all four parties will have the same view of project completion. Project managers must realize that they may have a very different stake in ending the project than the other three parties. Consequently, the project manager must prod, cajole, or offer inducements to those for whom completion is not obviously desirable.

Completion consequences are also influenced by the reasons for termination. It is certainly best to end the project because all the objectives have been satisfactorily achieved. It is a bad situation if one or more dimensions of the Triple Constraint have been missed substantially.

Everyone does not have the same stake in completion, and the project manager must understand the differences.

Personnel Reassignment

Project completion requires reassignment of people. We have now come full circle. The (temporary) project is no longer imposed on the rest of the (permanent) contracting organization. This frequently will necessitate a reorganization of the parent entity because the mix of remaining project work is such that the previously satisfactory organization is no longer appropriate.

The other crucial aspect of personnel reassignment is timing. If a person's next assignment is a choice one, he or she will normally be anxious to start and will lose interest in completing the present project. Conversely, if someone's next project assignment is undesirable, he or she may stall. When no assignment is obvious and layoff or termination is probable, personnel may even attempt sabotage to stretch out the present project assignment.

The project manager can cope with these tendencies to some extent by selecting the time he or she informs project personnel of their next assignment. But if the contracting organization has a reputation for terminating personnel at the end of projects, there is little a project manager can do.

A person's perception of what will happen when the project ends will affect his or her work as termination approaches.

There are several options for deployment of team members when the project ends.

The best situation is one in which all project personnel can count on their good work being recognized and appreciated and there being a selection of future assignments.

Even if no specific new project assignment is available when personnel need reassignment, there are still options. For example, personnel can write an unsolicited proposal, prepare an article for publication, work on an in-house development or software maintenance effort, or attend a short course or seminar. Temporary assignments such as these can be used constructively to fill in valleys in the project work load. They also can be used as a motivational tool if they are authorized so as to make participation a mark of recognition for a job well done.

Project personnel can also be assigned to the maintenance of the project after development has been completed. Their knowledge of the system should prove particularly valuable. However, maintenance projects often have a second class status. Many programmers, convinced of their superior design talents, with ego in their conceptualizations, feel there is not enough excitement in maintenance projects and resist assignment to them.

Organizational Changes Due to Project

When any project ends, for whatever reason, the organization is altered. Doing the project work adds a new body of knowledge to the organization. This is not just tangible information, but also new skills for many of the people. New working relationships have also been established, both within and outside of the organization, and these alter the informal organization, even if the formal organization is still unchanged.

INCREASING THE ODDS OF SUCCESS

There are both external and internal factors that influence how well a project satisfies its Triple Constraint.

External Factors

Customers for projects seem to be divided into two broad categories: knowledgeable and shortsighted. The shortsighted customers tend to emphasize the buyer versus seller relationship and to some extent create an adversary relationship between the two organizations. Conversely, knowledgeable customers and users realize that their stake in project success is ultimately just as great as that of the performing contract organization. Thus, a knowledgeable customer will become involved in the project in an effective, as opposed to a destructive, manner. Such a customer will specify expected reviews and include them in the original job definition. Beyond this, he or she will attempt to ask the tough questions and to carry out probing reviews of the contractor's work, not to embarrass but to help assure that all significant issues have been dealt with appropriately. Any required changes will be negotiated intelligently.

High priority projects inevitably seem to have better outcomes than lower priority projects because they tend to win all competitions for physical and human resources. This is not to say that low priority projects lack top management support; top management clearly wants all projects to succeed, but the lower priority projects are at a relative disadvantage.

A knowledgeable customer, high priority, and clear objectives aid successful completion.

Clear and stable project objectives are a sine qua non of project success. Objectives can and do change during the course of many projects, but not on a daily or hourly basis. Thus, committing these objectives to writing helps assure that they are fixed in everyone's mind, and revising them when they must occasionally change is also a clear requirement of success.

Internal Factors

A qualified, experienced, competent leader is vital, as is a balanced team. Having a team with a balance of skills and getting teamwork from it can be somewhat contradictory. People with very similar backgrounds tend to get along better; so it is easier to promote teamwork in a group composed entirely of, for instance, application programmers. Nevertheless, a successful project usually requires that a team be composed of more than this one skill. Thus, the project manager is confronted with merging people with diverse backgrounds into an effective and harmonious team.

A good leader, a balanced team, the right sized work packages, careful replanning, and orderly termination contribute to project success.

The natural phasing of the software development life cycle often places people responsible for a phase in an adversary relationship with those in a preceding or succeeding phase. For instance, analysts who defined requirements find themselves defending their specifications to the designers, who use the requirements specifications to define the general systems design and find, in that process, errors and omissions in the earlier documents.

Having the properly sized work packages helps you avoid two potential problems. Complex, difficult work packages should not be assigned to junior people and simple work packages should not be assigned to senior people, who will not be challenged by them.

Because projects will almost never be carried out exactly in accordance with the original plan, replanning is a constant requirement in project management. Project termination, especially the reassignment of personnel, requires active planning well before scheduled completion.

TYPICAL PROBLEMS

> Sometimes not only subordinate personnel but also the project manager must change during the project's life. This is a technique often used when a project is unable to successfully complete the design stage. The manager for the initial phases may be great at the inception but become stale with time or bored by routine wrap-up activities. The solution in this case is to change project managers, and both upper management and project manager must be alert to this possibility.

HIGHLIGHTS *Although the project starts with the definition phase and ends with the completion phase, project completion and customer acceptance depend on agreements reached during the definition phase.*

Personnel needs may change throughout the project staffing cycle.

It is best to end a project because all dimensions of the Triple Constraint have been satisfied.

The project manager must realize that project completion may not be good for all involved parties and plan for an orderly end well in advance of its scheduled time.

Both internal and external factors contribute to project success.

FURTHER READING

V. G. Hajek. *Management of Engineering Projects.* New York: McGraw-Hill, 1977.
   Chapters 19 and 20 provide a reasonable treatment of the completion phase.

S. F. Jacobus. "Dose of Rules Eases Documentation Headaches." *Information Systems News* (June 13, 1983), pp. 32–33, 36.
   This is a good article covering many detailed aspects of computer software documentation.

P. W. Metzger. *Managing a Programming Project,* 2nd ed. Englewood Cliffs, NJ: Prentice-Hall, 1981.
   Chapters 5, 6, and 7 give a detailed overview of the completion phase for programming projects, covering system test, acceptance, and installation and operation.

R. C. Tausworthe. *Standardized Development of Computer Software,* Part 1: *Methods* and Part 2: *Standards.* Englewood Cliffs, NJ: Prentice-Hall, 1977 and 1979.
   This is a complete presentation of aerospace documentation interrelationships and content.

20

What You Have to Do After You Thought You Were Done

Projects end with their completion, but there frequently are postcompletion activities that are necessary to the project and may be viewed as part of it. They are not, however, necessarily part of the basic contract. These are discussed in this chapter.

CONTINUING SERVICE AND SUPPORT

Some projects require postcompletion service and support.

Continuing service and support may be an obligation. If they are, it must be understood who is to pay for them and when. This is often left to be negotiated when the project is completed. Negotiating at this time may be desirable because of an initial inability to see what may be involved, but it leaves a potential Pandora's box at the end of the project. Good relations with a customer often dictate, however, that, in the hopes of getting additional jobs, you will continue to answer telephone inquiries and provide some support without fee.

Software maintenance is often done within the same company but by a separate organization. This organizational structure takes advantage of those types of programmers and analysts who prefer maintenance to development projects. Then the maintenance effort is treated as a separate project. An inherent danger is that the maintenance staff may call upon the original development programmers and analysts to assist in that effort and certainly to answer inquiries. Development programmers then face a conflict between their new assignments and the need to assist their co-workers. If the maintenance programmers are too demanding, the development programmers' manager on their new project will not have the resources he or she counted on to accomplish the project. The best arrangement is thus keeping original programmers for the maintenance project.

It is important for the manager of the maintenance effort to have the budget and personnel required to properly make the changes requested by the users, required by regulatory changes, and initiated by operating system updates. This is necessary to keep documentation and training up to date and to fine-tune the system over time.

Sometimes the customer organization will want to perform the maintenance in-house, which requires a knowledgeable and well-trained staff. From a customer relations point of view, if nothing else, it will still require knowledgeable contractor personnel to respond to the customer's inquiries. If customers are going to attempt to do their own coding, they will probably need more of the contractors' time than comes within the realm of marketing support, and it should be billed out by the contractor on an hourly basis.

Charge for continuation support whenever possible.

The contractor should view continuing service and support as an opportunity and not merely as an obligation. His or her employees will be working with the customer's personnel, providing continuing service and support, if it is included in the project. In so doing, they will have informal opportunities to explore ideas with the customer's personnel and hear about real problems the customer is facing. Thus, these contacts provide the basis for future business opportunities.

OWNERSHIP RIGHTS

Patents and special facilities required for contract performance have ownership value. In general, if it is a cost reimbursible contract in which the customer pays all the costs incurred, ownership rights revert to the customer at the end of the job. If it is a fixed price contract, ownership rights generally revert to the contractor unless otherwise stipulated in the initial contract. Ownership of code not developed directly for this customer but supplied by the contractor *must*

Patent rights and hiring policies must be outlined in the contract.

be clearly delineated in the original contract agreement. These can be points of contention unless they are discussed and clearly resolved in the initial contract. In any event, patent applications must be filed if any seem justified. The party of ultimate ownership must expect to pay for this activity.

Certainly one of the major issues facing the software industry today is the entire scope of the legal rights surrounding software. Legal clauses in employment contracts and signed nondisclosure agreements cannot prevent the transmittal of what is still essentially a conceptual product—software, not hardware. If an employee goes elsewhere and uses the basic architectural approach as before, how much must be changed before it is no longer your proprietary idea? These ideas and others are being battled out in the courts and will probably continue for the foreseeable future.

There is also the issue of people. Obviously, neither the customer nor the contractor owns any people. But "no compete" clauses in recruiting customer personnel into the contractor organization or vice versa are often in the initial contract. If they were not, the customers might hire the contractor's personnel to perform the continuing service and support the contracting organization presumed it was going to perform and be reimbursed for. Many computer vendors, however, do not have such a clause; the potential of hiring their employees is one of the benefits they offer their customers.

AUDITS

A project is not complete until the customer pays the bill.

There often are postcompletion audits, especially in contracts performed for governmental entities. It is therefore absolutely essential to retain records for the required duration and even more important to file and document them in an organized and thorough way. Many of the people who could explain some audited item may no longer be available when the audit is performed; so the contractor might lose an important claim if this is not done. Some portion of the final payment on a contract may be withheld until the audit is completed. Therefore, a final financial summary may not be possible until the audit is performed, and this can be months or even years after the other work is finished.

What can you do if your customer does not pay the bill? The responsibility for obtaining payment usually resides with the accounts receivable department and is thus outside the normal purview of the project manager. Nevertheless, an effective project manager who has assiduously maintained good customer relations may be able to help persuade a slow-paying customer to pay promptly. And the project manager, in considering the possibility of obtaining more work from the customer, will be concerned with the customer's payment history because that can influence the desirability of further work. Project managers do not want the accounts receivable department to take hostile action against a delinquent account for whom they hope to do further work. Thus, project managers and the accounts receivable department must discuss these issues and mutually decide on the mix of persuasion, cajoling, or legal action to take.

PEOPLE ISSUES

After being assured that all project personnel have been reassigned (or laid off or terminated if necessary), the project manager has two other things to do. First, send personal letters of thanks, appreciation, or praise to project personnel. Second, send a brief wrap-up report to management. It is smart to cite your own successful performance in this.

The project manager should also get, where offered by the customer and appropriate to the task completed, laudatory letters for the company and/or specific employees to assist with subsequent marketing and employee performance appraisals.

FEEDBACK

Throughout the project, you, as manager, communicated with users, designers, programmers and support personnel. Through reviews, documents, reports, and informal conversations, you received feedback as to progress against goals and performance. After the project has been completed, the need for feedback does not end. What does end is the formalized process for the feedback to reach you. If maintenance has been established as a separate project, feedback will occur within that project.

Feedback is important even after project completion.

If there is no ongoing maintenance project, then informal communication from you to the customer can help provide feedback as to the system's long-term usability and the customer's satisfaction and can possibly help identify additional work that you and your company can perform.

Internally—with those who worked on your project—even when there is an ongoing maintenance project of which you are not in charge, you can solicit feedback as to how the project proceeded, how it could have gone more smoothly, and how you performed as manager. That concern with others' feedback and maintaining contact with them after the project is completed can also be of value when you have to staff your next project.

TYPICAL PROBLEMS

> Basically, the problem here is simply doing it all. The press or excitement of new items to do often leads to the omission of some postcompletion activities. The solution is to recognize your responsibility in getting these things done.

HIGHLIGHTS

Continuing service and support activities may lead to future business opportunities.

Contracts often include assignments of patent rights and "no compete" personnel recruitment clauses.

Records must be carefully kept in case there is a postcompletion audit.

Managers should send letters of appreciation to project personnel and a wrap-up report to the boss.

FURTHER READING

R. D. Archibald. *Managing High-Technology Programs and Projects.* New York: Wiley-Interscience, 1976.
   Chapter 10 is a very short recap of some terminal activities.

J. J. Fialka. "Botched Benefits: Ailing Computers Give Social Security System Another Big Problem." *Wall Street Journal* (October 5, 1981), p. 1.
   This news report describes how twelve hundred programs that run the system have been amended to the point where no one really understands them anymore.

F. Greguras. "Software Protection: A Step Toward Copyright." *Computerworld* (December 12, 1983), pp. 25–32.
   This is a cogent discussion of the issues surrounding copyright and protection of proprietary software.

V. G. Hajek. *Managing of Engineering Projects.* New York: McGraw-Hill, 1977.
   Chapter 21 is a very brief recap of a few terminal activities.

M. Silverman. *Project Management—A Short Course for Professionals.* New York: Wiley Professional Development Programs, 1976.
   Chapter 10 briefly discusses phaseout, mostly covering the people issues.

H. Swartz. "Patents Should Be Good Medicine for Software." *Business Computer Systems* (December 1983), pp. 29–30.
   This brief article argues that the enforcement of patent protection law is the best protection against software piracy.

Part 6

OTHER ISSUES

Other Issues

21

Small Computer Software Projects

Relative to large projects, small projects have both advantages and disadvantages. Being smaller, they are easier to understand and less likely to get into difficulty. But there is less time and money to recover from anything that goes wrong and they inevitably lack high priority.

DEFINING SMALL PROJECTS

A software development project can be considered small on one or more dimensions: money, staff size, and time. However, small projects are also relative to the size along those dimensions of other projects within the same company. For example, a four-person, eight-week project might be considered small at a company where the normal project involves two hundred people committed for person-years rather than weeks, yet would be a normal sized project in a company where the projects all tend to be four-to-ten-week software maintenance efforts. A good rule of thumb is to consider anything measured in weeks or months (under a year) and with less than twenty people a small effort, taking into consideration its relation to the size of other company software projects.

Software project size is relative.

Small size relative to cost can be determined merely by comparing the budget to that for other software efforts. To a company committing $25,000 to writing its first accounts receivable system, the project reflects a very large commitment. To a company spending $200,000 modifying systems software to support a new hardware line, it might be considered small relative to the budgets for other projects that are reported in the millions of dollars.

Perception of project size may also differ between the customer and contractor organizations, based on the size of budgets in the respective organizations.

SIMPLIFIED MANAGEMENT

Small projects have a Triple Constraint to plan and control.

Figure 21-1 is a form that can be used to plan and control small projects. It shows the plan for the project. The form allows the work breakdown items and the schedule to be entered in either a network diagram or a bar chart form. The overall plan for labor and nonlabor cost may also be entered. As actual costs are incurred, they can be entered and variances can be noted. In this particular form, the labor categories do not exactly match those previously used, but the form is merely illustrative and could be changed to include any categories. Note also that the form uses months for the time horizon across the top. This could be changed to weeks, quarters, or any other convenient time frame. An alternate form, which lacks specific cost information, is illustrated in Figure 21-2.

PROBLEMS

There are four causes for the problems unique to small projects: tight schedules, tight budgets, small teams, and in many (but not all) cases, low priority.

Tight Schedules

A small project typically is planned to have a shorter schedule than a large project. Thus, the inevitable "getting up to speed" consumes a larger fraction of the available time. A one-week or one-month delay on a long program is less sig-

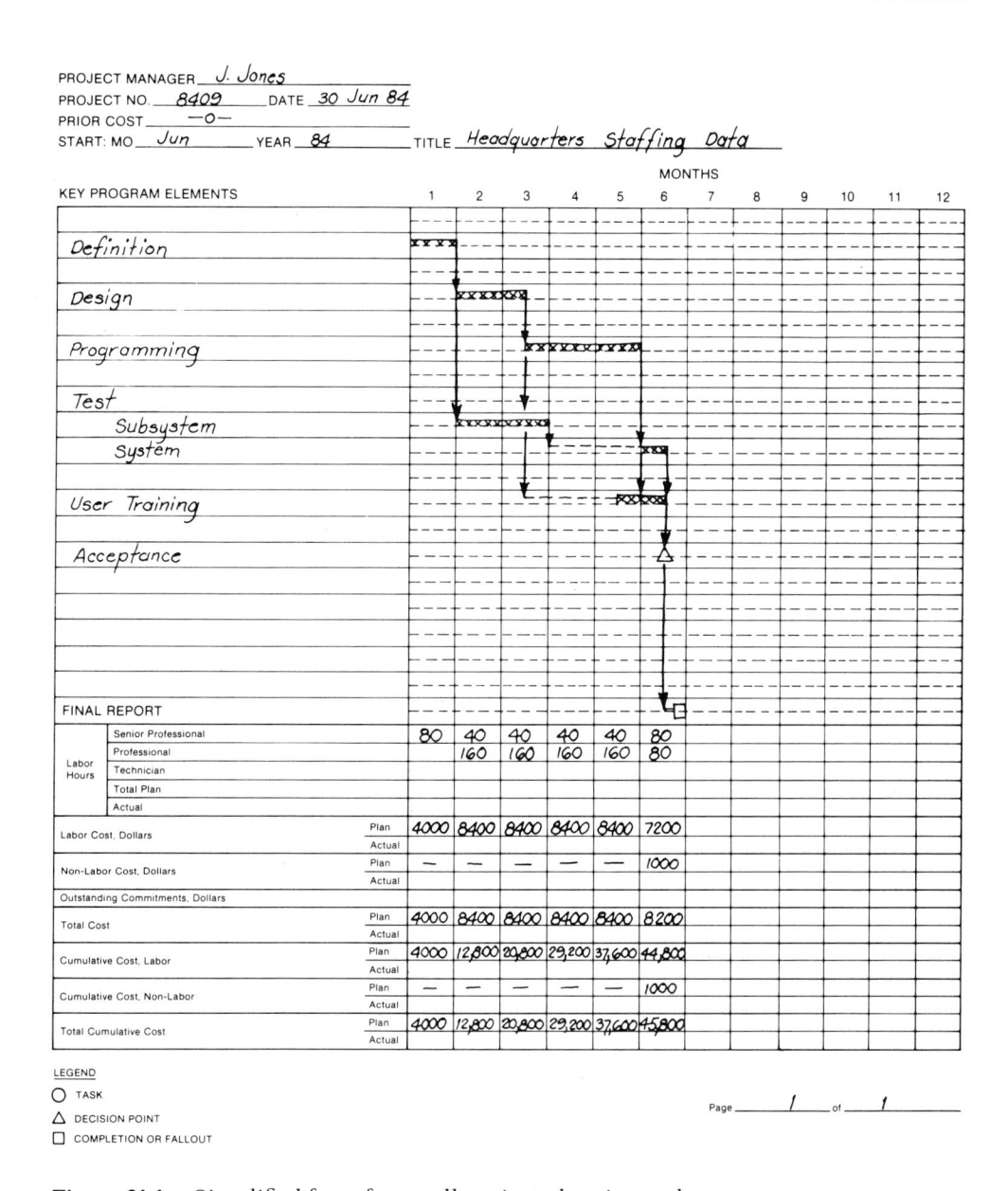

Figure 21-1. Simplified form for small project planning and control.

nificant than the same delay on a two-, three-, or four-month program, a typical period for a small project. The implication is that small projects must be initiated at the very first opportunity and the project manager must devote a relatively large amount of effort to assuring schedule compliance.

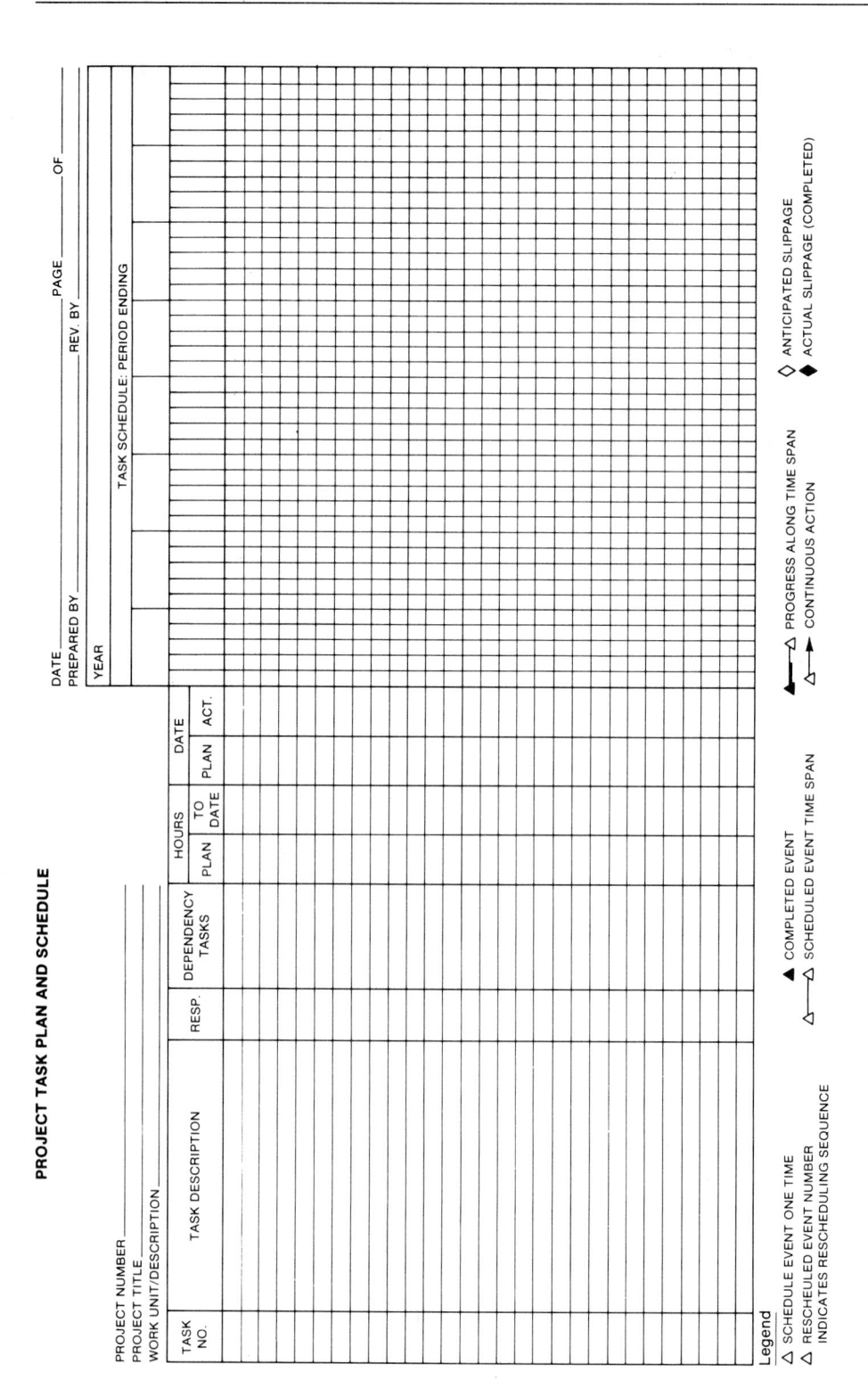

Figure 21-2. An alternate form for small project use.

Tight Budgets

A small project budget will be less than a large project budget. Hence, the absolute amount of money available for contingency must necessarily be less. In addition, the costs of administration and project management will consume a bigger fraction of the budget. When the inevitable revolting development occurs, there is less maneuvering room in which to cope with the consequences. The typical two-week lag in cost reports represents a significantly larger fraction of the overall project time and again leads to less reaction capability when some revolting development is discovered. Thus, extremely close attention to cost is required on a weekly, if not on a daily, basis.

Small projects lack time, money, personnel, and priority.

Small Teams

A large project can typically have the full-time attention of a functional expert (for instance, a forms specialist); whereas a small project must make do with the part-time assignment of such experts. Thus, the small project must compete against other projects for the specialists' time. In some cases, especially where computer programming is called for, this can be a major problem. Each time a person begins a particular programming task, he or she will spend a certain amount of time "getting up to speed." Thus, time is lost in reorientation. The problem may be worse with computer programming, but it is not confined to that specialty. Confronted with this reality, the effective project manager should attempt to bargain for full days whenever part-time resources are required.

Priority

Studies have shown that high priority projects are more likely than low priority projects to be completed successfully because they will normally win each competition for any key resource. If you have a low priority project and another person has a high priority project and you both request data entry for your projects, the person with the high priority project will have his or her needs satisfied first. And it is unlikely that a small project will ever have the same significance for an organization as a large project, which means low priority is more common on small projects than on large projects. Finally, small projects normally have less visibility, and therefore less chance for personal glory; so motivation can be less.

Imagine that you are spending half your time managing a small four-month project and the other half working on a much larger project. After two months, you discover that the small project is running late and will now require three-quarters of your time to complete it on schedule. There are at least four options to consider:

1. Be late on the small project.
2. Request that you spend only one-quarter time on the large project so you can spend three-quarters on the small one.
3. Request paid overtime approval for the small project.
4. Work unpaid overtime on the small project.

The choice among these, and any other viable options, can be aided by a decision tree or a qualitative matrix.

TYPICAL PROBLEMS

Beware that small projects do not escalate.

> There is another, insidious problem, namely, that of projects starting small and escalating. Again, "staying on top" helps, as does switching to more extensive, formal project management techniques as the project grows.
>
> The management of a small project should not utilize more resources than the project itself. Often, in a company with very formalized standards for software project management, the reporting is geared for large rather than small efforts. Although the management of small projects is no less important, the formal reporting methods might be somewhat relaxed so that the small project manager can spend his or her time managing and the technical staff can design and program.
>
> There are problems unique to small projects. Generally, they result from insufficient analysis of the scope of a problem, with inadequate resource allocation. This results in the manager having to spend more
>
> *continued*

time managing the more complicated situations that develop.

For example, with fewer people, a single person often performs many different tasks within the life cycle phases, such as establishing requirements and doing the systems design. There is thus a tendency not to be as rigid in documenting each phase because complete understanding is assumed. (After all, no communication interface occurred!) However, the documentation process itself often reveals design flaws, omissions, and other problems that need resolution.

Often user training is not addressed, or insufficient testing time is estimated. This is especially true when a small project consists of changes to an existing system; the impact of a small change can bring a formerly well running system to a halt because only a partial test was allotted in the budget.

Sometimes the repercussions of a small project on existing or planned systems are not thought out well enough and there is sizeable interfacing required by the technical staff and a great amount of management caucusing with other project managers.

Four causes of the problems unique to small projects are tight schedule, tight budgets, small teams, and low priority. **HIGHLIGHTS**

Another problem associated with small projects is a tendency for the project to grow.

FURTHER READING

B. N. Abramson and R. D. Kennedy. *Managing Small Projects.* Redondo Beach, CA: TRW Systems Group, 1975.
   Although somewhat specific to TRW, this short booklet has some useful pointers.

P. W. Metzger. *Managing a Programming Project,* 2nd ed. Englewood Cliffs, NJ: Prentice-Hall, 1981.

Pages 173–174 have a brief discussion of small projects.

M. Zeldman. *Keeping Technical Projects on Target.* New York: AMACON, 1978.

This is a graphic, manual system that may be helpful for controlling small projects, although the system illustrated in Figure 21-1 seems preferable.

22

Where Do You Go From Here?

In this chapter, we wrap up our discussion of the project management process with a summary of the key points you should remember as you put the tools and techniques discussed in this book into practice now or on your next project. Then we mention some trends we feel will impact how you can go about managing projects in the future. Finally, we list some sources for continuing your development of project management skills.

SUMMARY

The following list summarizes the five managerial steps for successful project management:

1. Define
   Project objectives
   Statement of work with output specifications
   Contract
2. Plan, with contingency
   Performance axis—work breakdown structure
      Project life cycle
      Milestone deliverables and reviews
   Schedule axis—network diagram
      Initial trial
      Activity times estimates
      Critical path calculation
      Adjustment

Cost axis—cost estimate by task and performing group
Each activity on network

3. Lead (or manage)
Organization
Staffing
Internal and external relations

4. Monitor (or measure)
Reports
Milestone documents
Reviews
Inevitable problems

5. Complete
Delivery
Acceptance
Personnel reassignment
Follow-up work

When you start a new project, you should review this list. Then you should turn to the chapter highlights, where appropriate, for a more detailed refresher. When necessary, you can review portions of this book or obtain some of the materials cited in "Further Reading." And always learn from your past experiences so that you can be a better manager on your next assignment.

OTHER SOURCES OF HELP

Sometimes you may still find that you are "over your head." In such a case, you may wish to retain a management consultant for assistance. Here are some sources of qualified consultants:

Associations that certify management consulting *companies:*

Association of Management Consultants
Suite 1400
500 North Michigan Avenue
Chicago, IL 60611
312-266-1261

ACME (formerly Association of Consulting Management Engineers)
230 Park Avenue
New York, NY 10017
212-687-9693

Associations that certify *individual* management consultants:

Institute of Management Consultants
19 West 44th Street
New York, NY 10036
212-921-2885

Society of Professional Management Consultants
16 West 56th Street
New York, NY 10019
212-586-2041

There are other qualified management consultants unaffiliated with any of these organizations. However, you have a better assurance of professional and ethical assistance if you choose a properly certified management consultant.

THE FUTURE OF PROJECT MANAGEMENT

We think it is likely that more project managers will have real-time project management status reports (technical, task status, labor hours, costs, and others) during the next decade. These reports may be provided on suitable terminals connected to mainframe computers, or they may come from microcomputer networks. Such real-time status information will allow project managers to recognize problems more quickly, which can reduce lost time if the project manager acts promptly.

In addition to real-time information, better graphic output devices (such as laser and color printers) will make it more convenient to keep network diagrams current and make them easier to read. These diagrams can be distributed electronically and be produced at remote work sites. Better software will also facilitate graphic representation of management data that is now presented numerically, thus highlighting areas of change.

Real-time project management status reports and better graphic output devices are upcoming.

We think it would be desirable (but less likely) for organizations to install an adjudicator function. This adjudicator would hear disputes about internal agreements, such as task work orders, and render a decision. This would institute inside the organization an analog to the external use of courts or arbitration to resolve contract disputes. This kind of mechanism could go a long way toward defusing internal corporate politics and the acrimony that accompanies it.

Many companies have already instituted user review boards to determine how the company will allocate its computer and associated human resources in an effort to reduce the competition for resources.

The software project manager's estimating task will be facilitated by the research results of the field of software engineering. The manager will be able to extrapolate results of projects similar in task and organization in making more meaningful estimates earlier in the project life cycle.

Software engineering will also facilitate the manager's tasks as automated techniques are implemented to tighten up requirements earlier in the project. Tools such as PSL and SADT, which are techniques to document requirements, hold great promise for minimizing, if not eliminating, the miscommunications that occur as software projects pass through their development phases.

User implementation of software will also affect the software manager's role and task. In many corporations, nontechnical managers are taking advantage of user-friendly software and microcomputers to implement their own systems, bypassing the traditional data processing service organization. As the other functional departments within an organization become more computer literate, they can be expected to play a larger role in the software development efforts in their organizations and may well become implementors as well as users.

The software project manager's role will change as the technology changes.

Lastly, with more and more packaged software available, software project managers can be expected to increasingly choose not to develop portions of a system that can be more cheaply obtained and more easily implemented. Their role will thus change to more interfacing with companies external to their own organization. They will need to have an up-to-date knowledge of the packaged offerings relevant to their industry and be facile with the buy/make trade-off decision-making process.

CONTINUING PROJECT MANAGEMENT SKILL DEVELOPMENT

There is no substitute for experience.

Reading this or any other book will not make you an expert project manager. It takes time and practice for the skills to become second nature—and you will have to develop your own style, consistent with your skills, interests, and personality. There is no substitute for your own experience. What works for one person may not be useful or appropriate for another. Thus, you should continue to experiment, read, and seek out other sources for continuing education in this subject.

Reading

The citations at the end of each chapter can be used to identify other sources available at the time this book was published. More will be published in the future; so you should watch for these.

In addition, you may want to read the *Project Management Quarterly,* published by the Project Management Institute (P.O. Box 43, Drexel Hill, PA 19026; 215-622-1796). This is the only journal devoted to project management, but unfortunately it is mostly dedicated to heavy construction projects.

The Institute of Electrical and Electronics Engineers (IEEE) has a number of excellent publications on software engineering and software management that contain worthy articles. The *IEEE Transactions on Software Engineering* is published quarterly (IEEE Computer Society, P.O. Box 80452, Los Angeles, CA 90080). They also issue the *Tutorial: Software Management,* which is devoted to many aspects of software project management. IEEE also publishes the proceedings of the International Software Engineering conferences.

Continuing Education

A consortium of universities called the Association for Media-Based Continuing Education for Engineers (AMCEE, Dept. MR, 225 North Avenue, NW, Atlanta, GA: 404-894-3362) has videocassette courses on project management. These courses can be leased or purchased.

Two sponsors of "live" project management training with which we are familiar are

UCLA Extension (CEEM)
Room 6266
Boelter Hall
University of California
Los Angeles, CA 90024
213-825-3344 and 825-1295

Industrial Relations Center
California Institute of Technology
383 South Hill Avenue
Pasadena, CA 91125
213-356-4041

Many other universities and commercial organizations offer seminars and extension programs of one-day to one-week duration. These vary in quality, teaching method, and subject matter; so you should determine who will lecture and lead these training programs. Then try to check out references by talking with prior participants.

Learn from other managers' experience.

The unique value of attending seminars or courses is the interaction with other project managers. No amount of reading or passive observation of videocassette courses—even if the materials are outstanding—can give you real practice with the development of human relationship skills, which are crucial when you must work with people.

If you cannot attend a university or commercial seminar, you may want to explore having such a seminar conducted in your own organization. Although you will not obtain the stimulus of interacting with personnel from other organizations, you will have a seminar customized to your own specific situation (perhaps using your own forms as examples). Such an in-house seminar can be much more cost-effective than sending many people to other seminars.

A FINAL THOUGHT

Good luck! May all your projects be successful.

Appendix 1

Abbreviations Often Used in Computer Software Project Management

The use of abbreviations seems to be peculiarly prevalent in the field of computer software. In fact, in many books and articles the abbreviations are never defined! Each contract within a contracting organization often has its own uses of terminology and special acronyms. The following list provides definitions of the most frequently encountered abbreviations in the computer software and project management fields. Appendix 2 provides a glossary of project management terms. Further amplification of the computer software terms can be found in these remarkably complete source books:

A. V. Stokes. *Concise Encyclopedia of Information Technology.* Englewood Cliffs, NJ: Prentice-Hall, 1983.

A. Ralston, ed. *Encyclopedia of Computer Science.* New York: Van Nostrand Reinhold, 1976.

Shorter but still helpful lists appear in:

G. B. Shelly and T. J. Cashman. *Introduction to Computers and Data Processing.* Brea, CA: Anaheim Publishing, 1980.

R. C. Tausworthe. *Standardized Development of Computer Software*, vol. 2. Englewood Cliffs, NJ: Prentice-Hall, 1979.

ACO -	Administrative Contracting Officer
ACWP -	Actual Cost of Work Performed
A/D -	Analog to Digital
ADA -	Ada, a structured language

ALGOL -	ALGorithmically Oriented Language (or ALGOrithmic Language)
AON -	Activity on Node
APL -	A Programming Language
ASCII -	American Standard Code for Information Interchange
AVS -	Automated Verification System
B & P -	Bid and Proposal
BAC -	Budget at Completion
BASIC -	Beginners All-Purpose Symbolic Instruction Code
BCWP -	Budgeted Cost of Work Performed
BCWS -	Budgeted Cost of Work Scheduled
BIT -	BInary digiT
BLISS -	A programming language
BUNCH -	Burroughs, Univac, NCR, Control Data, Honeywell (in distinction to IBM)
CAD -	Computer-Aided Design
CAE -	Computer-Aided Engineering
CAI -	Computer-Aided Instruction
CAM -	Computer-Aided Manufacturing
CCB -	Change (or Configuration) Control Board
CCDR -	Contractor Cost Data Reporting
CCN -	Contract Change Notice
CDR -	Critical Design Review
CDRL -	Contract Data Requirements Lists
CFE -	Customer Furnished Equipment
CFSR -	Contract Funds Status Report
CMO -	Contract Management Office
COBOL -	COmmon Business-Oriented Language
COM -	Computer Output Microfilm
CPCI -	Computer Program Configuration Item
CPFF -	Cost Plus Fixed Fee
CPIF -	Cost Plus Incentive Fee
CPL -	Computer Program Library
CPM -	Critical Path Method
CPU -	Central Processing Unit

CRT -	Cathode Ray Tube
C/SCSC -	Cost/Schedule Control System Criteria
C/SSR -	Cost/Schedule Status Report
CWBS -	Contract Work Breakdown Structure
D/A -	Digital to Analog
DAR -	Defense Acquisition Regulations
DASD -	Direct Access Storage Device
DB -	Data Base
DBA -	Data Base Administrator
DBCI -	Data Base Configuration Item
DBMS -	Data Base Management System
DDP -	Distributed Data Processing
DDR -	Detailed Design Review
DFD -	Data Flow Diagram
DOS -	Disc Operating System
DP -	Data Processing
EAC -	Estimate at Completion
ECN -	Engineering Change Notice
ECP -	Engineering Change Proposal
EDP -	Electronic Data Processing
EEPROM -	Electrically Erasable Programmable Read-Only Memory
EF -	Earliest Finish
EPROM -	Erasable Programmable Read-Only Memory
ES -	Earliest Start
ETC -	Estimate to Complete
FCA -	Functional Configuration Audit
FFP -	Firm Fixed Price
FORTRAN -	FORmula TRANslation
FOT & E -	Follow-on Operational Test and Evaluation
FP -	Fixed Price
FQR -	Formal Qualification Review
FQT -	Formal Qualification Testing
G & A -	General and Administrative
GFE -	Government Furnished Equipment
GPSS -	General Purpose System Simulation

HIPO -	Hierarchy plus Input-Process-Output
HLL -	Higher Level Language
HOL -	Higher Order Language
IBM -	International Business Machines Corp.
IC -	Integrated Circuit
IM -	Information Management
I/O -	Input/Output
IPO -	Input-Process-Output
IR & D -	Internal Research and Development
IS -	Information System
JCL -	Job Control Language
K -	Thousand (actually 1,024)
LF -	Latest Finish
LISP -	LISt Processing
LS -	Latest Start
LSI -	Large Scale Integration
MDS -	Microprocessor Development System
MICR -	Magnetic Ink Character Recognition
MIPS -	Millions of Instructions Per Second
MIS -	Management Information Systems
MODEM -	MOdulator-DEModulator
MP -	Modular Programming
MTBF -	Mean Time Between Failures
MULTICS -	MULTiplexed Information and Computing Service
NC -	Numerical Control
OCR -	Optical Character Recognition
ODC -	Other Direct Cost
OS -	Operating System
PASCAL -	A structured language
PCA -	Physical Configuration Audit
PDL -	Program Design Language
PDR -	Preliminary Design Review
PERT -	Program Evaluation and Review Technique
PL/1 -	Programming Language 1
PL/M -	PL/1 for Microcomputers

PM -	Project (or Program) Manager (or Management)
PMS -	Project Management Systems
PO -	Purchase Order
PR -	Purchase Requisition
PROM -	Programmable Read-Only Memory
PSA -	Problem Statement Analyzer
PSL -	Problem Statement Language
PWA -	Project Work Authorization
QA -	Quality Assurance
QC -	Quality Control
RAM -	Random Access Memory
RFP -	Request for Proposal
RFQ -	Request for Quotation
RJE -	Remote Job Entry
ROM -	Read-Only Memory
RPG -	Report Program Generator
SADT -	Structured Analysis and Design Technique
SCM -	Software Configuration Management
SCR -	Software Change Report
SNOBOL -	A high-level language
SOW -	Statement of Work
SPR -	Software Problem Report
SRR -	Systems Requirements Review
STR -	Software Trouble Report
T & M -	Time and Material
UDF -	Unit Development Folder
UNIX -	An operating system
VDU -	Video Display Unit
VLSI -	Very Large Scale Integration
V & V -	Verification and Validation
WBS -	Work Breakdown Structure
WO -	Work Order
WU -	Work Unit

Glossary

Terms Commonly Employed in Project Management

Activity A single task within a project

Actual Cost of Work Performed (ACWP) A term in the Cost/Schedule Control System Criteria (C/SCSC) system for the costs actually incurred and recorded in accomplishing the work performed within a given time period

Application Programmers Those programmers responsible for the development of function and industry relevant software that is determined by their employer's particular business (for example, banking, aerospace, stock brokerage, insurance, accounting, inventory)

Bar Chart A scheduling tool (also called a Gantt chart) in which the time span of each activity is shown as a horizontal line, the ends of which correspond to the start and finish of the activity as indicated by a date line at the bottom of the chart

Bid/No Bid Decision The decision whether or not to submit a proposal in response to a request for proposal

Bottom Up Cost Estimating The approach to making a cost estimate or plan in which detailed estimates are made for every task shown in the work breakdown structure and then summed to provide a total cost estimate or plan for the project

Budgeted Cost of Work Performed (BCWP) A term in the Cost/Schedule Control System Criteria (C/SCSC) system for the sum of the budgets for completed work packages and completed portions of open work packages, plus the appropriate portion of the budgets for level of effort and apportioned effort

Budgeted Cost of Work Scheduled (BCWS) A term in the Cost/Schedule Control System Criteria (C/SCSC) system for the sum of budgets for all work packages, planning packages, and similar items scheduled to be accomplished (including in-process work packages), plus the amount of level of effort and apportioned effort scheduled to be accomplished within a given time period

Burst Node In a network diagram, a node at which two or more activities commence after the completion of the preceding activity

Buy-In The process of making a cost bid in a proposal that is unduly optimistic or even actually less than the estimated costs for the project, which is done for the purpose of winning the job

Chart Room A room filled with planning documents displayed as charts, typically hung on the walls, used on large projects, and usually marked to indicate current status

Commitment An obligation to pay money at some future time, such as a purchase order or travel authorization, which represents a charge to a project budget even though not yet actually paid

Configuration Management Management of the methods used to control the software and hardware being developed; often used interchangeably with change control

Contingency An amount of design margin, time, or money inserted into the corresponding plan as a safety factor to accommodate unexpected and presently unknown occurrences that judgment suggests will occur during the project

Costed Work Breakdown Structure A work breakdown structure in which the costs corresponding to major elements of the WBS are also shown on the WBS

Cost Plus Fixed Fee (CPFF) Contract A form of contractual arrangement in which the customer agrees to reimburse the contractor's actual costs, regardless of amount, and in addition pay a negotiated fee independent of the amount of the actual costs

Cost Plus Incentive Fee (CPIF) Contract A form of contractual arrangement similar to CPFF except that the fee is not preset or fixed but rather depends on some specified result, such as timely delivery

Cost/Schedule Control System Criteria (C/SCSC) A planning and control reporting system devised by the Department of Defense for its contractors to use, intended to foster greater uniformity as well as provide early insight into impending schedule or budget overruns

Critical Path In a network diagram, the longest path from start to finish or the path without any slack, and thus the path corresponding to the shortest time in which the project can be completed

Critical Path Method (CPM) A type of network diagram in which the activities are labeled on the arrows

Customer Furnished Equipment (CFE) Equipment provided to the contractor doing the project by the customer for the project and typically specified in the contract

Data Entry Clerk Job category identifying personnel responsible for entering data into the computer via terminal or key to disc devices in a predefined manner as part of a processing operation

Documentation Any kind of written report, including such items as final reports, spare parts lists, instruction manuals, test plans, program code itself, all life cycle milestone documents, project history, and similar project information

Dummy Activity An activity in a network diagram that requires no work, signifying a precedence condition only

Earliest Finish In a network diagram schedule, the earliest time at which an activity can be completed

Earliest Start In a network diagram schedule, the earliest time at which an activity can be started

Firm Fixed Price (FFP) Contract A contractual form in which the price and fee are predetermined and not dependent on cost

Firmware Software programs contained in read-only memory

Fixed Price (FP) Contract Same as firm fixed price

Float Same as slack time

Functional Organization The form of organization in which all people with a particular kind of skill (such as engineering) are grouped in a common department, reporting to a single manager for that particular functional speciality

Government Furnished Equipment (GFE) The same as customer furnished equipment in projects where the customer is a governmental entity

Hardware Project A project in which the principal deliverable item is a physical product or functioning device of some sort

Latest Finish In a network diagram schedule, the latest time at which an activity can be finished

Latest Start In a network diagram schedule, the latest time at which an activity can be started

Matrix Organization The form of organization in which there is a project management functional speciality as well as other functional specialities, and where the project management function has responsibility for accomplishing the project work by drawing upon the other functional specialities as required

Merge Node In a network diagram, a node at which two or more activities precede the start of the subsequent activity

Milestone A major event in a project, typically one requiring the customer or upper management to approve further work

Module A self-contained unit of code that accomplishes a particular process

Network Diagram A scheduling tool in which activities or events are displayed as arrows and nodes in which the logical precedence conditions between the activities or events are shown

Periodic Review Any kind of project review conducted on a periodic basis, most commonly a monthly project review

"The Plan" A document or group of documents that constitutes all the plans for the project, frequently contained in a notebook or series of notebooks

Planning Matrix A matrix in which planned activities are listed on one side (usually the left), involved people or groups are listed across a perpendicular side (usually the top), and involvement of a particular individual or group in a particular activity is signified by a tic mark where the row and column intersect

Program Used interchangeably with "project," as in "program management" or "program manager" (In the case of computer software projects, "program" usually refers to a unit of computer instruction code that performs a specific function or set of functions.)

Program Evaluation and Review Technique (PERT) The form of network diagram in which events are displayed as nodes and where the connecting arrows indicate the precedence constraints

Programmer A computer software position with responsibility for writing (coding) a logical sequence of instructions to the computer to solve a computational, sequencing, or reporting problem using one or more computer languages

Program Analyst A computer software job category with responsibility for both coding (programming) and design (analysis)

Programmer Trainee A job category assigned to beginning programmers, usually with less than a year of on-the-job experience; the length of apprentice time varies by company

Progress Payments Payments made to the contractor by the customer during the course of the project, rather than at the end of the project, the terms of which are specified in the contract

Project An organized undertaking utilizing human and physical resources, done once, to accomplish a specific goal, which is normally defined by a Triple Constraint

Project Cost Accounting System A cost accounting system that accumulates actual costs for projects in such a way that total costs for all work in an organization can be allocated to the appropriate projects, normally providing monthly cost summaries; also used in cost planning to summarize the detailed task cost estimates

Project Organization The form of organization in which all or nearly all the people working on a project report to the project manager

Project Plan The entire plan for a project, consisting of the work breakdown structure, network diagram, and task budgets, but sometimes taken to mean only the network diagram

Project Team A term used in this book to designate the personnel working on a project who report to the project manager administratively, not merely for the work on the project

Proposal A document (sometimes accompanied by models) submitted to a prospective customer by an organization that describes work the organization is offering to do for the prospective customer

Request for Proposal (RFP) A document issued by one organization to another organization (or to several other organizations), describing work that the issuer wishes to have undertaken by the recipient(s) and inviting the recipient(s) to respond with a proposal

Request for Quotation (RFQ) Similar to a request for proposal, except that the desired items to be procured are stock or catalog items, and only price and delivery time need be proposed

Slack Time In a network diagram, the amount of time on any path other than the critical path that is the difference between the time to a common node on the critical path and the other path

Software Engineering That field within computer science responsible for the establishment and use of sound engineering principles and methods in order to economically obtain reliable and functional software

Software Project A project in which the principal deliverable item is a report or other form of documentation, such as a computer program

Statement of Work (SOW) That portion of a proposal or the resulting contract that states exactly what will be delivered and when

Subcontractor An organization, usually a company, working for another organization on some aspect of the project for which the other organization is under contract

Support Services The class of tasks ancillary to analysis, design, and programming that are required to accomplish a software development effort; includes documentation (technical publications), quality assurance, test and integration, and the data center operations

Support Team A term used in this book to designate the personnel working on a project who do not report to the project manager administratively

Systems Analyst The computer person responsible for analyzing users' needs and defining the functional requirements of the computer and procedural solutions to meet those needs

Systems Architect Job category of computer software personnel responsible for the high level systems design—the allocation of basic functions across applications and systems software and hardware

Systems Programmer Programmer whose primary responsibility is to write or modify operating systems, usually to customize them to the particular hardware used and software running at an installation for the application programmers' use

Task A small part of a project

Task Force An ad hoc group designated to cope with a project, similar to a project organization although frequently staffed with personnel on part-time assignment, usually adopted by a functional organization having only one project or at most a few projects at any given time.

Time Compression The act of reducing the planned time for an activity, accomplished perhaps by adding unplanned staff or using overtime.

Time and Material (T&M) Contract A contractual form in which the customer agrees to pay the contractor for all time and material used on the project, including a fee as a percentage of all project costs

Top Down Cost Estimating The approach to making a cost estimate or plan in which judgment and experience are used to arrive at an overall amount, usually done by an experienced manager making a subjective comparison of the project to previous, smaller projects

Topical Review Any kind of project review devoted to a single topic, such as a final design review or a manufacturing review

Triple Constraint The term used in this book to describe the three key project objectives that must be simultaneously accomplished, namely, the performance specification, the time schedule, and the monetary budget

Venture Organization The form of organization used in some large organizations where a three- or four-person team, itself functionally organized, is established within the larger organization to develop and commercialize a new product

Work Breakdown Structure (WBS) A family tree, usually product oriented, that organizes, defines, and graphically displays the hardware, software, services, and other work tasks necessary to accomplish the project objectives

Index

Acceptance 21, 266–268
Activities 87–88, 113
ACWP 142
Alternatives 251
Architecture 241
Arrow diagram 87
Audits 278–279
Authority 178–179
Authorization 34, 40, 79

Bar chart 84–86, 107–109
BCWP 142
BCWS 142
Brainstorming 193–194
Bubble diagrams 87
Budgets 6, 113, 121
Burnout 194
Burst nodes 89–90
Buy-In 124

Change control 71, 242–246
Changes 238–247
Chart room 70
Checklists 38–39, 82
Commitment 168–171, 217–218, 230–231, 294
Communication 182–185
Completion 7–8, 264–281
Computer 140, 144
Conflict 185
Constraints 129

Consultants 160–161, 294–295
Contingency 136–140
Contract 45–54
Contractors 46–47
Control 164–165, 201–203
Coordination 171–172
Cost
  accounting system 119–125
  estimating 111–125
  problems 19–20, 124–5
  reports 207, 216–217, 227–236
Costed WBS 80
CPFF 46–48
CPIF 46–48
CPM see critical path method
Creativity 192–194
Critical path method 86–109, 134–136
Critical success factors 208
C/SCSC 141–142
Customer 3, 30, 41, 45–51, 53, 119
Customer furnished equipment (CFE) 49, 54

Decision trees 252–256
Definition 7–8, 15–55, 293
Delivery 269–270
Design reviews 223
Documentation 51, 64, 222, 270
Dummy activity 89–90

Index

Earliest start & finish 100–102
Events 87–88

FFP 46
Feasibility 143
Feedback 183–184, 279–280
Float time 94, 100
FP 45–48
Functional organization 148
Funding 20

Gantt chart 84
GFE 49
Granularity 100

Hardware project 2

Implementation 117
Influence 178–180
Informal organization 154–5
Interdependencies 85
International projects 51–53

Latest start & finish 100–102
Leading 7–8, 147–196, 294
Life cycle 9, 69–72, 117, 212

Maintenance 23, 276
Management by objectives 191–192
Matrix
  array 255–258
  organization 151–152, 158
  planning 68
Meetings 186–187, 259
Merge node 90, 93, 101
Milestone 21, 86, 220, 224
Monitoring 7–8, 21, 201–261, 294
Motivation 162–163, 187–193
Multiple projects 207–208

Negotiations 21, 45–54
Network diagram 2, 4, 86, 88–103, 113, 128–132, 143, 172–173, 206

Organization 6, 147–155, 159
Overhead 119, 233–234
Overrun data 239

Parametric cost estimating 115–116
Patents 51, 277–278
Performance 16–17, 22, 48, 76–83, 117
Periodic review 215–219
Personnel 160–161
PERT 86–109
Phases 23, 35
Plan (The) 68–70
Planning 7–8, 36, 59–83, 213, 293
  cost 111–125
  documents 63
  matrix 68
  performance 76
Pragmatic estimating 105–106, 117–118
Precedence network 87
Priority 273, 289
Problem solving 249–260
Program management 5
Project
  cost accounting system 119–125
  defined 2
  life cycle 9, 69–72, 117, 212
  management 7
  manager 6, 105, 118, 157, 178–195, 271, 273, 296
  organization 148–149, 159
  origin 1
  plan 59, 61
  process 7–8
  reviews 211–225
  size 1, 5
  small 289–291
  staffing cycle 265–266
  team 157–166
Proposal 28, 31, 32, 36
Proximity 164, 184

Quality assurance 175–176, 223
Quasi-matrix 152–153

Reports 64, 203–207, 227–236
Requirements 82, 267
Resources 6, 127–144
Reviews 211–225
RFP/RFQ 21, 30–35

Risk 64–65

Schedule 6, 84–109, 127–132
Seminars 297–8
Simulation 36–37
Slack 94–100
Software engineering 296
Software project 2–3, 148
Sole source 31
Specifications 17, 22–23, 49
Statement of work 35–36, 49, 76, 81
Strategic issues 27–28
Structured walkthroughs 224
Subcontract 130
Subcontractors 7, 29, 121, 174–175
Support group 124, 169–170, 172–173
Support team 158, 168–176

Task 79, 105, 165–166, 202, 244
Task force 153–4

Task management 5, 113
Time
  earliest & latest 100–102
  estimation 102–106
  management 185–187
  problems 17–19
T & M 46–48
Topical review 219–224
Tradeoffs 134–135, 296
Training 162–291
Triple constraint 8, 10, 15–16, 24–25, 27, 33, 37, 49, 68, 84, 112, 170, 201, 218

Uncertainty 64–65
User 6, 21, 168–169

Variance 227–235
Venture organization 153

Walkthrough 224
WBS 37, 76–82, 96, 113, 119, 140